ROMANCE AND TRAGEDY

ROMANCE
AND TRAGEDY

*A Study of Classic and Romantic Elements in the
Great Tragedies of European Literature*

by

PROSSER HALL FRYE

Preface by Thomas M. Raysor

University of Nebraska Press, Lincoln

1961

To

PAUL ELMER MORE

Τοῦτο γὰρ μόνον, εἴπερ ἄρα, ἀνθεῖλκεν ἂν καὶ κατεῖχεν ἐν τῷ ζῆν, εἰ συζῆν ἐφεῖτο τοῖς τὰ αὐτὰ δόγματα περιπεποιημένοις

Marcus Aurelius

PREFACE

This book is a new edition of one of the most ambitious and able ventures in comparative literature ever published in this country. I believe that it deserves attention because it comes near to the attainment of literary purposes often professed but seldom achieved. We all recognize the unity and continuity in time and space of formal arts like music or architecture, painting or sculpture, and the consequent value for human culture of comparison and contrast in the analysis of the variety and the unity of human imaginative experience. But though we recognize the similar values in comparative literature, not only as far as literature is itself a formal art but in literature as a medium of interpreting experience and ideas, most of us cannot command Greek and German, French and Spanish, as easily and freely as Mr. Frye does in this book. And academic departmentalization, the necessary specialization of historical scholarship, the present academic rage for purely contemporary literature, and perhaps some intellectual nationalism or parochialism creeping insidiously into literary studies have all prevented us from attaining the wide range in space and time of such a book as this. Mr. Frye loses as well as gains from his breadth of knowledge and thought, but so do we from the narrowness of our specialization, and we can benefit from his qualities.

His qualities are not merely those of a student and critic of comparative literature with a very wide range, but of a classicist. His dedication to Paul Elmer More will remind older readers of the new humanists of the last generation. He shares their emphasis on intellectual criticism rather than specialized historical scholarship, he takes the side of the ancients rather than the moderns in the Battle of the Books, he is more interested in the ethical ideas of the work of art than in the psychology of the artist, he judges the work of art not in isolation but as an epitome of culture and tradition. But he was no polemic critic like Professor Irving Babbitt, and in this book at least he was fundamentally a genre-critic of drama and specifically in drama, of tragedy. In private conversation, the loneliness of his intellectual position sometimes betrayed him into defensive sarcasm, but as far as I can remember his conversation this was nearly always redeemed by the flashing zest of his wit and a kind of exuberant playfulness. To my mind it is a great pity that he always considered these tendencies too frivolous for criticism, but perhaps it is this side of his mind which restrained him from Babbitt's heavy-handed moralism. There is no mistaking his classical preferences in literature, but they are usually expressed in analytical argument, and not in dogma. I feel, therefore, that the scholar or critic of a different school or different background need not be on guard against Mr. Frye.

Preface

Without attempting to anticipate or summarize the book, I think that I may say something about its genesis. It is the outgrowth of nearly forty years (1896-1934) of teaching at the University of Nebraska, in which Professor Frye was first in the rhetoric and later in the English department, and also editor of the *Mid-West Quarterly* (1913-17) and one of the editors of *University Studies*. *Romance and Tragedy* was published in 1922 as a series of essays collected from the *Mid-West Quarterly* and *University Studies*, with the addition of two new essays on "Shakespeare and Sophocles" and "Structure and Style." In Mr. Frye's prefatory note on these bibliographical details, he expressed regret that his earlier essay on "Corneille: The Neo-Classic Tragedy and the Greek" had been published in his *Reviews and Criticism* (1908) before the idea of a series of essays on drama had come into his mind. I have accordingly included it in the present reprint in the place which Mr. Frye had indicated for it. At the suggestion of Mr. Eric Bentley, I have also included an essay on Calderon from a later book, *Visions and Chimeras* (1929), since it follows the line of thought explained in "The Terms Classic and Romantic" and briefly represented in the title "Romance and Tragedy." Mr. Frye takes his title from A. W. Schlegel's remark that "the great modern dramatists . . . must be judged on the principle of the romance," but he develops his thesis that "tragedy and romance become the typical *genres* of classic and romantic literature" so independently as a modern classicist that he is in opposition to Schlegel, not under his influence. The present book then is a study of classical and romantic elements in the great tragedies of European literature, and I have omitted an intrusive essay on Nietzsche to make room for the two earlier and later essays on drama which obviously belong to the series.

Thomas M. Raysor

CONTENTS

PREFACE . . . . .Thomas M. Raysor vii

I   LITERATURE AND CRITICISM   1

II   THE TERMS *Classic* AND *Romantic* 21

III   GERMAN ROMANTICISM 57

IV   THE IDEA OF GREEK TRAGEDY 92

V   CORNEILLE: THE NEO-CLASSIC
     AND THE GREEK 156

VI   RACINE 198

VII   SHAKESPEARE AND SOPHOCLES 270

VIII   CALDERON 305

IX   STRUCTURE AND STYLE 323

Translations of passages in Greek, French,
German, and Spanish are given consecutively
beginning on page 353.

ROMANCE AND TRAGEDY

Romance and Tragedy

LITERATURE AND CRITICISM

IN THESE days of "scientific method," when there is so little literary activity of a genuinely critical sort, it is a good deal easier to say in what such activity does not, than in what it does, consist. That literary criticism is not identical with a study of words or language, or yet of texts or "documents"; that it is not to be confounded with philology or with the exploration of origins or derivations, or the investigation of manuscripts, or a determination of the details of literary history — all this ought to be reasonably clear on the face of it, and when stated in so many words, would probably be conceded even by those who have done most to cause the present confusion. That such subjects and pursuits are very interesting, very important in their way, there is no gainsaying. The study of etymology alone has been of great, if indirect assistance in the comprehension of literature, although to an hundred etymologists there is probably no more than one good critic. But still literature is something more than words and lives with another life than theirs; they are but the appurtenances, and neither phonology nor phonetics will ever furnish the basis for a satisfactory criticism of literature, any more than a chemistry of pigments will suffice for a criticism of painting.

Nor is this general statement less applicable to the study of " literary " than of linguistic sources, rudiments, and developments, however useful the one, as the other, to the indirect appreciation of literature. Unfortunately it is only too easy to over-rate the importance of primitive and dialectic " literature " — of " communal poetry," for example, or the early Germanic " epic " ; or rather, to rate them in inappropriate and misleading terms. So when Dr. Sweet declares that *Judith* " combines the ' highest dramatic and constructive power with the utmost brilliance of language and metre '," he is obviously using a fabulous terminology which leaves nothing to be said for a Shakespeare or a Sophocles.

Even the name *literature* in such a connection must be taken in a cautious and qualified way; since it is just the want of a term to distinguish the " documentary " from the literary, which has confirmed, if it has not induced, the current misapprehension. That a piece of writing may have a relative or historical value without any absolute or literary value, is anything but an uncommon occurrence; indeed, most writing is of this kind. On the contrary, it happens only too often that this tentative and rudimentary " literature," these gropings and strayings of an immature or defective culture, which we are naïvely expected to admire nowadays, are perfectly indifferent to criticism — that is, to a better sense of the permanent significance of life, and are of interest solely to scholarship — that is, to a knowledge and reconstruction of the past. For such, after all, is essentially the difference between the functions of scholarship and of criticism: the former seeks to determine the fact; the latter, to interpret it. While scholarship endeavours to re-constitute the past in its habit as it lived, criticism attempts to liberate the idea, to set free the message it has to communicate. In this sense scholarship is " scientific," if one likes the word; it deals with facts, with the thing itself; it is impersonal and in its own manner final. Its results, when once obtained, are definitive and are taken up into the common stock of information, though their original form and method may be superseded and forgotten. On the other hand, criticism, as an affair of ideas, is necessarily individual and relative; for although literature is itself essentially in the nature of a permanent contribution to human experience, its application will vary from one generation to another and its interpretation will change with the age — to say nothing of the further circumstance that its meaning is always exposed to a personal reaction. How close the connection, then, between scholarship and criticism, is at once apparent. But though it is perhaps no wonder under the circumstances that the two offices of verification and interpretation should be confounded — particularly in view of the unwarrantable extension which has been given of late years to the province of philology; yet the two are, in reality, distinct, and the integrity of our thought requires that they should be kept so.

In this way the remains of Gothic, consisting of a few biblical translations and a legal instrument or two, constituted an historical find of some importance since they served to fill a gap in our knowledge of the Germanic dialects; but as literature they are naught, and may be neglected by a sound criticism without our suffering the slightest intellectual inconvenience or the smallest arrest of moral growth. Even *Beowulf* itself, that venerable monument of Teutonic ingenuousness, is, I believe, more interesting as history than as literature, though treated with exaggerated respect by our modern philological scholarship. At all events, it ought to be spoken of in other and more moderate terms than its admirers commonly use of it, as though it were in any sense comparable with the *Iliad* or the *Odyssey*. " Scientifically " they are both, no doubt, the products of a barbaric " culture "; but the inability to feel their moral incommensurability is in itself a sufficient critical disqualification for speaking of them at all. To the scholar, to the student, even to the critic himself, an acquaintance with these imperfect expressions of the human spirit is valuable, it must be confessed, after a fashion — as valuable as a familiarity with the history of his institutions to the statesman. But in the same manner that the one sort of knowledge is not statesmanship, so the other is not criticism. The critic should be thankful for every scrap of information, no matter how scanty or hardly gained, toward a better understanding of things as they are, of which not the least useful is that which informs him how they came to be so; but the means must not be mistaken for the end — a grasp of the facts for a comprehension of ideas. It is all very well to know the recipe of the pudding; but if we are to avoid mental bewilderment — and that is perhaps as much as we can expect to do in a world where truth is largely a matter of convention — we must remember that its enjoyment is quite another thing and requires for its expression an entirely different set of terms.

On the other hand, just as it is necessary to guard against mistaking philological or historical for literary inquiry; so, too, it is equally necessary, in the interests of intellectual clearness, to beware of a like confusion between criticism and some ingenious analogy or illustration of the " natural " sciences. That the course of literary development furnishes a suggestive example of the principles of organic evolution, is undeniable. But undeniably, too, though so serious a mind as Brunetière has failed to see it, the illustration is biological, not critical. To be sure, though a doctrinaire by disposition, Brunetière never succeeded in finding quite so imposing a doctrine and building quite so hard and fast a system about it as Taine did; but something of the sort at least he tried to do with evolution. He observed that the history of literature is, in reality, the history of a succession of ideas of a certain kind, and like every succession of phenomena, may be made to take on a resemblance to the processes of organic evolution. That is to say, if a number of things occur in succession, the human mind is bound to make a series of them, supplying the necessary connections and transitions, and generalizing the results in one way or another. In the same manner that a child invents a fairy tale to go with the pictures that interest it, so we, children of a larger growth, make up a story, sooner or later, about the amazing panorama of existence. And it was Brunetière's special attempt to fit this story of evolution to literature. And after this fashion, just as he delights to recognize in letters the familiar phenomena of the differentiation and modification of *genres*, the growth and transformation and degeneration of species, so we may too, if we please, exercise our ingenuity in trying to show how Dickens's novels grew out of the work which preceded him and how they mingle the romance of Fielding with the sentimentality and realism of Richardson. But after all, that is not what we read Dickens for — if, indeed, amid the constant solicitations of modern scholarship we have sufficient literary virtue left to read him at all. Or again, we may amuse ourselves in thinking to surprise the origin of the English novel as a whole in a kind of cross, such as Brunetiere has so much to say about, between the comedy of manners and the social essay, such as Addison wrote, cleverly deducing from the former its turn for modern detail and from the latter its moral seriousness. But to say nothing of the fact that such transitions or transformations are in themselves quite unintelligible and explain nothing, this sort of thing yields no just sense of the tragic import of a *Clarissa Harlowe*.

And the case is no better with the " psychological " interpretation of literature than with the " physiological." To be sure, a work of genius is, in a manner, a psychological product as, in another, it is a physiological one. But while such a scientific study of genius, as it is pleasantly called, may throw a good deal of light upon the processes of composition and may even establish a kind of extrinsic mechanical order among the phenomena of literature, it fails dismally to express its essence or spirit; and leaving such a residuum, it can not be properly reckoned as criticism. For though literature is to some extent a physical and psychological product, it is to a much greater extent a moral one, of which in the exact sense of words there is no science possible. It is an affair of principle, not of law. What are known nowadays, ridiculously enough, as the moral sciences have to do, as far as they are capable of exact formulation, not with the moral order proper, but only with certain physical manifestations or accompaniments of the moral nature. In other respects they are purely descriptive and hence essentially literary in character. How much of the effect of Professor James' *Psychology,* for instance, depends upon the dexterity of his phrasing! And how much of the contents of any modern psychology consists of ordinary commonplaces done over into a kind of special jargon or cant — a sort of perverted rhetorical exercise, a misty intellectual algebra!

For this reason it fares little better with the sociological criticism represented by Hennequin, and in a modified and milder dose by Leslie Stephen:

" If we allow ourselves," says the latter, " to contemplate a philosophical history, which shall deal with the causes of events and aim at exhibiting the evolution of human society . . . we should also see that the history of literature would be a subordinate element of the whole structure. The political, social, ecclesiastical, and economical factors, and their complex actions and reactions, would all have to be taken into account, the literary historian would be concerned with the ideas that find utterance through the poet and philosopher, and with the constitution of the class which at any time forms the literary organ of society. The critic who deals with the individual work would find such knowledge necessary to a full appreciation of his subject; and conversely, the appreciation would in some degree help the labourer in other departments of history to understand the nature of the forces which are governing the social development. However far we may be from such a consummation and reluctant to indulge in the magniloquent language which it suggests, I imagine that a literary history is so far satisfactory as it takes the facts into consideration and regards literature, in the perhaps too pretentious phrase, as a particular function of the whole social organism."

In extension of the same principle Hennequin would transmogrify criticism to the following effect:

"A work of art," he says in *La Critique Scientifique*, "is a collection of æsthetic means and effects tending to excite emotions which have the following special signs: they are not immediately followed by action; they are formed of a maximum of excitation and a minimum of pain and pleasure; in short, they are disinterested and an end in themselves. A work of art is a collection of signs revealing the psychological constitution of its author; it is a collection of signs revealing the spirit of the admirers whom it expresses, whom it assimilates to its author, and whose disposition it modifies to some degree either because of its nature or species. Æsthopsychology is the science which, making use of the first of these definitions, develops from it the second, third, and fourth; which, starting out in this way, arrives at the analysis, then at the synthesis, then at the complete understanding of one of the two orders of great men, the great artist, and at a vaguer understanding of the vast social groups gathered around him by admiration and similarity. "

And further, if I may; it is so curious, and so symptomatic of a kind of modern mind:

" Æsthopsychology is, therefore, a science; it has an object, a method, results and problems. An æsthopsychological analysis is composed of three essential parts: an analysis of the components of a piece of work, namely, of that which it expresses and of the manner in which it does so; of a psychophysiological hypothesis which by means of the elements previously disengaged, constructs an image or representation of the consciousness of which they are the sign, and which establishes, if possible, the physiological in correlation with the psychological; and finally a third step in which the analyst, setting aside the insufficient theory of the race and *milieu,* which is exact only for primitive literary and social periods, and considering the work itself as a sign of those whom it pleases, while remembering that it is also a sign of its author, infers the former from the latter. "

To Hennequin's mind, therefore, and to some less extent to Leslie Stephen's also, literature is merely a form or mode of social expression, in which society, working through the individual author, records its own psychology at a particular moment or period of its history, so that criticism becomes a kind of *Volkspsychologie,* as the Germans call it, and the author himself a mere transmitter or mouthpiece. In measure, of course, the contention is correct. In some manner a book is undoubtedly the outcome of a certain society and may be explained to some degree in function of the society contemporaneous with it. Such was Taine's idea, which, narrow and inelastic as it was, was at least more liberal than the dogmas of most of his successors. At best, however, society is but the condition, and like all conditions, does not originate but influences. To say nothing of the merely empirical objection that it is often the author who is, in all seeming, the first to divine and rescue truth and is frequently obliged to impose himself upon his audience if he would be heard at all, so that he appears rather to form his public than to be formed by it — it is evident, in addition, that a work of literature in the strict sense of the word is something exceptional by its very nature. It is the difference — or as we still say, rather condescendingly, the genius — which gives the book its value. It is not the newspapers which constitute the literature of a period. Mere unison, what everybody is saying, as well as imitation, reproduction, repetition, fail to count. "There is nothing in the drama of Rotrou," says Brunetière, "which is not to be found in that of Corneille; if the work of the former did not exist, there would be nothing lacking to the history of our theatre . . . and that is why his tragi-comedies may interest a few of the curious, but have not a place in the history of French literature." Only the contribution, the distinctively personal vision, is of any permanent importance — and it is the work of permanent importance alone which is properly literature, since literature is obviously literature by virtue of its message to us who read it and not by virtue of its expression of local and temporal peculiarities. Pope is still poetry, not because he voices the ideals of Anne — it is just in as far as he follows the fashion of his day that he has been repudiated — but because he voices certain ideas that humanity would not willingly forego:

> " And sure, if aught below the seats divine
>   Can touch immortals, 'tis a soul like thine,
>   A soul supreme, in each hard instance tried,
>   Above all pain, all anger, and all pride,
>   The rage of power, the blast of public breath,
>   The lust of lucre, and the dread of death. "

It is sentiments like these, the sense of human dignity, that still constitute Pope a poet, not the *Dunciad*; while, on the other hand, Addison, the image of his time, is only less of a classic by that very fact.

Of this theory Paul Albert, himself one of its more unsystematic advocates, has such an amusingly inadvertent refutation that I can not refrain from quoting it. " Before all," he says of criticism, " the first thing to seek in a work is what makes its life, what is the soul of it. But how to discover this without replacing the work in the *milieu* where it was produced, without reconstructing the religious, social, and political life of the peoples who saw it born? It is because the work was in intimate harmony with the society for which it was made that it is thought beautiful." Very well. But in another moment, when brought face to face with the reality, how easily and unconsciously he relinquishes a contention untenable in fact! *A propos* of Molière he declares that "genuine art is a happy mixture of the particular and the general, of the real and the ideal. By many traits of detail Harpagon and Tartuffe properly belong to the seventeenth century; the total of their physiogonomy consists, however, of types of all times and all countries." Precisely so. That is the distinction to which the "sociologist" himself is finally driven between great literature and small — its relative persistency. It is still literature by its appeal for us who read it now, not by its appeal for those who read it in the past. Indisputably Sophocles is an Athenian as Shakespeare is an Elizabethan; and their plays are full of local and temporal allusions and insinuations that we nowadays find it difficult or even impossible to understand or detect — for it is extremely doubtful whether we ever see in the past, with all the assistance that scholarship can give, just what was seen by its contemporaries; so that if Sophocles and Shakespeare were nothing more than Athenian and Elizabethan, they would not be literature. While, on the other hand, it is more than probable, that we have come to admire them for many a quality which their own generation and, indeed, they themselves never suspected. For it is only as they yield a meaning or significance for posterity, as they assist their successors to a better comprehension of life, that they continue to be literature. They are literature only as they are explicable, not in terms of some other subject or interest, but immediately and for themselves, and as they have succeeded in surviving the society in which they arose, while their literary characteristics are those which remain when the peculiarities of such a society are abstracted. Even Taine himself is compelled in the end to grade the arts in accordance with the duration of the fashions which they commemorate. In a word, literature is literature by virtue of some exceptional and permanent significance; any discussion which fails to bring out this appeal or which, instead of bringing it out, substitutes other concerns, such as philology or evolution or psychology or sociology, is irrelevant from the point of view of criticism. I do not say that such a discussion may not be fruitful — that it may not assist us in understanding Sophocles' significance or Shakespeare's; but the main thing critically is that significance, and whatever is not concerned immediately with that significance, is not criticism.

In a sort, no doubt, the biographical criticism, so much affected by Sainte-Beuve, is in much the same case:

"In the range of criticism and literary history," so he expresses himself about it, "there is no reading, it seems to me, more entertaining, enjoyable, and at the same time instructive in every way, than good lives of great men; not shallow and dry biographies, scanty and yet pretentious notices, where the writer thinks only of shining and where every paragraph is pointed with an epigram. I mean broad, copious, even diffuse histories of a man and his works; biographies that enter into an author, produce him under all his different aspects, make him live, speak, move as he must have done in life; follow him into his home, into his domestic manners and customs, as far as possible; connect him on all sides with this earth, with real existence, those everyday habits on which great men depend no less than the rest of us; in short the actual foundation on which they stand, from which they rise to greater heights at times, and to which they fall back constantly."

To be sure, a study of the author's life comes nearer to the springs of his inspiration than does any of the other studies that I have mentioned. But all the same the impertinence, though more subtle, is still impertinence. In any case, what gives the writer his sole interest for criticism is his book. If he happens to be more remarkable as a character, he belongs on that side to history, not literature. Otherwise, the light by which he shines is reflected and has its source in his writing, where it may best be sought, not in his life. I am tempted even to say that a book which requires a knowledge of its maker for its enjoyment is necessarily of an inferior order. It is no particular recommendation that so much of Swift's work begins and ends with Swift. Even Goethe himself is open, in many instances, to the same reproach; to some extent he has allowed himself to become subdued to the tyranny of his own being. But then Goethe is by all odds a more significant figure as a human being than as an artist. An intimate acquaintance with the personal peculiarities and doings of authors is recognized, and correctly so, as the property of the special student rather than of the general or cultivated reader. There is felt to be something technical and professional about it. To think otherwise is to confound literature with life. The hero, the statesman — and the poet too, it may be — belong in part to the world, whose recorder and critic is the historian; the poem alone belongs to literature. And while it is well that the literary critic, zealous of every side-light, should know his man too, yet his task is largely a special one and requires an amount of scaffolding quite incommensurate with the size of his edifice when finished. And so it is — to put a term to my enormity at once — that there are times when in reading Sainte-Beuve I am filled with impatience at the frequent obtrusion of the writer's private preoccupations and the constant exhibition of the critic's workshop.

Nevertheless, I would not go to the other extreme, as many do, and because literature can not be wholly contained by an exact terminology, protest that criticism is nothing more than an account of the manner in which a book happens to strike us individually. In this view — the view of Anatole France and Walter Pater — the taste for literature is entirely an affair of personal liking; criticism is altogether capricious, illogical, and unreasonable — a story of adventure in a library; the only thing that can be said with certainty about a piece of writing is that we do or do not care for it. But not only is this impressionism as erroneous as any of the other conceptions of which I have spoken, it is, if anything, more vicious because it is more licentious and unprincipled. For even though literature is not amenable to scientific formulation, it does not follow by any means that criticism is wanton and unscrupulous.

Life, for instance, eludes as a whole the symmetrical categories of science for the reason that it belongs in large part to another order — to the moral, not to the physical order with which science deals. And yet the irreducible discriminations of the individual consciousness are subject after a fashion to principle though not to law — so much so that there is nothing more contemptuous than to call a man unprincipled. At all events, though our actions may be unprognosticable, we are able at least to give them some kind of consistency, to justify or excuse them on general considerations after the fact. But our impression of a book is, after all, only a portion of our mental life, as the book itself is of its author's, and is naturally constituted in the same manner as the rest of the experience to which it belongs. While literature, further, is a representation or more broadly a treatment of life as a whole and consists of the various conceptions or visions or interpretations, not of the life of a particular time or age exclusively, but of the life of humanity at large, including not merely its active or objective life — its manners, customs, and usages — but also its inner or conscious life — its thought, emotion, and reflection; and its author's merit is measured by the value which his view of these matters has for the race. Is his view of life conformable with moral experience, is it elevated and sustaining, does it help to free us from the tyranny of appearance and of the phenomenal, does it aid us to bear misfortune and prosperity, injustice and flattery, does it strengthen and confirm our spirit and save us from ourselves; then it is good literature and a permanent contribution to human culture. For however it may be with the physical world with which science undertakes to deal — whether its order be inherent or imputed; it has been necessary at all events for man to organize for himself the moral world, the world in which he lives the most. The knowledge of himself and of his proper aim and activity, the distinction between the human and the brute, the sense of a social nature, of principle and duty, of right and wrong, even the feeling for seemliness and beauty — all these acquirements have been the result of a long and uncertain development, the contribution of many hands. To be sure, there is confusion enough as it is. But these acquisitions of the human spirit, these partial dispersals of chaos, have been confirmed and perpetuated by literature, which, even if it has not created the moral illusion, has given it form and currency.

It is for this reason that any serious discussion of literature should have to do, first of all, with the conception of life included in the work — not with life alone, for literature is not life itself but its reflection in a consciousness essentially moral; and not the book alone, for the book is merely the record of a reflection — but with the relation between the two, or in other words, with the attitude of literature to life. Should this relation be broad and general, as in the case of an entire national literature like the Greek, or rather more restrictedly, of some large literary movement like German romanticism; then the criticism will be broad and general too and will aim to show the manner in which this national literature as a whole or this literary movement as a whole has confronted the problem of existence. Or the relation may be narrow and particular or even individual, as in the case of a single author like Shakespeare; and under these circumstances the criticism, adapting itself to the subject, will become individual too and will have to show what Shakespeare answered to the most pressing questions which life proposes.   Naturally, such a criticism will not expect of literature a replica or pastiche of actuality. It will look rather for the harmonious adjustments of the human spirit, the establishment of a rhythmic conscious order among the promiscuous elements of experience.   And in so doing, it will have no hesitation in calling in assistance from any department of investigation that is likely to throw a light upon the matter — whether physiological, psychological, sociological, or what not; though it will try to avoid mistaking such answers as it may get from these sources for answers to its principal inquiry.   And inasmuch as the life which is both the subject and object of literature, is neither scientific nor yet unprincipled but broadly moral; our criticism will be neither scientific nor impressionistic, but will consist in a free play of the intelligence just as life does.   It will be based on general principles, which, though elastic, are broader than the observation of a single case, and which are capable of being explained and justified, as our conduct is, rationally and intelligibly, if nothing more.

Now, if these considerations are just, though only in a limited and partial measure, it would seem to be high time that criticism were busying itself with the foundations of such a study — or were at least

establishing certain common grounds or postulates to which its conclusions might be referred with the effect of ending all critical divergencies or at least of justifying their existence.   In comparison with the age and the pretensions of the subject is it not astounding that there is yet so little substantial agreement with regard to the significance and rationale of the simplest literary phenomena?   To all appearance it is still impossible for any two critics to agree as to the proper relation in general of literature to life, as it is to appeal to any accepted canon by way of settling their disputes.   One opinion proceeds on the assumption that literature and life are or should be identical; another, that they are diverse, though without venturing to define the difference.   Of the former party, one assumes that it is the closeness of the imitation that makes literature; another, that it is the technical skill, the trick of style, the verbal coquetry of the rendering. Of a stanza of Browning's *Lover's Quarrel,* which retails the heroine's costumes, Mr. Chesterton observes that it " would almost serve as an order to a dressmaker and is therefore poetry," while a reviewer cites the remark as an amusing illustration of Mr. Chesterton's ignorance of the very nature of poetry.   But Mr. Chesterton is either right or wrong.   If he is wrong, there should be some way of bringing him to terms.   If he is right, there should be some way of silencing his detractors. It is scandalous that at this time of day a man may make any statement about the rudiments of literature without fear of shame or ridicule.   Is there another subject of consequence in which such recklessness would be tolerated, much more applauded as though it were an admired qualification in an authority?

And yet this is a problem which lies at the very roots of criticism; for how is it possible to determine the merits or even the character of a piece of work while the aim and intention of its existence are uncertain?   How can we form an opinion about a literary product before we know what literature in general ought to do — or at all events what it actually has done?   Nor is the problem insoluble, much as the factiousness of modern criticism may have embroiled it.   At least there ought to be comparatively little difficulty in stating it fairly, even though it may not be possible all at once to reconcile individual prejudices or preferences for one literary position rather than another.   Community of opinion in all such matters is, like every work of construction, an affair of slow and laborious cultivation.   Right reason gradually prevails; a canon finally develops. But it must be preceded by copious discussion, by a clear recognition and exhibition from every side of all the facts in their proper character.

THE TERMS CLASSIC AND ROMANTIC

IN THE "Postscript" to his *Appreciations* Walter Pater has undertaken, albeit rather light-heartedly, a task of the first importance. Not only does he pretend, like most modern critics, to distinguish literature in a loose and general way as classic and romantic, and to explain its most violent contrasts as the expression of an irreconcilable antinomy in human nature; he also proposes to examine the two parties to the dispute in hopes of determining their essential character and significance. As for the division itself, that is patent, he considers, on the very surface of literature in a stricter and more traditional tendency and a freer and more innovating or radical one. The poetry of Pope is very different from that of Shakespeare; the former is marked by an instinct of contraction, the latter by an instinct of expansion. And it is not difficult to see that every author, taken as the term of a similar comparison, is actuated by one impulse or the other. Racine, to be sure, is not very much like Pope; but as contrasted with Calderon, he evidently practises a severer and more formal art, he is more restrained and forbearing. While in the same way that one writer is less exuberant than another and assumes a more reserved attitude toward life, so too one literature or one period of literature will evince the same disposition more strikingly than some other literature or period. French as a whole has always been more cautious than English; while in English the age of Dryden was much more contained than that of Tennyson and Browning, and in French again the age of Louis XIV was one of reservation *par excellence*.

To be sure, such instances do not go very far or burrow very deep. It is true that the writers of modern times may be readily grouped into two classes as they have looked at life more directly and immediately and as they have looked at it through the medium of books and previous interpretation. At the same time, it is difficult — or rather, impossible — for any one to write nowadays without being conscious of his predecessors and without being seriously affected by their example. The ghosts of our ancestors haunt and coerce us; and almost imperceptibly we find ourselves yielding to their silent but persistent influence. It is we who are the ancients; and at first thought it would seem as though we were fatally bound over to authority by virtue of our historical position, in spite of the startling accumulation of new fact which works constantly to distract and dilate our minds, while the contrary appears the case with Æschylus and Sophocles — they had not to resist the tyranny of tradition, even though life might have been in itself less varied and clamorous for them than it is for us. At all events, they saw it as independently as Shakespeare and Calderon, and what they saw was equally perplexing and disquieting. And yet it is they who have come to be reckoned the representatives of literary conservatism.

But superficial as these examples may be and far as they are from touching bottom, they do at least serve to illustrate what is so much a matter of general consciousness that every modern critic of any competence has recognized it in whole or in part, under one name or another — ancient and modern, naïve and sentimental, objective and interesting, pure and ornate, expressive and suggestive, Apollonian and Dionysian — the existence, namely, of two distinct and contradictory views of the poet's function and its exercise, dividing the field of literature, regardless of minor irregular bickerings, into two opposed and irreconcilable camps, which have finally come by common usage to be distinguished, rather loosely if conveniently, as classic and romantic.

To the continued use of these current terms in such a broad and inclusive sense to denote a universal distinction, not as between an uncertain better and worse, but as between two more or less incommensurable literary denominations, there is at present one serious drawback. Like most handy and suggestive words which are not the peculiar property of some technical study these terms have been appropriated to so many partial and particular uses, to say nothing of their laxer and more popular employments, and have finally developed so many implications and associations that they have become a kind of intellectual stumbling-block and source of misunderstanding, not only in ordinary speech, but also in criticism. And as Pater, in spite of something like an implicit promise, has failed to disentangle the snarl of meanings in which they are now involved

— has been, indeed, like most critics, less interested in doing so than in adding another kink of his own, and setting out to clear up the confusion, has, if anything, further embroiled it; it may be excusable, under the circumstances, to attempt the task anew in the mere hope of dispelling a little of all this verbal perplexity and without the pretension to increase the number of definitions with which the subject is already encumbered.

I

DERIVATIVELY, classic signifies obviously enough that which forms a class or order; and hence as applied to literature, it comes to refer to any acknowledged model or example of excellence. In this broad and general acceptation, which may be designated for convenience as the popular meaning of the word, every literature has its own classics irrespectively — English, French, German, and Spanish, as well as Greek and Latin; and Shakespeare and Calderon are, without further reserves, as fairly classics as Sophocles and Virgil, although they differ so widely in spirit and method. And however the word may be applied, or in whatever connection it is used, it still raises, to the prejudice of romanticism, a faint but perceptible reminiscence of this primary notion of standard and pattern merit, as when Goethe remarks simply that classic is sound, romantic unsound literature.

In order to understand the secondary meaning of the term in literary usage it is necessary only to remember that modern literature is a flower of recent growth. Three hundred and fifty years ago there was little or nothing of it in existence. Or if there were standing a few of those great monuments which now loom so gigantic on our horizon, they were by no means the objects of deferential admiration and emulation which they have since become. To our earlier critics as to those of the Renaissance the standard, the class-forming writings were Latin and Greek. They were the classics, the paradigms of all expression. As such they have formed, until recent years, the basis of study in college and university, and have perpetuated this particular sense of the term so that still among students and scholars and even among the intelligent general public classic is used of Greek and Latin literature as much as of anything. Whence this may not be improperly styled the academic acceptation of the word.

But the conception undergoes a further change. By a natural abstraction the same term comes to be applied, not merely to Greek and Latin literature in particular, but to the spirit in general illustrated in these literatures. It refers, not only to Sophocles' tragedy and Virgil's epic, but also to such qualities, wherever found, as are characteristic of these works — notably an extreme susceptibility to the moral significance of the subject, resulting externally in a sense for order, balance, moderation, measure, and the like — in short, to a certain easily recognizable manner of conceiving and rendering life. For these general characters, as disassociated from any particular age or race, *classic* becomes a handy designation and may be appropriated to any writer or group of writers so marked, no matter what the period or language. In this, which may be labelled the critical sense of the word, it has become permissible to say in a general way that Pope and Addison in English, Racine and Voltaire in French, and Goethe in German are all classic, because they display more or less consistently certain peculiarities which find their clearest expression in Greek and Latin. And it is permissible also to add that French literature is, on the whole, more classic than English or German, because it has made so much more of these qualities. And it is permissible even to speak of Shakespeare himself as classic in some respects and of Goethe as sometimes classic and sometimes not according as either seems animated by this spirit or another. And finally it may be said that a given period or a given school is classic as it is remarkable for such a disposition, like the age of Anne in English or Louis XIV in French.

Of course, it is a misrepresentation, though not an uncommon one among romanticists, to speak as though Pope and Goethe and Racine were classic because they imitated the Greeks or the Romans, or even because they wrote something like them. That is not the idea. A writer is classic, not because he writes like some one else, but because he writes in a certain spirit, because he maintains a certain attitude toward life. Whenever this spirit makes itself apparent in an author or a period or a litera-ture, there we have a classic author or period or literature. To be sure, the writings in which this spirit attains its purest and most perfect expression belong to the past — as do Shakespeare and Calderon for that matter; though the romanticists have not been slow to emphasize this suggestion of age and decrepitude, to which the word so easily lends itself, as an offset to the notion of standard perfection implicit in its popular use. Properly, the classical character is intermittent; it is neither archaic nor obsolete, but reappears at every revival of the great tradition of culture, though since the French Revolution it has ceased to influence any important portion of our civilization. And further, since every modern classic has looked to Greek originals or their Latin reflections for encouragement or inspiration, it is the modern habit to speak as though imitation and conventionality were invariable principles of classicism. Such an imputation, however, belongs to the word only in certain of its narrower and more controversial definitions. The classicism of Dryden and Pope was undoubtedly imitative and conventional pretty nearly by definition; so were almost all the romantic recommencements, which threw back to Shakespeare much more impudently than the classicists to Sophocles or Euripides. It is infinitely amusing to find Stendhal reproving his countrymen for their slavish imitation of Racine and exhorting them in the same breath to mimic Shakespeare. After all, imitation and convention are partly unfortunate effects of chronological position and generic decadence, and do not affect the essential nature of either party; for I suppose that it will be readily conceded that Shakespeare and Sophocles are as original the one as the other, while Calderon illustrates the process of con-

ventional petrifaction as convincingly as Dryden or
Pope, if not more so.

To distinguish a little more carefully, therefore,
the assumption of the term by those who have undertaken of set purpose to imitate or reproduce the
models of Greek or Latin literature or what they
have regarded as the essential qualities of these literatures or of classicism in general, must be considered as a kind of misappropriation. In this use
the word is identical with what is more properly
known as pseudo-classicism and covers not only such
tragedy as Ponsard's and Delavigne's but much of
Voltaire's also. Undoubtedly, an excess or abuse
or misapplication or falsification of classicism, inclining to dryness, rigidity, and stultification, were
to be viewed as pseudo-classic in a close discrimination. In any case, these deviations of classicism
have their pendant in the various schools of romanticism, each of which has insisted in a somewhat similar fashion upon some one set of romantic characters
to the exclusion of others and has given in this way a
particular turn to the romantic spirit. At the same
time there is always something romantic in every romantic school. They are both estuaries of their respective oceans. And bad as pseudo-classicism may
sometimes be, it contains at worst a little classic
leaven, as the romantic schools at best are always
infected with the general romantic virus.

The word *romantic* has suffered a series of vicissitudes even more bewildering than those of *classic*.
Popularly it designates whatever succeeds in com-
bining with a certain charm or fascination the un-

usual, the irregular, the striking, and the exceptional. In the first instance, it seems to have derived this popular significance from its association with the corrupt dialects of the Latin and the vernaculars which grew out of them, in exact parallelism with the modern philological use of romance. Any writing composed in one of these vernaculars would be romantic in distinction from a composition in classic Latin. But from the very character of these " romances " with their lax sense of moral reality and their vagrancy of imagination the adjective comes to cover the abstract qualities so embodied, as in the popular use of the word; while on the other hand, it would naturally be transferred to any writing or group of writings which might cultivate such a general manner or propose to imitate or revive the spirit of these productions. Such is A. W. Schlegel's account of the matter: " By the word *romantic, romance,* were designated the new dialects which arose from the mixture of Latin with the tongues of the German conquerors — hence the compositions written therein were called romances; whence is derived the term *romantic*, and the character of this poetry consists in the amalgamation of old German with the later or christianized Roman, so that its elements are already indicated by its names." In such fashion the name was assumed by the romantic school in Germany, which aimed more or less deliberately at a resuscitation of mediævalism — or better, perhaps, at a substitution of national antiquity and tradition for a foreign and humanistic one — as well as by those of France and England — if England may be said properly to have had a romantic school — which had their eyes to some extent on mediæval subjects if not on mediæval ideals.

And still further, on the strength of a similar etymology, the German romanticists, under the leadership of Friedrich Schlegel, tried to make out an affiliation between romanticism and romance in the later sense, *Roman,* and to establish the more romantic forms of the novel, itself the putative successor of the " romance," as the type and pattern of romantic literature. " And so," in the words of A. W. Schlegel, " the romance [*Roman*] . . . stands foremost in the newer poetry — a *genre* which is capable of representing the whole thereof. We shall see that the great modern dramatists — yes, the entire form of our drama, must be judged on the principle of the romance." Nor is the relation solely a fanciful one, if the attention is fixed on what we now call romance as distinguished from novel, which has been sobered and " classicized " to a great extent by the influence of the drama, something as the rough comedy of the Greeks was chastened by the example of their tragedy.

On the other hand, the French critics have come to consider that the perfecting of their classic tragedy consisted in the retrenchment of romantic elements and a consequent separation from romance with which it was at first entangled. To speak exactly, then, and with the double shading of the word *romance* in mind, there is, as a matter of fact, only one tragedy, the French itself and the Greek, which arrived at the same result in another way. All other tragedy contains a greater or less admixture of romance, in the shape at least of epical,

" chronicle," or " heroic " elements. To be sure,
the dramatic *genre,* even at its loosest appears in
itself more classical, by virtue of its superior organization, than does narrative or " story " of any kind,
as is evident from a comparison of *As You Like It*
with Lodge's *Rosalind,* or of *Julius Cæsar* with
North's *Plutarch,* or even of Fielding's comedies
with his *Tom Jones.* But still irregular tragedy —
or for that matter romantic drama as a whole —
represents a relatively undifferentiated form.   In
Shakespeare and Calderon, for example, the essential character of chronicle and heroic poem is often
so obtrusive that it can not be overlooked, even
with the best will in the world, not only in scenario
but in movement and plot, to say nothing of theme.
Indeed, in Calderon the play is regularly nothing
more than a romance cut up into lengths for the
stage; while this is exactly the direction of Shakespeare's decadence in *The Winter's Tale* and *Cym-
beline,* which like our current dramatized novels have
lost again the sense of a partly achieved distinction
and relapsed into an imperfectly differentiated rudi-
ment. In this way tragedy and romance become the
typical *genres* of classic and romantic literature, re-
spectively, and serve by their varying proportions to
indicate the prevalence of one spirit or the other.

Such, then, is what may be called the controversial
significance of the term *romantic;* for in some or all
of these meanings it has been used by the promoters
of certain programmes, to whose efforts, particularly
those of the Germans, is due much of the confusion
with which the word is covered. Such programmes
find their counterpart in special classic movements

like that of Dryden and that especially against which Lessing raised the banner of revolt. The point is that they are all aberrations as well of the romantic as of the classic spirit. In spite of the similarity of the name, the work and the significance of these schools are quite different. And since in the case of romanticism in particular each has used the term irresponsibly to clothe its own notions, there has resulted a bewildering and contradictory set of associations connected with a single word.

On the whole, however, it has always been the disposition, if not the immediate purpose, of a movement of this kind to break with the great tradition of human culture and to reassert the merely national and popular extraction. Indeed, with A. W. Schlegel *eigentümlich* and romantic are synonyms. And as the tradition of culture originates with Greece and as the purely national and popular genealogy has its roots in mediævalism, romanticism as an eccentric movement comes sooner or later to appear as the opponent of humanism and a restorer of barbarism. Such a performance is strikingly illustrated in the *volte face* of Friederich Schlegel, who began as a classicist and Grecian and ended as a mediævalist and Roman Catholic. In the case of German romanticism as a whole this attempt to revive mediævalism was from an early date comparatively self-conscious and perverse, and resulted in a certain carelessness of the permanent acquirements of human culture and a discontent with the real basis of human sanity, which was as dangerous as it was un-Greek. Though in France, on the other hand, romanticism has always preserved a specious air of relative sanity and moderation — it is necessary only to contrast the comparative lucidity of Rousseau with the turgidity of the Schlegels to see the difference — I doubt whether its influence has been any less mischievous. And while both schools may be considered dead as such, they have infected the literature and criticism of posterity to such an extent that they are still the most active elements of our intellectual life to-day.

Indeed, it is just this insidiousness which makes the danger of a vigorous romantic propaganda — the encouragement it gives to the barbaric and chaotic elements latent in every civilization — the vagueness, disorder, and turbidity into which humanity is liable to relapse but of which the Greek was the most obstinate enemy that has ever existed. As a matter of fact, every interruption or suspension of his culture has been followed by a romantic upheaval. I need hardly mention mediævalism itself; I need only take the most formidable shock which culture has suffered since the Renaissance — the French Revolution, succeeded as it was by the romantic agitation of Europe. Nor does it require very keen eyes to see that we ourselves are menaced by three apparitions which look like so many *revenants* of the three great institutions of the Middle Ages and which are in fact nothing but the three great rivals of humanism whatever form they may happen to take from time to time. In the first place our incipient socialism is a kind of transmogrified feudalism, a reincarnation of the principle that the individual exists for the state rather than the state for the individual; for it is indifferent after all what kind of tyrant we serve, king or demos, whether we build great communistic cathedrals or railway stations. Our technicality, too, or specialism, with its distrust of the free intelligence and its reduction of every interest, even history and literary criticism, to the exercise of rigid methodism, is only another manifestation of the spirit which once expressed itself in scholasticism. And finally our religiosity as exemplified in spiritism of one kind and another, what is it but a survival of the mortal superstition which formerly found sanctuary in the mediæval church with its myriad hagiology and wonder-mongering? If there were to be to-day a serious outbreak of romantic fervour, it is these elements that we should find vigorously exploited and glorified as we do find them feebly and ineffectually celebrated in our present feeble and ineffectual literature.

But however this may be, it is clear that these several romantic schools agree in one respect — in their opposition to classicism of any kind, so that the name becomes still further generalized, particularly under the criticism of the Schlegels, to include any work of literature or any writer who is opposed to classicism, just as the romance languages are contrasted with classic Latin, either by temperament or on principle. Hence, if classic be supposed to resume the spirit illustrated by ancient literature, then romantic will embrace all that literature which has grown up in independence or in ignorance or in defiance or in neglect of that spirit. In some such fashion, the word comes finally by one détour and another to denote the antithesis of classic and to imply another disposition of spirit altogether. Such

is what I should like to call the critical significance
of the word. A susceptibility to irregular beauty,
a fondness for the striking and the unusual even at
the expense of regularity and order, a preference
for fascinating detail above symmetry and proportion, a predilection for the coruscations of style —
for the glittering word and phrase, for the exotic
and exquisite epithet, for everything that touches
and thrills and dazzles, a hunger for sensation, even
when these desires lead to a dissipation of the attention — such are its external qualities as far as it is
profitable to analyse them at present.

II

FINALLY, then, if the various side-issues and incidental associations raised by the words be
disregarded, classic and romantic in their broadest
and most fundamental usage, that which I have ventured to call the critical, are seen to involve the
recognition of a single great split or cleavage affecting in a general way the whole body of literature
and dividing it into two factions or parties. Whatever confusion, ambiguity, or vagueness may be
noticeable in their special or narrower attributions
or in their conflicting suggestions and implications,
they still testify to the underlying consciousness of
an irreducible opposition of poetic temper and attitude into which all differences of literary conception
and manner finally resolve and which is illustrated
most clearly at its extremes in a comparison of
Greek and modern literature and their representa-

tive authors and *genres,* Sophocles and Shakespeare, tragedy and romance.

With the bare recognition of the fact, however, unanimity ceases. As far as it is seen to imply a principle of literary classification and discrimination, the authority of criticism has been exerted, on the whole, for the greater part of a century, to trouble and obscure the clear perception of its real character and significance. In spite of the bankruptcy of the school, it is amazing how much of its present capital criticism owes to the German romanticists without even seeming to be aware of the character of the debt or even the circumstance of the obligation. In the words of a German man of letters, " the history of literature can sum up its judgment of the Schlegel brothers by saying that they are the parents of modern criticism." And yet what could be more preposterous to an independent mind unswayed by a traditional superstition than the monstrous inversion by which the literary successor of mediævalism has been made to appear a representative of infinite and illimitable ideals, the literature of the idea *par excellence,* in contrast with the narrow and soulless perfection of the Greeks, whom Renan calmly declares to have been utterly destitute of moral seriousness? And since many of the gravest errors of the movement have succeeded in perpetuating themselves in this way, piecemeal and disguised, as they never could have done naked and integrally, it may not be amiss to consider briefly what new elements of confusion have been introduced into the case by the critic who has posed it systematically and *à parti pris,* from the romantic point of view, as an organic law of artistic development, and whose conclusions, modified and transformed to suit a later spirit, still serve as the basis of most of our critical distinctions   I mean Hegel.

Of all these confusions one of the most insidious, to which is due in great part the current identification of art and literature — or more exactly, the arbitrary discrimination against every variety and process of literature which fails to conform to the misleading analogy of the fine arts, together with all the vexatious corollaries which have been deduced therefrom — lies at the very roots of Hegel's theory and is assumed in his initial definition.   According to the terms of that definition the essential character of art — of poetry and literature no less than of sculpture and painting — is form.   Not that Hegel fails to recognize that no piece of writing offers a sensible presentment in the same precise corporeal manner as a statue or a painting — but his notion is, just the same, that the author is bound to be as concrete and plastic in the realization of the idea as the sculptor, who is obliged actually to materialize it under a substantial figure with definite members and features set in a particular pose and expression.   In itself language does not suffice to substantiate the idea artistically any more than the stone of the sculptor; they are both but the rude unfashioned material, the stocks and stones and blocks out of which is constructed the tenement that finally lodges the idea.   It is only as they are used in this way to fix the idea in a particular shape in which the idea is implicated that they come to assume a formal artistic significance.   In the one case the form is evoked, in the other it is represented; but it is equally important in both — so much so that in literature as in sculpture the absence of intermediate image is conclusive evidence of want of art. By definition, therefore, it becomes impossible for literature to express its ideas immediately in words — it is no such simple and popular confusion of literary form with style into which Hegel falls; on the contrary, they must be submitted to a kind of preliminary projection before their final reduction to language, so that when they eventually reach us it is as the result of a double precipitation, the one verbal, the other figurative. Such a conception, it is interesting to notice in passing, tallies with Schlegel's doctrine of poetry as a *zweite Potenz* — imagination to the second power — the effect of language being squared, as it were, with that of this secondary exponent. Any writing in which the idea is not masked in this particular manner, is not art; in Hegelian phraseology it is only a case of the absolute becoming self-conscious.

From this definition of the essential character of art it results, not only that idea and image are inseparable, but that the relation between them affords a means for its discrimination historically and absolutely. In this way arise three stages or classes. In the earliest and lowest of all, which Hegel calls not very happily symbolic, the idea is overpowered by the matter with which it is invested. The peculiarity consists, not so much in the excess of bodily substance, as in the grossness of its organization. Either the inspiration is too dull thoroughly to fuse the materials through which it seeks to manifest itself, or else the cast is so rude and clumsy that it hardly seems to be informed by any idea at all. Of course, in literature the statement must be understood, not merely of the verbal composition, but of the sensuous suggestion, the spectre of reality raised by the artistic use of language, as in a laboured and impenetrable analogy like the second part of *Faust*. Of such art in general architecture absolutely and Egyptian architecture relatively are the types; for every art, while it represents, as compared with others, some one kind or class exclusively, one being superior to another, has yet its own historical evolution and does also in its several stages illustrate all three, so conforming to the cyclic or corkscrew scheme affected by the German romanticists. In this hierarchy of art, then, architecture occupies the lowest rank. In proportion to its bulk its significance is contemptible. For its size and outlay it expresses less and expresses that little less clearly than any other art whatever, while it is in Egyptian architecture that this sense of obstruction and obscurity is at its strongest. Something it does seem to suggest — some presentiment of dark and riddling fatality, but suffocating under an incubus of meaningless masonry. In such a case, indeed, it is impossible to speak of expression in any proper meaning of the word. The production is not really expressive at all; it acts at best as a kind of sign, a hieroglyph, or in Hegel's words, a symbol of the idea. And as there is an almost ludicrous incongruity between the sign and what it signifies, like a child's drawing of reality, the effect of such an art is inevitably grotesque.

The second or classical order or degree of art arises when the idea and the form are in some sort of equilibrium. There must be a perfectly clear conception and a thoroughly adequate realization so that neither the physical nor the spiritual is in excess of the other. On the one hand, such art does not attempt to express more than its materials are capable of rendering; and on the other hand, these materials are thoroughly informed and animated by the thought. Sculpture is the generic example, with its substantial but shapely proportions, its limited but sufficient import. In music, in painting, even in literature there is felt to be a want of firmness and solidity, a deficiency of body, in the media of expression. But in sculpture, and more specifically in Greek sculpture, which Hegel looks upon as the formal perfection at once of the *genre* and of art as a whole, the idea itself is just suited to corporeal representation; while the stone, though saturated with the idea, is still capable of holding it in suspension like a clear transparent solution. Evidently art like this, illustrated relatively for literature by Greek tragedy, which critics still persist absurdly enough in comparing with a frieze or a bas-relief, supposes a double adaptation, not only of image to idea, but also of idea to image. It is the result of a felicitous compromise between spirit and matter — an inglorious concession, Hegel seems to think, on the part of the former. Spiritualize the conception never so little and the marble is no longer able to do it justice. The harmony of the statue is impaired; you have one of those gnarled and gristly colossi of Michelangelo's, part seraph, part prize-fighter, agonizing tempestuously in a paroxysm of thwarted aspiration. Or the medium changes; your Apollo becomes a cramped ascetic languishing ineffectually on a strip of painted canvas. In any case, the integrity of the association is destroyed; the soul has hopelessly outgrown its physical habitation; and the result is a new manner or development of art, the romantic, which Hegel designates as distinctively supreme and modern.

It is not only that modern life is fuller and more varied than was ancient, it is also more profound and mysterious. On the one hand, the mere spectacle and outward show of things, which constitutes the subject of artistic representation, is vaster and more bewildering than ever; on the other hand, the problems it suggests, which supply the artistic theme or motif, are infinitely more baffling and inscrutable. We are no longer concerned exclusively with the present visible world of the ancients; we have become rummagers of the past, *antiquitatis perscrutatores,* and peepers upon the future. To our properly human cares and anxieties we have added the world to come, the life everlasting. Small wonder that our minds have grown over-curious, refined, and subtle; that our spirits are perturbed and troubled. Under these circumstances, the artist finds himself in the presence of an accumulation of experience, emotion, conjecture, and speculation so prodigious that it is impossible for him to reduce it to any definite and palpable form of being. Since he can apprehend it himself only darkly and furtively, as it were by indirect vision, so he can communicate it only by way of suggestion or similitude. Hence the need of a more ethereal, a less earthly medium, like painting or music, or a more tenuous *genre*, like lyric poetry, for the characteristic manifestations of romantic art.

Such is, in outline, Hegel's classification and philosphy of art; or more narrowly and relevantly, such is his contribution to the definition of classic and romantic. Nor is it difficult to see, even from this hasty sketch, why the *Æsthetics* should have made its critical fortune. At its touch matters diverse and disparate seem to draw together and coalesce and take on meaning as though by enchantment; the illusion of method is complete. In this wise it appears to account for the sense of ease and satisfaction and finality in Greek art; for the feeling of lack, the longing and nostalgia of modern art— and to do so in the most agreeable and flattering manner by ascribing the perfection of the former to a mere nicety of technical adaptation while condoning the very incapacity of the latter as a trifling physical infirmity significant only of excessive soulfulness. In such manner, it takes advantage of an easy confusion between evolution and development, and assumes the latest of an historical series for the greatest, regardless of the fact that decadence is as much a term of the vital series as gestation. How seriously such an oversight has affected Hegel's general conclusions I am not prepared to say. To criticize his theory as a whole would not only lead me too far afield, it would be beyond my powers. I would notice only in the application to literature one or two errors which still continue for all their gravity to perpetuate themselves in contemporary criticism.

In the first place, Hegel assumes that art and literature have to do with the same sort of ideas. He takes it for granted that the idea of a picture, a sonata, and a book are all of a single denomination. But not only is such an assumption absurd, it also introduces into literature an arbitrary and artificial distinction by confusing its manner or method too with that of art. Not only is it evident on the face of it that neither a painting nor a sonata expresses the same order of ideas as a book, but it is evident that neither expresses its proper idea in the same manner — if indeed a painting or a sonata can be said to express an idea at all. To believe otherwise is to leave one kind of literature out of account altogether. On such a supposition only that kind of writing in which the idea is disguised in concrete circumstance in such a way as to lose resemblance to itself and become fixed in the mind under some particular physical aspect, belongs to art. All writing, on the contrary, which attempts to give an account of its ideas without the assistance of such an intermediary, is not art; it is the resolution of art. To speak exactly, then, literature, in as far as it is art, would exist in the first instance, not for the expression of ideas at all, but for the evocation of images. Such a hard and fast distinction drawn straight through the body of literature I for one can not admit. I can not group the drama, the epic, the novel on one side of such an imaginary line; and the essay, criticism, history, oratory, it may be, on the other. Without further reason I can not applaud Thackeray when he narrates and condemn him when he reflects. I can not reserve my admiration solely for the figure and my contempt for the *mot propre*. It would be better to withdraw literature from under the wing of art altogether — nor is the name of such favourable literary augury these days that any serious-minded critic should stickle for it — for literature is all of a piece and indivisible by virtue of the exact identity of its materials and its intention.

And here again, though it amounts to much the same thing in the end, Hegel fails to make a second vital distinction. The materials of the artist — the stone of the sculptor, the colours of the painter, the notes of the musician — are not naturally suitable for the communication of ideas. In themselves they are not properly expressive. They serve only as the groundwork of a physical contrivance in which some sort of idea is at best implicit and which serves to suggest the idea vaguely and uncertainly — or rather, certain of its circumstantial characteristics. It is almost as though the idea were accidental, or at least incidental, in art — so much so that many modern artists, notably writers so styled like Gautier and Maupassant, have denied its existence altogether.

But the function of language, on the contrary, is precisely the immediate identification and definition of ideas. Its significance resides solely in expression. Hence the curious transfer whereby the term has come to mean in literature, not the purport or sense of a certain detail of execution as in the fine arts, but the phrase itself. As a result, literature is explicit by its very constitution. To be in character it is bound to be intellectual. When it ceases to be so, it becomes inferior or worthless. Even emotion must be rationalized if it is to agree with the structure of language. In short, literature is quite another thing than art, not only in method but in spirit. It does not live, as painting and sculpture do, in the world of physical forms at all, but incorporeally and in the idea. And consequently, it is only by a kind of license that it can be said to exist, as is so often glibly repeated, for the creation of the beautiful. Since it is deprived of anything like substantial figure or material contour, the epithet *beautiful* has no exact and literal meaning when applied to it. In a strict use of terms an idea is neither beautiful nor ugly; it is true or false. Or if it is beautiful in any sense, it is so only in an applied and secondary one by the fineness of its truth. While as for poetry, though I hope I appreciate its sensuous charms as much as any man, yet they are at best but ancillary to the thought and even in themselves, again, are beautiful, not in a precise definition, but merely figuratively and by way of a trope. Such is the mischief that results from the attempt to convert an innocent manner of speaking into a hard and fast formula that many have unthinkingly accepted as a scientific specification what has but an approximate and descriptive value, to the detriment of the whole conception and theory of poetry. The manner of literature, like its matter, is proper to itself; it has attractions of its own comparable after a fashion with those of music, with whose general movement and development it corresponds much more closely than with

painting or sculpture, but by no means identical with
them even in that limited sense which makes perfection of style an art or beauty, as well as an end,
in itself.

As a matter of fact, what Hegel has done, is virtually to raise a prejudice against all literature which
is expressive rather than suggestive — that is to say,
which is not romantic. Since art is incapable of
conveying an idea except indirectly and by means
of an image, it is a natural inference that a perfectly
clear and explicit literature, inasmuch as it is inartis-
tic, is in some degree inferior. And this impression
is deepened by a recognition of the following corollaries of the theory.

Since romantic art is characterized by a disparity
between conception and expression, it must approach
in effect the first and most primitive manner of art,
the symbolic. To be sure, Hegel implies that the
one is over-spiritualized, while the other is under-
spiritualized. But his classification is based entirely
upon the relation of form to idea; and both cases
are marked equally by a disproportion between the
two. To all intents and purposes, the result is the
same; both are imperfect art. And since in the one
case as in the other the realization is hardly more
than a sign of the idea, a hierogylph more or less
arbitrary and inadequate, a mere intimation rather
than an indication, romantic art is essentially as
symbolic as its predecessor. Such a consequence,
indeed, Schleiermacher makes no bones about accepting, though with a slight distinction — it is
hardly a difference — in defining romantic art as
allegorical — a definition which Heine adopts and

elaborates, after his own fashion, in his *Romantische Schule,* though his approval has by no means the force of a concession. And finally, in consequence of the discrepancy between the idea and its expression there arises in both instances the same sense of almost ludicrous incongruity, the " grotesque," which Hegel himself remarked in " symbolic " art and which Hugo in his preface to *Cromwell* recognized as a note of romantic art too — a declaration which Schlegel had in a manner anticipated with his " transcendental irony."   Hence, thanks to a question-begging definition, the highest manifestation of literature, by force of being romantic, becomes identified with a kind of writing originally symbolic or allegorical in character, in which the idea tends to shrink farther and farther behind the material incident and circumstance with which it is at first incorporated, until it virtually disappears altogether.

From these considerations it would seem as though Hegel must have divined the character of romanticism very imperfectly — at least in its relation to literature. In particular, he has failed to detect the circumstance — perhaps he was too unfavourably situated to do so both from the literary and the historical point of view — that this romanticism which he has celebrated as a literature of boundless aspiration, is characterized in principle by an almost slavish subservience to sense.   And yet his system logically contains the whole formula of *l'art pour l'art* and of " naturalism."   The insistence upon the value of form, upon the sensuous garniture of the idea, is sufficient to motive the former movement;

while the indifference to clearness of expression in comparison with the importance he attaches to concrete and objective realization — or rather, materialization —seems to make it inevitable that what was at first a mere medium or vehicle for the transmission of thought, should gradually lose its ulterior significance, like a painted window with the light gone out of it, and become an end in itself, like any other opaque and impervious surface. So it is pertinent to observe that the French " neo-romanticists " — Gautier, Flaubert, the Goncourts — though but sectaries and representative only of a local and limited romanticism, were virtually realists — however they might resent the imputation — at the same time that they professed to be " artists " exclusively and preoccupied solely with " form." From them to the " naturalists " was but half a step, as is indicated by their intimacy and sympathy with Zola, who at once riotously impressionistic and meticulously documentary seems to unite the two extremes of the movement in his own person. In short, it is towards actuality that the current of romanticism, in its main waters as in its several branches, steadily sets. In principle, the romanticists have always found their affair, not exactly in representing things as they are, but in reproducing the sense of headiness and intoxication, the giddiness and *Rausch* with which the excitable spirit of the poet is affected in the immediate presence of life — rather than in fathoming its significance and rationalizing its apparent inconsequences. Or more accurately, they have pretended to find this significance in the sensations proper to existence. Hence the characteristic

suggestiveness, the romantic " wonder," generated
by the imitation of nature and explicable by the absence of definite intellectual content, as a shadowy
corner looks the more mysterious the emptier it is.

This connection between romanticism and what
we are accustomed to call by another name and to
think of erroneously as something quite different, is
expressed by the Spanish critic and scholar, Menen-
dez y Pelayo, himself a romanticist by the fatal im-
pulsion of blood and nationality, in so clear and final
a fashion that it would be mere pedantry not to
quote him *literatim:*

" At the bottom of every first-rate work of art there is,
in our opinion, a multitude of ideas which have never
perhaps crossed the mind of the poet in their abstract
and general expression, but which actually underlie the
concrete and palpable forms of his work, as they underlie
life itself, of which every dramatic work worthy of the
name is an idealized transcript. And the richer and more
complete the reality reflected in the work of art, so much
the greater is the number of ideas which, thanks to it, are
revealed and made manifest to the eyes of the readers."

Precisely. In spite of the deceptive solidity of its
pretensions naturalism so-called is only a variant of
romanticism — romanticism on all fours, if you like,
but still romanticism. Minor differences aside, they
concur essentially in asserting the substantial identity of literature and life. To the one as to the other
the cardinal virtue of art is to lend itself, like nature,
to an unlimited variety of interpretations in pre-
senting a surface which produces virtually the same
order of sensations and involves the same order of

ideas. The rest is merely a matter of relative emphasis. If the interpretation seems transcendental to the romanticist and scientific to the naturalist, it does so because the significance is indefinite, as a cloud may resemble anything as long as its figure remains undefined.

Candidly, it can hardly be said that Hegel himself blinks this kinship altogether, whatever derivative criticism may do; he divines it, to be sure, but very imperfectly. " In the representation of sensible forms," he observes, " art is no longer afraid to take to her bosom reality with all its imperfections. Beauty has ceased to be indispensable; the ugly has come to occupy a prominent place in her creations." But though this formula seems, after the event, to provide for the contingency, it is doubtful whether he himself would have been prepared at the time to open his arms to such a portentous apparition as Zola; for the point is, he fails to conceive of romanticism in any but its more local and secular manifestations. To its broader aspect as a characteristic product of modernism, the summation of a series in which " naturalism " is but a single term, he is pretty well blinded. If anything, he appears to regard the research of actuality as a symptom of romantic decline and is disposed to terminate the movement, whose very being is the cult of sensation, at the moment when it begins to come of age and declare itself for what it is.

On the whole, then, temerarious as it may seem to say so, the greatest objection to which Hegel's conclusions — or rather, the criticism which derives from them is liable from the point of view of liter-

ature, is superficiality. And indeed, in treating literature substantially as an affair of form on the
same footing with the arts he himself is not guiltless
of confounding the essential with the incidental. In
such arts as painting and sculpture it is hardly going
too far to say that it is the form which solicits the
idea; in literature, on the contrary, it is the idea
which appropriates the form. In art, that is to say,
the idea is accessory — and even then it is mainly an
idea about form and material; while in literature it
is paramount and principal, the form merely receives
and contains it. Literature, then, as far as it is true
to itself and its own character, is not so much concerned to image life as to commemorate some idea
about it — or in other words to interpret it. Hence
any satisfactory classification of the subject must
proceed, not from form or yet from the relation
between form and idea, but solely from the ideas
which alone give significance to its interpretations.

Now, as a matter of fact, the interpretations of
classic and romantic literature seem in a broad
and general way to be informed by two distinct ideas
or conceptions of life. To the former life is at
bottom an illustration of moral principles, whose
main interest is human and rational. To the latter,
as far as it illustrates anything at all, its interest is
" natural " and " scientific "; it is an illustration of
physical law. From the literary point of view life
has always presented itself to the romanticist as
a subject of powerful if impermanent sensations, a
spectacle of inexhaustible variety and brilliancy,
capable of an indefinite amount of emotional stimulation. It is so to Zola and Tolstoï as truly as to

Victor Hugo and Shakespeare. As far as their re-
ports yield any clear and consistent idea of it, they
yield only such an idea as is proper to actuality itself
— an idea of " natural " or mechanical congruity.
In other words, while the classicist found his motive
of literary order in the integrity of the human spirit,
the modern seeks for his in the uniformity of nature.

To Sophocles, for instance, the course of human
events would seem to have been regulated exclusively in accordance with some abstract principle of
absolute justice, which provided automatically for
the correction or suppression of the offender in proportion to the gravity and danger of his guilt. An
offence once committed, it was as impossible for the
offender to evade the moral responsibility by plead-
ing the purity of his intentions as to escape the
physical consequences; indeed, they were one and
the same. The act itself was sufficient to imperil the
moral order, as a civil crime is now felt to imperil
our social order; and it was visited accordingly upon
the transgressor, not with the discretion of a human
arrest but with the same relentlessness and impassi-
bility as what we speak of loosely nowadays as an
infringement of " natural " law. Indeed, Sophocles'
providence or fate or whatever it may be called, appears in its workings singularly like our " nature "
save that it is thoroughly and inherently moral and
relevant, for to such a conception there was naturally no accident. Character as such had no more
to do with the one law than it has to do with the
other; the child who holds his hand to the fire is
sacrificed as inevitably as Antigone, no matter how
amiable his disposition. Man was all of a piece;

what he was and did, was as much a part of him
as what he purposed. Happiness was, therefore, a
moral issue; success, an evidence as a result of
virtue.

Naturally such a position is no longer tenable.
With the modern notion of physical causation consequences have become in themselves morally irrelevant. Guilt or innocence is but an imputation.
What happens is merely a term in a mechanical
series and without moral significance of any kind.
Let the statue of Mitys fall upon the murderer's
head as it may, it will never quicken our conscience
a jot. When the religious man like Nicias goes to
the wall, we conclude only that he has failed to
hit things off somehow and we call him superstitious
for his pains; his piety is beside the mark. Such
a philosophy, however, if logically enforced, as it
is in science, is felt to be fantastically superficial;
it fails to satisfy the heart, it is dramatically impossible. In spite of such prepossessing names as
" utilitarianism " and " Nietzscheism," the effort to
dissolve humanity in nature has had but a partial
success as yet; and where it has most succeeded,
literature has most suffered. On the whole, the serious drama has attempted to save the moral issue by
a kind of compromise in transferring human responsibility from act to intention. Hence the tragedy
of character. But even in this view happiness is
nothing more than a clever adjustment to " environ-
ment " and illustrates nothing one way or another
— except Darwinism. The unscrupulous may succeed; there is no power interested in frustrating
them — indeed, they are more likely to do so than

not, they are the least handicapped. And so, as a matter of fact, they do in Shakespeare's historical plays, where he was unable to tamper with his materials. On the other hand, the scrupulous may go to the ground, as in a drama of the general type of *Hamlet*. From this dilemma, again, tragedy tries to extricate itself with greater and greater difficulty. We still have moral prejudices and we occasionally withdraw our situation from the domain of nature to that of conscience. We like to show occasionally that the villainous arithmetician may bungle his calculations like Iago. Or after all, like Claudius, he may not be so prosperous as he looks. But then, unless we do violence to our logic of nature — as Shakespeare is not always averse to doing when he can and as there is always great temptation to do — such a man's unhappiness must be subjective and so more or less unfit for dramatic exhibition. And so from all these compromises and concessions there results a kind of fundamental inconsistency and insincerity about our serious romantic drama — it is not tragedy at all, but a nondescript; for tragedy is impossible without an unflinching moral vision. The sole relief is to save our sympathy for the virtuous but unhandy hero and his cause and to cover his adversary with contumely. The resolution is purely human, it is a kind of *argumentum ad hominem;* there is no vestige of divinity about it.

But such speculations are premature. They only illustrate in the persistent *genre* of drama the two different conceptions of life and its significance which determine romantic and classic literature.

That this difference of idea may have occasional differences of form in the only sense in which the word has any meaning for literature — that is, of style and structure — I am far from denying. But the latter sort of difference is merely a secondary characteristic.

The principal and primary matter is the difference of view. And in the determination of this essential difference modern criticism, riddled as it is with the misconceptions and misrepresentations of romanticism, gives us little assistance. And yet with this uncertainty fastened upon it, without a clear understanding of the character of the fundamental interpretations which literature undertakes, how shall criticism hope to arrive at any final conclusion on any subject? Indeed, this is the reason that all our criticism is so uncertain, groping, and tentative the moment it abandons pure description and undertakes to deal with anything larger than an isolated phenomenon, a mere biographical or philological detail; it lacks the elementary generalization, the basis of classification.

For these reasons I can not help thinking that one of the first requisites for a sound criticism in the future is a general rectification of values founded upon an examination of the ideas at the bottom of Greek and modern literature — not a squabble over classicism and romanticism in the narrower and sectarian sense of the words, but a comparison of the two dispositions of spirit illustrated by the two orders of literature as a whole. In a single breath, what we need is a fundamental literary criticism which shall differ from philology and history in

being a criticism of principles and from æsthetics
in devoting itself to the peculiarities of literature
as distinct from the fine arts — that is to say, as a
medium of ideas.   And in this task it seems as
though comparative literature might find its most
useful occupation at the present time.   I can not
believe that it is by a confrontation of verbal or
conceptual borrowings, or by a juxtaposition of haphazard parallelisms, much less by a nosing of recondite analogies through a maze of barren dialects in
which a flower of poetry never bloomed, that comparative literature is going to quicken our gratitude
or justify its high pretensions.   But rather, it is by
the definition of certain universal ideas and principles which are appreciable only by contrast, much
as our sensation is itself a matter of variety.   And
not only is the task I have ventured to propose of
such a sort — not only is it in itself a worthy and
desirable work — but it is also one well worthy of
the breadth, the learning, and the disinterestedness
to which comparative literature lays claim.

Such a task is hardly to be accomplished or even
undertaken by a single writer or all at once.   But
it may be performed little by little and by many
hands.   Every critic who attempts, however small
his scope, to exhibit the vital connection between
literature and life, who eschews mere formal and
verbal eristic to elicit his author's ideas, who keeps
a sure hold on reality and illustrates his subjects by
his experience, who judges not by caprice or convention but by principle — such a critic is contri-
buting his share to the making of such a criticism.

GERMAN ROMANTICISM

Welch ein Unfug! Welch Geschrei!
FAUST

THE German romantic movement was the result of defective culture, of bodily and mental derangement, of spiritual and nervous disorder. It is a work of degeneration, deformation, and disease. And it bears on its front the stigmata of its infirmities — absurdity, folly, inanity, and confusion. There is Hardenberg, the pattern of the school, who falls in love with a chit of thirteen and at her death a year or so later dedicates himself to the grave, an unblemished sacrifice of love, unblighted by sickness, violence, or sorrow, the cheerful victim of his own regret. In the meanwhile he begins a new era and dates his note-books from the epoch of her decease. By the end of the following twelvemonth, however, he has sufficiently vaporized his emotions in various scribblings to choose another bride and is reduced to " faking " metaphysical nonsense to pass off an infidelity which would never have been cast up against him but for his extravagant protestations. Sophie and Julie are two, such is his magic arithmetic, only in the land of phenomena; in the land of fulfillment, where all differences are reconciled, they are but one. There again is Friedrich Schlegel, grubber of ideas for the whole party, proclaiming in sublime paradox that formlessness is the highest form of art; the fragment, the consummate *genre* of literature; the dissolution of poetic illusion, the signet of poetic genius. Prophet of transcendental buffoonery and irony, of *Freiheit* and *Willkür*, he has ended his days in the service of the two narrowest *Autoritätsprincipien* that ever were, Austrian imperialism and Roman Catholicism. There is Tieck too, after an education little better than an emotional and intellectual debauch, writing dramas backwards and demonstrating the identity of poetry and music by " transposing " notes into words:

" Die Farbe klingt, die Form ertönt."

There is Schleiermacher, the priest, the *Geistlicher* preaching free love and the " emancipation of woman," making himself, in Walzel's words, " the forerunner of the modern French novel," the gospel of lubricity and license. And finally there are poor Hölderlin and Wackenroder, the one crack-brained at thirty or thereabouts, the other fretted out at twenty-five between his duty and his inclinations. Nor are their friends and lovers much better. On the whole they are pretty much of a piece with Dorothea Veit, the daughter of Moses Mendelssohn, who deserts her husband and two children to run after Friedrich Schlegel, and Caroline Michaelis — Dame Lucifer, Schiller called her — Böhmer's widow, Gallic agitator, inmate of a German prison, mother of a nameless child, who accepts Friedrich's brother Wilhelm, as a *pis aller* and under his nose carries on a *liaison* with Schelling, for whom she finally leaves her husand.

I

BUT enough of personalities. The thoroughly significant thing about German romanticism as a litterary phenomenon is its sterility. It has almost no works, literally next to nothing to show for itself in the way of literature. A little vapid verse, two or three staggering dramas, a few rickety *Märchen* and twaddling rhapsodies, several dilapidated novels, or rather romances, to sustain the claims of a school that pretended to derive from the *Roman* — this is just about all its literary capital, the greater part of it unreadable, inexpressibly childish, silly, and dull. In itself it were all equally harmless, though for different reasons, because all equally ineffectual. If there is something almost disarming about the naïveté which could seriously busy itself with a performance like *Heinrich von Ofterdingen,* the preposterous crudity and flatulence of a *Sternbald* is no less disabling. Both were alike negligible, had it not been for the impudence of their exploiters. Indeed, as a general thing the illustrators of the movement were not in the first instance responsible; they were merely " let in " for it. In its inception the school consisted virtually of a pair of doctrinaires and theorists — Wilhelm Schlegel, dilettante and eclectic, and his brother, Friedrich, pedant and *mauvais tête* — who attempted to create a criticism *a priori* and who, impotent to illustrate it themselves, were forced to have recourse to what they were able to pick up elsewhere. After a fashion it resembled those institutions which are universities in name but

in fact are nothing but examining boards. It criti-
cized the productions of others, and if pleased there-
with, graduated them romantic. It lived on foreign
conquest and annexation, and made capital of the
fruit of other men's labours. In such wise it cannily
took possession of Tieck, who was at bottom an
independent man of letters, a free lance, even a
journalist in the sense that with him literature was
before all a business and a livelihood. In a word
Tieck was too much of a Dryden to be a romanticist
by vocation. The significant thing about him is that
he outgrew his romanticism, which in his case was
only a malady of adolescence, a distemper or kind
of green sickness. It was merely one of his manners
and no more permanent or final than that which
marked his period of " enlightenment."

In particular, however, romanticism found its
most advantageous affair in the inadvertencies and
indiscretions of acknowledged genius. So it laid
hands upon certain work of Schiller's and Goethe's,
and insisted upon making them romantic leaders in
spite of their protests. To be sure, Goethe was in
some sense romantic and not wholly irresponsible
for many of the positions his name was used to
cover. But the capital fact of his life, after all, was
his conversion from romanticism, even after his own
kind, which was at worst of quite another complex-
ion than that of the School's. What importance he
himself attached to this change of colours, is shown
by the circumstance that he is constantly preoccupied with it during the. latter part of his life — end-
lessly affirming, explaining, justifying, and comment-
ing it. Unfortunately, however, for a just perception

of the facts it is the romantic Goethe with whom we are better acquainted, partly on account of the currency which he himself has given his earlier years in *Dichtung und Wahrheit* and partly on account of the assiduity with which the romanticists have continued painting his portrait after their own likeness. But for all the seduction of his youth and the apotheosis it has received, the significance of his manhood, of his intellectual being, should not be overlooked — and that was irreconcilably at odds with the romantic error.

And yet it must be acknowleded in the same breath that whatever his principles, Goethe was always inclined to coquette with romanticism more than was good for him. Personally I fail to see much choice, as literature, between the second part of *Faust* and Tieck's *Prinz Zerbino*. As a system of philosophy, metaphysics, or *Symbolik* the former may be vastly superior; that is a question to be decided by those who understand it. But at all events it was by no means difficult for the romanticists to find in him excuse or precedent for some of their worst follies. So it was in particular with the gigantic egotism which underlay their pretensions to artistic vocation. There is something almost *bête* in the complacency and open-mouthed stupefaction with which Goethe — and even Schiller, who had less reason for it — contemplate their own productions, as though they were some great and inevitable work of nature, to say nothing of the exaggerated respect which they have for their own occupation. And while perhaps the frequent fatuity of the romanticists was less innocent as it was less excusable, they might have pointed to this common trait among others as a plausible evidence of kinship.

Nevertheless, the lesson to be drawn from the careers of Goethe and Tieck as a whole is perfectly obvious. The notions of the Romantic School are, in the most favourable interpretation, those of youth and immaturity; it is impossible for any sane man to grow old, not to say ripe, in them. Their very begetters abandoned them in later life — or rather, the other way about, their ideas abandoned them, and they went out one after another like draughty candles. Even the two Schlegels became, the one a functionary of authority and tradition, the other a literary *cicisbeo* or factotum. In short, there is about romanticism nothing permanent or achieved. It is not a state of attainment in which it is possible to rest content, as Goethe rested in his classicism. It is not even a stage of development; it is a mood, an aberration of spirit, to which youth, together with periods of dissolution and transition, is particularly liable.

No wonder, then, that the existence of German romanticism was parasitic; it lacked the constitution to live independently and relied upon other sources for its sustenance and support. Hence in part its mischievousness. It deranged the intellectual economy and impaired the moral health of the whole age and its posterity by disturbing the natural circulation of ideas and stimulating a set of abnormal and artificial appetites and reactions. The ideas which it appropriated, the work which it approved, were seldom their authors' best or sanest. To be sure, there was at the time little enough that was excellent to choose from; still of what there was, it failed to take the best. Or if by any chance it did, the reasons for its choice, as well as the use it made of its selections, were anything but judicious. Naturally, its acquisitions were exceptional and accidental when considered with reference to the entire work of the author from whom they were extracted; and since they formed no *ensemble* of themselves, they were frequently inconsistent and incongruous one with another. In this way arose endless difficulties — multiplied explanations, reconciliations, compromises, adjustments, extenuations — and in general an impression of confusion and inconsequence about the whole ingeniously tessellated fabric. This is the explanation too of that inextricable mixture of truth and falsehood in the romantic doctrine by which so much that is erroneous has succeeded in passing current in the past until our criticism and appreciation are honeycombed with it and by which the wariest critic is liable to be disconcerted still.

Upon this confusion it was inevitable that the intellectual sterility peculiar to the movement should react disastrously. As a matter of fact, the two characters are hardly separable, and it would be difficult to say whether the romantic confusion is a result of literary impotence or *vice versa*. It is merely a case of action and reaction. Inasmuch as its promoters had few ideas of their own, they were thriftily disposed to make these ideas go as far as possible by applying them to all sorts of subjects indiscriminately. So Friedrich Schlegel transferred to current criticism the principles he had originally derived from the study of Greek. He judges *Wil-*

helm Meister by the same criteria as the *Iliad* and the *Odyssey* and arrives, as might be expected, at an insanely jumbled estimate of both. Nor did the school, under his able tuition and that of his brother, proceed otherwise with such general subjects as art, nature, religion, and philosophy, as though to justify Schleiermacher's saying, " *Es gehört zu dem sich noch immer weiter bildenden Gegensatz der neuen Zeit gegen die alte, dass nirgend mehr einer eines ist, sondern jeder alles.*" So little sense had they of the just measure that they seldom touched an idea without spraining it. They broke up wholes into parts and erected parts into wholes. They isolated single factors and treated them as complete in themselves. They mistook means for ends and ends for means. They added and subtracted unlike denominations to make a desired product. They slurred distinctions and ignored resemblances. They invented such hybrids as the " religion of art " and the " religion of nature," terms which they took literally, not metaphorically. " Any man is a priest," says Schleiermacher, " who under a form original and complete has developed in himself, to the point of virtuosity, the faculty of feeling in any mode of representation." With Schelling they turned poetry into philosophy and with Novalis they turned religion into poetry. For the latter, indeed, the gospels derive their authority chiefly from the fact that they have to do with the dissolution of a spell (*Verzauberung*) and hence resemble a *Märchen* or fairy tale, the favourite romantic *genre*. In a word, confusion — chaos they themselves define as the romantic element — is, with futility, the constant char-

acter of the movement, and our present universal
deformation of ideas is but an heirloom of the School.

Capital, in particular, for its critical temper is
the crass eclecticism with which it sought to run
the arts together, into a kind of indiscriminate medley, without regard for their natural differences of
aim, effect, material, and method. With the phenomenon itself we are only too well acquainted nowadays, when our critics are still discoursing as though
the *Laokoön* had never been written, while our poets
are industriously creating pastels in prose and symphonies in verse, to say nothing of the painter's
marvels in tone and the musician's miracles of colour.
But appalling as it is to observe how quickly a distinction once achieved may be totally obliterated,
it is not we in this case who are the first offenders.
Friedrich Schlegel, Novalis, Tieck, and " many more
whose names on earth are dark " — they are all
with one accord for the promiscuity of art. " Hence
it is desirable to bring the arts together again and
to seek transitions from one to the others. In this
wise statues may rouse into paintings, paintings
become poems, poems music, and who knows what
noble church music will mount once more like a
temple into the air! " So the elder Schlegel; and
to much the same effect Novalis: " In general it
is impossible for the poets to learn enough from the
musicians and painters. . . . They should be more
poetic and as who should say more musical and
picturesque." While the younger Schlegel in his
own very best manner raises distraction to its highest power: " Romantic poetry is a progressive universal poetry. Its mission is not merely to unite all

the separate varieties of poetry and to reconcile poetry with philosophy and rhetoric; it will and must also now blend, now fuse poetry and prose, genius and criticism, art-poetry and nature-poetry." As for Tieck, it must be acknowledged, he is by no means so universal a spirit; he is merely an advocate for the poetry of music and the music of poetry: " What! is it not permissible to think in tones and to make music in words and thoughts? "

In all these quotations, it should be noticed, the word poetry has come to have a meaning so vague, shifty, and ambiguous as to be incapable of supporting any conclusion — or what amounts to the same thing, as to be capable of supporting any conclusion whatever, an advantage which Wilhelm Schlegel finally pushes home in his Berlin lectures on *belles lettres* and art by substituting the term " poetics " for the " theory of art " (*Kunstlehre*) in general.

All this has a very familiar ring. It is quite in our own way — so much so as to seem rather trite and hardly worth consideration save for the sake of its genealogy. But then, which of the romanticists' errors is likely to appear novel in the eyes of their heirs? At the same time, I may be pardoned in the interests of completeness for calling attention to still another obsession and that the most striking and significant of all. I mean that which at bottom a disciple of Freud's might be disposed to think responsible for the whole romantic neurosis. To be sure, there is ever a disposition at periods of ecstatic agitation to confound love erotic with love charitable. But in this instance the symptom is particularly important because what seems to result from a study of the romantic doctrine of passion, is the suspicion that a great part of the disorder of the school was the result of nothing more or less than sexual unrest. The manner in which this sensual ground of uneasiness appears and reappears at frequent intervals, like a shoal under ruffled water, is startling. How much of Novalis' piety is due to the loss of his Sophie it is hard to say; but its kind or quality is unmistakable — it bears the marks of a thwarted or perverted desire, a momentary vacancy of the senses. In his own words, " the exaltation of the beloved object to a divinity is applied religion." And equally characteristic of the confusion between Eros and Charity is the jotting in his note-book, " *Christus und Sophie.*" But it is Schleiermacher in his *Reden über die Religion* who puts the official and theological seal upon this notion that " *die Lösung aller Rätsel im Geheimnis der Liebe liege* ":—

" For him who stands alone the all exists in vain, for in order to take up into himself the life of the Universal Spirit (*Weltgeist*) and to have religion, man must first have discovered mankind, and that he finds only in love and through love. For this reason are the two things so intimately joined; longing for love, ever fulfilled and ever renewed, comes at once to constitute for him religion. . . . Therefore religion withdraws into the still more confidential intercourse of friendship and the dialogue of love, wherein face and figure are plainer than words and even a sacred silence is intelligible."

With these tenets it is hardly astonishing that the promoters of the movement should be, on the whole, so little edifying in their relations with the sex. One and all they were dominated not by women but by woman. The gallantry of Wilhelm Schlegel is notorious. For the riotousness of Friedrich his *Lucinde* is sufficient evidence, not to mention his early letters to his brother. But why multiply examples? The lubricity of *Ardinghello* seems to have awakened a response in every one of them, even Tieck. And not only this, which might be paralleled in more robust natures; but about all their love affairs there is invariably something morbid and uncanny. Caroline was eleven years older than Schelling; she was thirty-five and he was twenty-four, when he first fell in love with her. Sophie von Kühn was a mere child of twelve or thirteen when betrothed to Hardenberg. I have already spoken of Wilhelm Schlegel's inglorious conquest of Böhmer's widow after her experience in Mainz and her political incarceration. He seems to have borne with exemplary equanimity her infatuation for Schelling, which took place under his very nose, and to have accommodated himself to the *liaison* with a complaisance in no wise short of ignominious. Even after Dorothea's divorce from Veit Friedrich Schlegel insists upon keeping up the irregularity of their relationship as long as possible in sheer delight apparently in his own depravity. Characteristic too is the well-known passage of his *Lucinde* in celebration of the transposition of the masculine and feminine *rôles* in love. Schleiermacher himself must needs fall in love with a married woman to begin with and finally marry the widow of a friend. But something too much of this. Touched as lightly as may be, such matters are unpleasant to the English genius; were they stressed according to their actual importance for romantic psychology, they would be offensive.

II

In itself, therefore, with all its borrowings and ascriptions, its errors and confusions, its lack of literary integrity and moral consistency, German romanticism was something wholly factitious and affected. It could be kept alive only by successive stimulation and galvanization. Hence its cravings for nostrums of all kinds — literary, philosophical, scientific, theological, and mystical. Hypochondriac as it was, it had tried all the doctors in turn — Herder, Schiller, Goethe, Kant, Fichte, Schelling — only to abandon them sooner or later for quacks like Böhme, Baader, and Ritter. By its very nature it was condemned to be forced and excessive, or lose its *raison d'être* altogether. Like a wrong headed disputant, it must keep itself in countenance by abounding obstinately in its own bad sense and relying upon the violence and the extravagence of its asseverations. In order to justify its own existence it had no alternative but to browbeat truth and brazen out its own absurdity. For this reason it was always refining, subtilizing, alembicating its own dicta, until it became involved in issueless mazes of paradox and hyperbole.

As a matter of course the folly and perversity to which it was conditioned by its mode of existence had their roots in the bosom of its founders and their desperate determination to shark themselves up a celebrity, whether or no, by bolstering out their own character to heroic proportions. To this circumstance is due very largely the notion of genius as of something akin to delirium and madness which reigns to-day — or at least divides unequally the honours with the older conception of well-balanced, though exceptional, power. This modern idea of an irresponsible, insensate fatality — *" une force qui va,"* in Hugo's favourite phrase — an impulse at once spasmodic and irresistible, a sort of throe or convulsion of nature, may be taken with due allowance as a self-characterization of the romanticists. It was the deification of their own character; and in delineating their heroes they have but portrayed themselves, for their " art," such as it was, had nothing impersonal or dramatic about it. Life was a gigantic mirror in which they saw their own figures a thousand times repeated and of colossal dimensions. *" Mich führt alles in mich selbst zurück,"* confesses Novalis. Or if it failed to admit their pretensions to magnitude, they shut their eyes to it and denied its competence altogether:

> " Ich komme nur mir selbst entgegen
> In einer leeren Wüstenei."

As a matter of fact they all had been spoiled in the nursery, and spoiled children most of them remained all their lives. The work with which they won a hearing was almost uniformly unfit for publication; in France it would never have got into print at all. It was only the abject poverty of German letters at the time which allowed them to pose as writers, and precocious one at that. Tieck's origins are incredibly crude and mawkish. Friedrich Schlegel's first critical efforts are execrably written and composed, and reek of intellectual coxcombry and pretension. Novalis is jejune and silly. The best of them all is Wilhelm Schlegel, and he is commonplace and foppish. But finding themselves indulged in their whimsicalities and mannerisms, and flattered by their ability to dumbfound the respectable Philistine, the Nicolais' and other *Aufklärer* of the day, they had no incentive to correct themselves and clarify the ferment of their youth. And particularly so, since there was no authority capable of impressing or overawing them. For a graphic picture of the spiritual conditions at the time as they appeared even to the romanticists themselves, whose very element was confusion, I can do no better than quote Schleiermacher:

" It is a time," he says, " when nothing human remains unshaken; when every one sees just that which determines his place in the world and secures him to the earthly order, on the point not only of escaping him and falling into another's possession, but even of perishing in the universal maelstrom; when some not only spare no exertion of their own powers but also call for help on every side in order to keep fast what they consider the axes of the world and of society, of art and of science, which are by an indescribable fatality upheaving as though of themselves from their deepest foundations and are leaving to destruction what has revolved about them for so long; when others with restless impetuosity are busy in clearing away the ruins of fallen centuries in order to be among the first to settle upon the fruitful soil which is forming underneath out of the rapidly cooling lava from the frightful volcano; when every one, even without leaving his own place, is so greatly agitated by the violent convulsions of the universe that amid the general vertigo he must needs rejoice to see a single object steadily enough to hold by it and gradually be able to persuade himself that there is something still standing."

Amid the universal trepidation Goethe and Schiller alone exercised some sort of steadying influence. But even Goethe and Schiller, as I have already remarked, were not invariably level-headed. And by the time the youngsters might have profited by their better example the mischief was done; they were confirmed in their folly to the point of resenting criticism and admonition. They quarrelled with Schiller and even with Goethe, and consorted only with those like-minded with themselves, " *Brüder im Geiste*." From their early corruption, therefore, they never recovered. If they were not thwart and perverse from the start, they soon became so under the process of deliberate self-cockering and mutual admiration which was the breath of their life.

Psychologically, their leading motive was egotism. From this one characteristic it would be possible to derive pretty nearly their whole activity. " *Das Ich soll sein*." The self was their favourite, their exclusive pursuit; *Selbst-beobachtung*, their darling study. It is with utter rapture that Schleiermacher describes the glorious moment when he first discovered his I, unique and unmatchable — like Childe Roland's dark tower, " without a counterpart in the whole world " — and recognized it for the foundation of all morality and religion. Eminently representative too is the letter written to her husband by Rahel Varnhagen, their disciple, when the cholera was raging in Berlin: " What I want is a death of my own. I won't die of an epidemic like a blade of grass in a field, parched by malaria among its companions. I will die alone of my own disease — that's the kind of woman I am."

As a result the whole history of their ideas is individual; it is a part of their biography, not of the history of thought. In this sense it is almost physiological, like their figures or their faces. In spite of the liberty about which they were always prating, they lay themselves under the very worst of tyrannies — the tyranny of self. Their intellectual and moral life was as completely subdued to the accidents of their own persons as was their digestion or bodily health. Their mental and ethical tone was as exposed to the weaknesses and disorders of their own temperaments and as helpless before them as was their physical tone to the weaknesses and disorders of their constitutions. Tieck had romanticism just as he had rheumatism — as passively and as unintentionally — however much he may have brooded over it when he once came down with it. So it was that they never succeeded in abstracting their thought — there is nothing universal or even general, impartial, and inevitable about their ideas.

In no respect, perhaps, is their egotism more strikingly shown than in their attitude towards literature and art in general. As *littérateurs,* ergo artists, at least in intention, they were so deeply immersed in their own profession as to be incapable of seeing

anything else. Not only was it the one serious concern of life, it was also the standard or norm of all
other concerns whatever. Even in Goethe the importance attached to æsthetics strikes us nowadays as
rather naïve, if not actually silly — at all events as
beside the mark. The kind of artistry which runs
through *Wilhelm Meister* as the sole preoccupation
of every character of any account and which indeed
is the one touchstone of character, is quite in the romantic vein and belongs to the same order of things
as the *Sternbaldisieren* with which Goethe himself
reproaches Tieck. But though Goethe may have
given a kind of currency to the idea, it was reserved
for the romanticists proper to complete the confusion
between art and morality, between the conception
of life as an accomplishment and as a duty. As for
so many other of our vices we are indebted to them
too for the disposition to " literatize " and " arti-
cize " life. Indeed, so far did they carry the practice, so impotent were they to think outside of their
own categories, so inflated with their own assumption that they must needs make existence a play and
God an artist also because they, forsooth, were themselves second-rate literary men. Even Schelling is
so carried away with the draught created by these
ideas as to place æsthetics above morals, to find the
consummation of philosophy in a work of art, and
to justify metaphysically the conception, which is
represented even by Schiller and Goethe, that the
only complete man is the poet — " *die Poesie das
Höchste und Letzte sei.*" Heaven forfend! What
a world this would be if all of us were artists! But
with this conception, at all events, the distinction

between philosophy and poetry, between art and life is wiped out at one stroke; and reality and fancy mingle in graceful phantasmagoria. "*Was wir Natur nennen ist ein Gedicht, das in geheimer, wunderbarer Schrift verschlossen liegt.*"

Subdued as they were to the spell of their own being, they never discovered in all their aspirations after freedom that the only liberty is the liberty of self-restraint. They failed to perceive that life was constantly spreading its snares to involve them in a coil of fatal consequences, in a chain of determinations where their independence would be irretrievably lost and they themselves would become but creatures and slaves of circumstance. Friedrich Schlegel's *Lucinde* is to all intents and purposes a panegyric of sexual passion — or love, as he preferred to call it. Its thesis, as far as it can be said to have such a thing, consists with the conviction that the realization of liberty, of the infinite, *das Unendliche,* is possible through the unbridled gratification of this appetite alone. With pitiable shortsightedness he seems never to have reflected that the moment he yielded to his passions, he had become enmeshed in a network of influences over which he had no control whatever, that he had committed himself to the conditioned and given hostages to fortune. Only by an act of self-control and denial, only by standing aloof and refraining would it be possible to affirm his ego in withdrawing it from the consequences of its activity.

" Von der Gewalt, die alle Wesen bindet,
Befreit der Mensch sich, der sich überwindet."

But consequences was the last thing they thought of; they were totally devoid of discipline. And when they philosophized, they were merely trying to talk themselves into believing what they wished. Their freedom was the freedom to do as they liked; their liberty, the liberty to indulge their own caprices.

Whether the romanticists consciously recognized the discrepancy between their profession of liberty and their actual subjugation to self, it would be hard to say. In any case their whole dialectic was directed to the problem of reconciling just these two different notions; though it was only by a kind of sophistry, in invalidating the authority of achieved distinctions, that they succeeded in doing so. By obliterating the line of demarcation between the outer and the inner order and reducing the former to a tributary of the latter, by such means alone was it possible to make it appear as though the gratification of impulse, which makes man the slave of circumstance, was after all only a sort of self-determinism. It was for this reason that they welcomed with enthusiasm the philosophy of Fichte, which justified their existence in representing the universe as the creation of a glorified and transcendental ego. No doubt Fichteanism was in the air, and it was of these cobwebs that Fichte spun it. But it was as symptomatic of romanticism as acceptable to it.

For this reason their attitude toward nature becomes extremely interesting. It was to nature that they resorted in the first instance because her passivity had no embarrassments for their self-esteem.

They sought to her as they did to those of similar mind with themselves. With her they could be themselves, unrebuked and unabashed. They were rid of the clash of wills, of the constraint of human intercourse, of the elementary decency which compels even the most obstinate and wilful in society to have some small regard for the rights of others, if for no better reason than a fear of the unpleasant consequences which result from neglecting them. Before nature they could flaunt their own personality as arrogantly as they pleased. Above all, they might have of her the supreme satisfaction which the egotist finds in the conviction that his influence is irresistible; they could make her over in their own image so that she should bear their very seal and impress. That they never saw her as she is — passionless, irrational, meaningless, a pure illusion — is clear from their account of her. They saw her only as they were; they discovered in her only what they brought to her. It is after their example that we have learned to identify the moral and the natural world. Cramped as they were by their own limitations, they were incapable of conceiving another order distinct and remote from that with which their own consciousness acquainted them. Like Novalis they took nature to be the " systematic index or plan of our spirit " just as we ourselves are " *Analogien-quelle für das Weltall*." And in that consciousness of theirs they found little that was not sentimental. They had no principles, no criticism — hardly a purpose; they were moved by accident and caprice. Such is the sense of every word they wrote. Heinrich von Ofterdingen falls in love with Mathilde because he happens to feel, on seeing her, as he did in a dream on seeing the little blue flower. It is circumstance alone which determines them in one direction rather than another — circumstance and mood. And as they were themselves, so they thought of nature — as something equally moody, capricious, and passionate. *" Das grosse Weltgemüth "* Novalis calls her. It was a later and different turn of romantic thought which by an analogous error made her out a being essentially intellectual, while by an inevitable reversal of the original confusion it is man who has become a creature of nature's, a natural product, instead of nature's being an achievement of consciousness, a sentimental creation, a gigantic *Kunststück* or transcendental *tour de force* — or in Novalis' words, *" ein Universaltropus des Geistes."*

The *volte-face* is noteworthy. But after all, the two attitudes are only counterparts and are in reality so represented by Schelling, who finally gave a philosophical organization to all these indefinite ideas that were crossing in the air. " It is our view of nature," he says, "not that it accidentally coincides with the laws of consciousness . . . but that it necessarily and originally realizes as well as expresses those laws, and that it is nature and is called so only in as far as it does this." It follows that " the system of nature is at the same time the system of consciousness "; that " nature is visible mind and mind invisible nature." While, further, " nature thus appears as the counterpart of consciousness, which consciousness itself produces in order to return thereby to pure self-intuition or self-consciousness." "Hence in everything organic there is something symbolic, every plant bears some feature of the soul." And he ends by transferring the whole scheme of consciousness to external nature, using his metaphysical principles to fill in the gaps in the positive knowledge of the physical universe which existed in his day, exactly as Novalis advises in the *Lehrlinge zu Sais:* "The careful description of the history of this inner world of consciousness is the true history of nature; through the consistency of the world of thought in itself and its harmony with the universe is formed of itself a system of ideas for the accurate representation and formulation of the universe."

At this point the confusion has culminated in the complete identification of the law for man and the law for thing. Such is the fallacy of the romantic conception of nature past and present: with Schelling it offers man as the measure of nature or else with Renan it offers nature as the measure of man. How much clearer, or at least how much less prejudicial is the Greek idea of nature as of something in itself indifferent or inert, as a decoration or accessory of voluntary action or a machine which requires intelligence to move! It is responsible for the whole marvellous Greek mythology. Between the modern and his landscape there ever swims a haze — the fume of his own distempered imagination:

> " Die Wesen sind, weil wir sie dachten,
> Im trüben Shimmer liegt die Welt,
> Es fällt in ihre dunkeln Schachte
> Ein Schimmer, den wir mit uns brachten."

With Tieck he is like a man in a trance, a somnam-
bulist in a limbo between night and morning:

"It often happens that the world with all its tenants
and occasions reels before my eyes like a flimsy phantasmagoria. And I too seem but an accompanying phantom,
which comes and goes and comports itself amazingly
without knowing why. The streets look to me like rows
of mimic houses filled with silly occupants, who simulate
human beings; and the moonlight, shimmering pensively
on the pavements, is like a light that shines for other
objects and has fallen upon this wretched and ridiculous
world by chance alone."

In this particular, it must be confessed, the hands
of the romanticist were again strengthened by the
example of Goethe, in spite of his superior clarity
of vision and his sterner sense of actuality. For his
own part he was never able to conceive of nature,
in the passive sense otherwise than as a work of
art or in the active sense otherwise than as an artist,
for his pantheism involved the one with the other.
As such it must exhibit, on the one hand, the same
sort of design as any other artistic product, a poem
or a statue; at the same time it must proceed, on
the other hand, in accordance with certain ideas
similar to those which determined his own work.
His investigations of nature, therefore, consisted in
a series of attempts to explain that design by penetrating to the ideas behind it. In other words, the
universe was an artistic illusion, whose significance
resided in the motif which it realized — just as a
novel is an illusion whose only principle of coherence
resides in the author's conception. Practically,

therefore, since it was a mere mode of artistic expression, the problem was to find the animating and creative ideas which as artist it was trying to communicate. It never occurred to him that it might be nothing more than a mechanical what-not — a something which had fallen together and operated, not in virtue of a set of ideas, but in accordance with a set of formulæ, that it might be something in and for itself, independent of the consciousness and without reference to it. Hence Schiller's perfectly just objection to his *Ur-pflanz*, " that is an idea, not a fact.'" In short Goethe was, in reality, not scientific, but literary. While art begins by assuming that nature is an illusion, science begins by assuming that it is a reality. While the former endeavours to discover an idea that will give it significance; the latter endeavours to discover a formula which will express the manner in which it works. For this reason the mathematical theory of light was simple nonsense to Goethe. It was not an idea, a creative conception at all; it was a mere *modus operandi*. On the other hand, in those cases where our organization of the universe is nothing more than the interpretations of the human spirit — or in those sciences which consist largely in classification, which are little more than arrangements of data, in accordance with our own notions, and in which the generalizations are in a sense only categories of the human intelligence — in sciences like botany and biology he was quite at home. But even there, notwithstanding his profounder divination, he was virtually at one with the romanticists.

As a result of their exclusive and consistent egotism, when they came to write, they had naturally nothing to write about but themselves. That was all they knew, even if anything else had happened to interest them, as it seldom did. With one or two unimportant exceptions they had divorced themselves from all the active and practical concerns of existence. At the one end Tieck had disassociated poetry from life and reflection; at the other Schleiermacher had disassociated religion from virtue and morality — " everything with religion, nothing for it." Their forms were almost devoid of content — in short, the form was the content; hence the famous definition of transcendental poetry as the poetry of poetry and their curious doctrine of second powers or the multiplication of a subject into itself. The French Revolution alone of all the stirring historical movements that were eddying around them, seems to have roused them to a faint flutter of excitement — mainly because they saw a way to turn it over to the account of their own subjectivity. " The French Revolution, Fichte's *Theory of Knowledge,* and Goethe's *Meister,*" declares Friedrich Schlegel, " are the greatest tendencies of the century." In consequence, their own novels are all autobiographies, revamped and redated, but cribbed, cabined, and confined by the writers' own limited experience of themselves. It is so with *Sternbald* and *Heinrich von Ofterdingen,* with *Lucinde* and *Hyperion.* Indeed, this is Friedrich Schlegel's definition of the romance — an individual confession. And it is equally so even with their philosophies; of Schleiermacher's *Monologen* Haym remarks: " He talks as a man would do to his most intimate friend." In a word, all their writings are personalities and indiscretions.

It is only natural, therefore, that from the literary point of view their work should be as poverty-stricken as it is. But it was not only so, it was muddled too. As they were puppets of mood, without genuine character, all impressions were indifferent. Just as their criticism was destitute of principles, so their creative work, their *Dichtung,* was destitute of selection. What marked it most conspicuously was the raw eclecticism which is the note of romanticism everywhere — a seated contempt for the discrimination of a sane and disciplined taste. Hence a mishmash of motives, costumes, cults, civilizations — Hellenism and Mediævalism, Paganism and Christianity—jumbled together in inextricable medley. In this respect the elastic dream-economy of *Heinrich von Ofterdingen* is remarkable and amply justifies by its conveniency the *Märchen* or fairy story as the romantic type *par excellence.* All their *Dichtung* is essentially inchoate, as were the two products which served them as paradigms — Goethe's *Meister* and Tieck's *Genoveva.* And amid all this ferment and clutter only one distinctly discernible purpose — the desire of these young hotheads to reproduce the impressions made by life upon their feverish and excited imaginations.

III

EVIDENTLY, an existence of such unremitting self-exploitation must have been extremely fitful and spasmodic. It must have had its moments of exaltation, of reckless intoxication and *Rausch*. But these moments must have been succeeded by intervals of desperate reaction and disillusion. Hölderlin alone is sufficient proof of it. As a result of this emotional insecurity, no doubt, originated the doctrine of Transcendental Irony. The title, ostentatious as it is, covers nothing more than an attempt, on the part of Friedrich Schlegel in the first instance, to pass off one's mortification at one's failings and shortcomings by being the first to ridicule them when they were too conspicuous to escape general attention. It is a common enough shift in every walk of life for those who are embarrassed by the discrepancy between their pretensions and their performance to make a virtue of necessity, and by anticipating detraction and taking sides against themselves, to vindicate a kind of critical or intellectual superiority over their own practical activities. In such manner the romantic ego had at least the advantage of appearing to know better than it could do and of restoring its authority by a characteristically unprofessional intrusion or supervention upon its own work. Like Victor Hugo's theory of the grotesque the transcendental irony was a tacit confession of the writer's powerlessness to produce a perfectly congruous and satisfactory piece of work and an attempt to make a merit of the fact by erecting his weakness into a quality. In other words it was an effort to insure the romantic poet against the mediocrity of his own gifts. As Haym, who is usually so reserved in his strictures, remarks in another connection: " This is perhaps the most striking index of romantic poetry — that what is elsewhere an evidence of impotence and banality [*Unpoesie*] it construes as an indication of beauty and perfection."

From the point of view which has been gained at present it is impossible to mistake the nature of the transcendental conception of self engaged in these speculations — as of something distinct from all that is tangible, palpable, or in any way apprehensible or accountable. It is something quite noncommital and irresponsible. It is uncompromised by a man's actions; it is as evidently unprejudiced by his character; nor has it apparently any manifestations by which you can bring it to book. You can not corner it, try as you will. Whatever he is or does, no matter how *bête* or fatuous or futile he may be, the romanticist has only to reply to your censures: " Ah! you are quite mistaken; that is not I. See, I have quite as much contempt for that sort of thing as you have." Verily, it was a dabster at evasion, this transcendental self. In every instance it eludes you and by a like expedient. It " dematerializes " like a " spirit " under your very eyes and leaves you gaping foolishly at vacancy.

Upon morality the effect of such a doctrine was bound to be fatal. This retirement of the real man from his character and occupation, this moral absenteeism, provided a ready excuse for all sorts of irregularities, which could be represented as merely impertinent to the genuine self. By this means it was possible to excuse any atrocity as transcendentally irrelevant and indifferent. And as a matter of fact, the romanticist soon came to understand by morals nothing more than the uses of human nature in its laxest and most inclusive sense. The study of morality was the study of humanity; and it was a consequence of his eclecticism that he embraced in the term the animal as well as the spiritual, the earthly as well as the ethereal. And since the ponderable, if once admitted, is likely to weigh the heavier in the balance, it happened more often than not that his morality was, in the ordinary acceptation of the word, very immoral indeed. In fact, Schleiermacher makes no bones about proclaiming " the immorality of all morals." While further, as humanity is infinitely various, it will follow that there are as many moralities as there are human beings. It is again Schleiermacher who with great complacency makes the flattering discovery that the ego possesses a morality as unique as its individuality. Perhaps *Lucinde* is as good a map as we have of human nature after the romantic morality, where humanity is likely to display itself very much as it is. But alas for Schleiermacher, who went to the pains of defending it! it is not only a nasty book it is also a stupid one.

> " Der Pedantismus bat die Phantasie
> Um einen Kuss; sie wies ihn an die Sünde.
> Frech, ohne Kraft umarmt er die,
> Und sie genas von einem toten Kinde,
> Genannt Lucinde."

And its viciousness as well as its stupidity, like that of the school behind it, consists in its licentiousness, in the rejection of every principle of restraint or control. The conception of obligation as such seems never to have dawned upon this gentry. As Goethe said of the Schlegels, " Unhappily both brothers lack some sort of inner check to hold themselves together and keep them fast " (" *Leider mangelt es beiden Brüdern an einem gewissen innern Halt der sie zusammenhalte und festhalte* "). About their conduct there is always something shifty, unreliable, incalculable — it is subject to a kind of aberration which seems to withdraw it from the province of morals altogether and relegate it to that of whim, caprice, and haphazard. It hardly belongs with the rational and providential at all. It very nearly substantiates their own claim of identity with nature.

It is in this respect that German romanticism differs most strikingly from New England transcendentalism. The parallelism between the two is too close and obvious to be overlooked. To read Tieck is, in many cases, like reading Hawthorne translated into German, or *vice versa*. I am disconcerted by the similarity every time I reread them. Not only is there a resemblance of general tone and spirit between Hawthorne's sketches and such stories of Tieck's in particular as the *Blonde Eckbert* and the *Runenberg;* but there is also a resemblance of style and treatment, as is obvious from comparing the opening of *The Great Stone Face* with that of *Die Freunde* or *Die Elfen.* And so, likewise, with Novalis and Emerson there is in both the same characteristic sententious, fragmentary manner, the same

brachylogy.   And what is so amazing, is that the
scholars and literary historians would have us believe that there was no direct discipleship on the part
of the Yankees.   But however this may be, the
leading ideas of the two schools or movements were
much the same; their philosophy of life was, as a
philosophy, identical.   What New England transcendentalism amounted to in the end, as we have
had a chance to see in this generation, was, like German romanticism, the apotheosis of a purely ideal
and sentimental ego above character and conduct at
large, and the arbitrary elevation of the dicta of
this ego into a code of morality.

   To be sure, Emerson was himself a man of character and he assumed the ego to be possessed of
such character because he was.   But it was just the
weakness of Emersonianism that in its adoption by
others it was bound to take on the peculiarities of
those who adopted it — and they might have character, or more frequently, as it has turned out, they
might not.   In other words, there was nothing in
the original doctrine to guarantee or ensue character.
And it is on this account that transcendentalism has
again become the philosophy of an age and a country
in which the general level of moral action is conspicuously low.   It is just the philosophy for a race and
a generation with our notions of liberty and self-
interest — for a race and generation which wishes to
be free to defraud its neighbors in the morning and
boast of its moral elevation in the evening.   It
affords a sentimental refuge for self-esteem in any
emergency.   It enables us in the handiest way in
the world to redeem the baseness of our practice by

the nobility of our sentiments. No matter how low our behaviour, how contemptible our acts; our genuine self remains untouched. Herein lies the explanation of the curious anomalies of our civilization — our unscrupulous and oppressive money-getting on the one hand and our ostentatious and munificent benevolence on the other; our sordid living and our grandiose declamation — the morose might call it hypocrisy; we call it idealism.

To make Emerson and the romanticists responsible for all these consequences seems at first thought unfair. In his own case there is present one idea whose absence is thoroughly indicative of the German transcendentalists as well as of contemporary idealists. Emerson was still animated by a sense of duty. Whether it was a survival of his descent or an independent acquirement of his own, the consciousness of responsibility and guilt had not yet faded from his mind. Though this conception does not appear explicitly in his work, perhaps, it was implicit in his character. It is virtually taken for granted, even though it may never be mentioned; and it is in this particular that his utterances have an immeasurable superiority over those of the Germans. The transcendental idea of liberty had succeeded in retrenching the categorical imperative altogether. Liberty consisted in following your own bent. Whatever gave the self range and opportunity was moral. In short, morality was egotism. Into this error Emerson never slipped. But it must be remembered that it was romanticism pure and simple that he preached; and that in preaching it at all, he is justly accountable for the results.

In other respects Hinduism too offers an edifying contrast with transcendentalism. In one sense they were both systems of the ego. While the latter, however, is optimistic; the former, on the contrary, is pessimistic. It all lies in that. The note of romanticism is eclecticism — indifferency, promiscuity. The note of Buddhism is discrimination, distinction, reservation. What saves Buddhism, in short, is its dualism; that is, its freedom from confusion. To the transcendentalist nature was but an extension of the ego; human nature was but " sister to the mountain " and " second cousin to the worm "; the insentient was but an *alter ego* of consciousness. To the Hindu nature was a derogation to the genuine self. And with nature we must understand all that part of human nature which was liable to " natural " law. Hence liberty for the Buddhist lay in the self-restraint which enabled him to withdraw more and more from the influence of the fleeting, the impermanent, and the earthly until he should emancipate himself wholly from the law for thing, the mechanical determinations of a material cosmos, and ensue the higher and spiritual, the true self. Whereas Hinduism would make religion consist in a recognition of the distinction between the eternal and the impermanent, the one and the many, and in an effort to establish the former; romanticism in the person of its evangelist, Schleiermacher, would find the infinite everywhere and in everything and would swallow up both the one and the many in a miscellaneous all. " The meditation of the pious is only an immediate consciousness of the universal, of all that is finite in the infinite and through the infinite, of all that is temporal in the eternal and through the eternal. To seek and find this in everything that lives and moves, in all that grows and changes, in all that acts and suffers and to have and know life itself only in immediate feeling as this being — this is religion." An illimitable diffusion, a boundless dissipation, an unceasing flux of sensation and emotion in which all distinction and definition melt away in shifty confusion — such is the last word of the romantic religion as it is of the romantic ethics — endless dissolution.

THE IDEA OF GREEK TRAGEDY

Ἐγὼ δὲ τέχνην οὐ καλῶ ὃ ἂν ᾖ ἄλογον πρᾶγμα.

GORGIAS

IT IS not infrequently objected to the practice of generalizing on literary topics that it tends to transform what is properly a creature of flesh and blood into a lifeless, if symmetrical, figure of abstraction. In some respects the charge is just. To suppose that Sophocles wrote the *Antigone* in conscious illustration of a dramatic formula, would be totally to mistake the process of literary creation. He wrote it because he liked the subject and found it suggestive: as we say nowadays, he saw something in it. But even in this case it is perfectly legitimate to analyse and define the kind of thing that appealed to him and the kind of thing that he succeeded in making out of it as far as his impressions and methods are uniform. In other words, it is possible to determine the character of his work as a whole even at the risk of neglecting the specific play of feature and circumstance which lends every individual performance its own peculiar vivacity. And the same sort of treatment is equally feasible with the body of Greek tragedy — or for that matter, with tragedy considered as a universal *genre*.

And further, even though the Greeks, like other tragedians, worked freely, according to their own genius, in the stuff that pleased them, without reference to rule or prescription; even so, it is none the less certain that they proceeded in accordance with certain general ideas and habits of thought. At all events, in order to understand what they have done, we should naturally have to take it up in some general expression, which at most would represent, not necessarily their manner of creating it or our manner of enjoying it, but merely our manner of disposing of it. No one pretends, I suppose, that the physical or mechanical principles which help us to make sense of the rainbow, offer any adequate equivalent for our joy in it, or even that it was ever made in deliberate demonstration of such principles. And while I should hardly care to institute a comparison between scientific and critical generalization, there is sufficient analogy between the two cases to illustrate the fact that as the sole condition of dealing intelligently with a number of details, we are obliged to gather them into our minds in a broad and systematic way. And while, again, I would not be so rash as to say that any dramatist ever harboured any such views as I am about to utter concerning Greek drama; yet I do believe that some such conception — if not mine, then that of another more happy — is involved in that drama and is a fair expression of the manner in which it arranges itself, when it does arrange itself, in our heads. For after all it is necessary to remember that the creation of a play and its comprehension are two very different things.

On the other hand, I am as far from pretending to say anything novel as I am from expressing the the visions and raptures of genius. Not only has

Aristotle occupied this ground before me; but he has in some sense told the whole story once for all. Not that every just remark, which has since been made on the subject, derives directly from Aristotle. But while it would appear ridiculous to father all subsequent ideas upon him, yet it is true that whatever is justly said in this matter does array itself naturally under his authority, almost as an explanation or extension of his teaching. If I can only classify the facts, therefore, from a single point of view so that they will all hang together and take on that air of intellectual consistency which results from the possibility of considering a number of particulars in one light and under one angle, I shall think my purpose satisfactorily accomplished. The aim of criticism must always consist, in the first instance, in making its subject intelligible by reducing it to a single set of relationships.

I

LIKE every other work of literature a tragedy is the product of two factors. There is, first, the crude stuff or substance, fact or invention — the " myth " or " fable," as it used to be called, the " story," as it is called nowadays — which serves as the foundation of the action; and second, the handling or treatment, the " art," which gives this raw material its literary value. It is only by a kind of license that we can speak of an event, whether real or imaginary, as a tragedy. In such a case we are merely availing ourselves of a handy theatrical figure. Literally, we are justified in saying at most that such an occurrence might possibly yield a tragedy if properly worked up and presented. Even in the common manner of speaking the force of the figure depends on a recognition of the necessity of dramatic elaboration for genuinely tragic effect. In other words, a tragedy is not a work of nature but of art.

Like the treatment, however, the myth or story itself, upon which the tragedy is founded, should have a special character of its own. It is probably a vague recognition of the circumstance that every transaction indifferently is not proper material for tragic handling, which confines the popular application of the term to certain occurrences in real life, however capricious and inexact this application of the word is likely to be. In short, tragedy is not wholly an affair of manner any more than it is wholly an affair of matter. The substance must be suitable; and it can be so only when it is of a sort to violate our feeling of moral congruity or fitness. That is to say, the tragic story or fable should involve a discrepancy between our sense of fact, as illustrated in the incidents of the action, on the one hand, and on the other, our conception of justice and right reason. And it is just this disheartening consciousness of inconsistency, implicit in the perception of the dramatic data, as between our knowledge of things as they are or seem to be and our vision of them as they should be, which it is one of the duties of the tragic dramatist to reinforce and deepen by his treatment.

At first sight it may seem something of a paradox

to rest tragedy upon the same general basis, the appreciation of incongruity, as that upon which it has become usual to rest comedy. And yet it has been observed again and again that as far as the mere dramatic substratum is concerned, there is no essential difference between tragedy and comedy: the same premises may serve for either according to circumstances. As Vinet, for one, has pointed out, the subject of *Mithridate* is identical with that of *L'Avare* — the fifth scene of the third act in the former play utilizing exactly the same situation as the third scene of the fourth act in the latter; while between *Mahomet* and *Tartuffe*, and *Andromaque* and *Ricochets*, to mention only obvious instances, there is an unmistakable likeness of the same kind. And yet how different the effect! The truth is, incongruity may stir very different emotions under different circumstances.

In the case of comedy it is the sense of decorum and convention, rather than any graver feeling, which is offended. A violation of the proprieties, an inconsistency of character, a contrariety of circumstances — of such is the fabric of comedy. In spite of its tragic possibilities *Le Misanthrope* arouses, as a matter of fact, no profound distrust, it stirs no serious misgivings. That a prig of Alceste's stamp should so far belie his professions as to fall in love with a trifling flirt like Célimène, arouses much the same feeling, under Molière's management, as that a man in irreproachable evening clothes, to borrow an example from Professor Sully, should slip and fall into the mud. To the intelligent observer the one experience is, of course, much more interesting than the other. The latter is wholly superficial and fortuitous. The former is rooted in human nature and furnishes a better pasturage for that sort of intellectual curiosity and amusement which it is the business of the comic poet to elicit from his themes as it is the business of the tragic poet to elicit from his the motifs proper to his own *genre*.

In the case of tragedy, on the contrary, the incongruity is such as to shock profoundly the moral prepossessions of the race — to shake, if not to unsettle, confidence in the moral order, in the moral reality of the universe. The sacrifice of a girl so innocent and ingenuous as Iphigenia to the indirections of her father's ambitious policy or that of a woman so elevated and disinterested as Antigone to state's reason and municipal convenience, is in itself a direct attack upon the observer's faith in a supreme equity, in a just apportionment of human lots. Nor is it otherwise with *Mithridate* as compared with *L'Avare*. The spectacle of a ravenously avaricious character like Harpagon in the throes of a passion so extravagant as love, presents an extremely curious and amusing case of ethical casuistry — nothing more; while the exposure of Monime in her maiden decorum to the jealous inquisition of her tigerish master is enough to confound belief in the equitable regulation of mortal affairs.

It is this sort of thing that I should like to call the tragic qualm — this feeling of insecurity and confusion, as it were a sort of moral dizziness and nausea, due to the vivid realization, in the dramatic fable, of a suspicion which is always lurking uncomfortably near the threshold of consciousness, that the world is somehow out of plumb. Herein lies the genuine " clash " of tragedy, as it has been called — not in a mere collision of persons or interests or even of ideas within the confines of the play itself, but rather in the contradiction life is perpetually opposing to our human values and standards.

To be sure, our sensibility for this sort of thing is rather blunt at present. This is not a tragic age. Nor is it essentially a moral one. But for all that there are times when the tragic qualm, inherent as it is in the nature of things rather than of art, obtrudes itself irresistibly. The wanton assassination of the most inoffensive of our presidents is a case in point — as is the senseless obliteration of an entire population by earthquake, volcanic upheaval, or other cataclysm. I grant that even these tremendous catastrophes are beginning to lose their terrors for the popular imagination in the rapid extension of a civilization preponderantly material. But at the same time, though such matters are not of themselves proper for tragedy for a reason that I shall assign in a few minutes, yet they do still stir in thoughtful natures the kind of feeling peculiar to the tragic fact as such; they raise again the horrifying old distrust of nature and her dealings with her creature. Like every lapse of reason, like every intrusion or irruption of the irrational or the unintelligible into the sphere of human interests, they threaten again the security of man's dearest illusions, they trouble his spirit and fill him with nameless apprehensions for the sanity and good faith of that order in which humanity with its quivering and importunate conscience is helplessly and irre-vocably involved. For after all the tragic qualm is perhaps nothing more or less than a sudden and appalling recognition of our desperate plight in a universe apparently indiscriminate of good and evil as of happiness and misery.

Without the tragic qualm, then, in the dramatic data there is no tragedy. But this is not enough; it is but preliminary — in Plato's words, $\tau\grave{\alpha}$ $\pi\rho\grave{o}$ $\tau\rho\alpha\gamma\dot{\omega}\delta\iota\alpha s$. It is necessary that the qualm should be allayed, that the quarrel between the certainties of experience and the exactions of conscience should be composed, and that confidence should be restored. In addition to making sure of the emotions proper to his stuff in itself, the poet must also manage in such a way as to answer the question mutely pro-pounded by his fable: if such things can be, what becomes of the law of eternal righteousness as given in the heart of man? Such is the question which the drama, as " the imitation of an action," forces re-lentlessly upon the attention of the audience. And the whole function of tragedy, as a literary *genre,* is to resolve this doubt, in one way or another, through the medium of the action but of the action as a dramatic, not as an actual, performance. Other-wise, there is no art — nothing but a dull dead stere-otype of reality with all its contradictions, incoher-ences, and inconsequences — and with all its resultant incredibility. Senseless assassination or aimless annihilation may indeed present a problem, but the problem is insoluble. And where there is no solution, either by fault of the circumstances or by fault of the poet, there is no genuine tragedy.

If I may venture for a little while into the thicket of critical exegesis, this or something very like it seems to me to be what Aristotle had in mind in speaking of the " purgation of the passions " as the end of tragic poetry. The eventual relaxation of the emotions of pity and horror, which were characteristic of the tragic qualm as it affected the sensibilities of the Greek by reason of certain conditions which I shall have the temerity to discuss before long — the eventual relaxation and alleviation of these emotions by some adjustment or other, after their violent excitation by the representation of the action, appears to satisfy the Aristotelian definition of tragedy, as δι' ἐλέου καὶ φόβου περαίνουσα τὴν τῶν τοιούτων παθημάτων κάθαρσιν as accomplishing through pity and horror the purgation of these selfsame passions. But in any case — and this is the point after all — what is indisputable is the sharp distinction drawn by the *Poetics* between the myth and its handling, between the action as an imitation and an initiation — or in other words, between life and literature. And in the light of the distinction it can hardly be denied that Aristotle regarded as indispensable some such final accommodation as I have tried to indicate. Without some such reconciliation of experience with conscience, without some adjustment of the course of events to the principles of human nature he could not have conceived of a tragedy in the proper sense.

It is through this solution, as I have called it in customary fashion, that tragedy acquires its significance, as it acquires its poignant sense of reality through its presentation of the tragic problem im-

plicit in its imitation of an action. While it is by the
latter avenue that life enters tragedy, ideas enter
it through the former. In this manner verisimilitude
on the one part and moral consistency on the other
become necessary attributes of the tragic poem.
But even in the first case, in the case of the fable
itself, it is as much the dramatist's vision which is
involved as his observation. The success of his
action, even as imitation, depends mainly upon his
eye for the problem. What affects the audience is
his fidelity, not so much to a certain order of phenomena, as to a certain order of emotions. In a
word, the verisimilitude of his drama, and hence its
reality, is measured, in the last resort, not by the
exactitude with which he is seen to reproduce the
spectators' own sensations, but by the justice with
which he is felt to have voiced the tragic qualm.

II

Of the technical elements of tragedy in general I
have said nothing. I am concerned with what may
be called its intellectual bases alone. I have assumed
the dramatic *genre* with all its appurtenances and
and properties. And I have taken for granted as
sufficiently obvious of itself that the rational premises of tragedy are expressed and to a certain extent
conceived in terms of sensation and emotion. The
kind of story in which the problem is sensibly embodied and through which the tragic qualm is emotionally communicated, together with the manner
of treatment whereby the solution is intimated, will

depend upon the character of the drama and its inspiration. Naturally, too, the specific feelings to which the tragic qualm is determined, will vary with the dramatist's sense of the tragic problem — as will the pacification with his convictions religious or otherwise — as these may be affected by his natural disposition and the civilization in which he finds himself. If the tragic problem of Shakespeare and the Elizabethans is compared with that of Sophocles and the Athenians, it will be found to arise from quite another notion of the fatal incongruities of life and to be differently constituted with respect to its emotional notes, while the solutions tacitly proposed by the two dramas will naturally diverge to an equal extent.

With Shakespeare the tragic dissonance or " clash " would seem to engage as between man's possibilities or pretensions and his fate. The incompatibility of his desires and aspirations, which are illimitable, with the conditions which actually dispose of him — mean, trivial, absurd, belittling as they may be, but always at odds with his higher nature and impulses and frequently ruinous of his life and happiness — something like this would appear to be what moved Shakespeare most in his graver moods. The contrast between what humanity might or should be and what as a matter of fact it may become by the accidents of existence — herein lies the discord at the root of his tragedy. A being of inexhaustible capacity, noble in reason, infinite in faculty, godlike in apprehension, reduced to a mere quintessence of dust — a Hamlet whose world is out of joint or an Othello "fall'n in the practice

of a damned slave," such is the Shakespearean protagonist.

> " This man so great that all that is, is his,
>   Oh, what a trifle and poor thing he is! "

In short, Shakespeare's tragedy, like romantic
tragedy in general, is a tragedy of circumstances;
hence the " low " and " comic " elements with which
pseudo-classicism used to reproach it. To regard
a business like the graveyard scene in *Hamlet* as a
side-issue or a sop to the groundlings, as apologetic
criticism was once fond of doing, is to miss the point.
There may be some excuse for disliking it when done,
but Shakespeare knew what he was about when he
did it. In its violent affront to the ideal dignity of
Hamlet's situation at the moment when he is totter-
ing precariously on the edge of his own grave as of
Ophelia's, in its fantastic contradiction of the Hamlet of abstraction by the Hamlet of fatuity it is
of the very essence of Shakespearean tragedy.
The objection that such a scene is out of
keeping with the seriousness of the emergency
is true enough; but it is equally pointless, for the
tragedy consists in just this affront to human dignity, this outrage to the sacredness of the individual.
That such an objection should ever have been made,
argues a gross misunderstanding, not only of the
manner in which he conceived the tragic problem,
but also of the nature of his tragic irony, so different
from Sophocles'. " That is the glory of Shakespeare," Tennyson is reported to have said, " that he
can give you the incongruity of things." Even about

his comic characters in their more sober aspects hangs the atmosphere of fortuitous calamity. It is what gives Falstaff his grip upon our sympathies; he ought, it seems, to be so much nobler than he is. For Shakespeare's mixture of comic and tragic is not confined to a mere intermingling of scenes of one sort with those of another; it resides in a kind of duplicity of conception, which is, perhaps, humourous rather than comic. Just as the lighter characters like Falstaff may catch a reflection of pathos from being in some manner the victims of untoward circumstances, so his tragic characters too may be slightly ridiculous for the same reason, like Othello gulping Iago's innuendoes or Macbeth gaping at the witches. At all events, from the nature of the case his tragic heroes, for all their wilfulness and violence, are always a little pitiable as well as pathetic, like poor old Lear. About them all is a little something of Coleridge — one reason, perhaps, that he is able to speak of them with so much intelligence and sympathy. Such is, no doubt, the unavoidable weakness of a drama in which fatality has been displaced by necessity. If there is a principle presiding over the course of Shakespeare's action it is the law of causation, in accordance with which the quarry is finally run down by a pack of consequences, more or less incidental, with whose inception his own character has little or nothing to do, however it may appear, as the only constant and predicable element, to determine the outcome, very much as the duration of the hunt might be said, regardless of the hounds, to depend upon the endurance and cunning of the fox. After all the problem set by Shakespeare is simply how a man of such and such possibilities could go to the ground. The answer consists in tracing the circumstantial conspiracy, the causal succession by which he has been brought to such a pass, together with its effect upon his character. Transfer Hamlet and Othello, and the tragedy becomes unthinkable. How long would it have taken the former to unmask Iago or the latter to settle with Claudius?

Hence the curious result, as compared with the Greek, that whatever their fortunes, Shakespeare's protagonists are morally accountable only for their intentions. It is impossible, of course, to deny that Hamlet pays the penalty of his acts, such as they are, in the sense that he endures the event; but he is in no wise answerable to the audience for the predicament in which he finds himself, as is, for example, the Hippolytus of Euripides. On the contrary, not only does Macbeth suffer the consequences of his conduct, he participates in their odium as well, on the strength of the malevolence of his motives. The latter is adjudged a criminal, the former is not. At the same time, there is a striking want of concurrence between verdict and sentence. Inoffensive as he is, Hamlet comes off no better than Macbeth. The tragedy is the same in both cases — the ruin of a promising career. In the one instance justice is felt to have been done; in the other not. Why, then, the identical issue? In short, for the tragic problem implicit in his representation of life Shakespeare has no moral solution. He seems to say: Such is the way of the world; to be sure, it offends your sense of fitness that humanity should be liable to these wretched contingencies, but what would you have?   Life

> " is a tale
> Told by an idiot, full of sound and fury,
> Signifying nothing."

In default of a final impression of moral consistency as between the hero's deserts and his apportionment, the consternation of the spectators is composed by a feeling which is left with them of the sympathetic superiority of the victim over the forces to which he succumbs.   In spite of his insufficiency it is impossible not to rate Hamlet or Lear above the whole conspiracy to which he falls a victim.   In this way the tragic qualm, as I have called it, is allayed after a fashion; the audience is reconciled to the catastrophe — otherwise there would be no tragic effect at all.   Such a conclusion, however, is purely sentimental and lenitive; there is no reassertion of the moral order, no catharsis of the passions to which the qualm is due.   It is not by his solution, to speak exactly, that Shakespeare is great. Perhaps the kind of incongruity on which he based his drama is incapable of moral reconciliation.   At all events, it is, as a matter of fact, to the terrific vividness with which he pictures the plight of humanity in a world of unscrupulous eventualities and draws its consequences for the character of the individual that his greatness is due.   Hence the individuality of his drama and its title to the common designation, tragedy of character.

Such, as I conceive the matter, are the fundamental ideas of Shakespearean tragedy, which is in most respects a fair type of romantic tragedy in general. By comparison, the problem of Greek tragedy has to do with the effect of an action, as such, in promoting human happiness or misery; while the solution seeks to justify the issue by attaching to the action concerned a corresponding moral quality of good or evil. It is not a concern for happiness in itself which differentiates the Greek tragedy from the Shakespearean; on the whole, it is rather a concern for the correlation of happiness and righteousness. But as far as the representation itself goes, all tragedy, as a matter of fact, is alike eudæmonistic in referring immediately to the instinct of happiness as sole umpire of the *dénouement* or *metabasis*. If life were suddenly to be conceived as a discipline of suffering, a school of character alone, without reference to the welfare of the individual, our tragedy would have to be recast. I do not see how Lear or Œdipus could be regarded, on such a supposition, as a tragic figure. Indeed, in the *Œdipus Coloneus,* where Sophocles has taken this view to some extent and has modified the postulates of tragedy in some measure to suit it, the impression produced is not wholly a tragic one. The shock to the sensibilities upon which depends the effect of the action in tragedy, as distinguished from that of its resolution, consists capitally in seeing humanity fail, by some outrageous *contretemps* or other, of the well being to which it instinctively thinks itself entitled. And the peculiar feeling or quality of feeling which makes the qualm of one tragedy differ from that of another is due, not to a care or a neglect of such a natural expectation, but to the particular manner in which it is raised to be disappointed — that is, finally to the character of the two parties to the collision, that which serves to raise the hope or expectation and that which serves to disappoint it.

Now in Shakespeare this collision or clash was seen to grow out of an inconsistency between the fairness of human promise or appearance and the dubiousness of mortal performance — or in terms of feeling, between the expectations raised by the hero's personality and the disappointment caused by his subsequent career. In Greek tragedy, on the other hand, preoccupied as it is with the ends of action and its relation to prosperity, the collision originates in a discrepancy between the hero's conduct and its consequences — between the favourable expectations raised by his action and the deplorable results that actually ensue from it, as when an act calculated to ensure success is in reality productive of calamity But of the probable outcome of an act there is morally only one prognostic — the intention or purpose of its author. Acts of which happiness may consistently be predicted, whose termination ought to be prosperous, are those whose intentions are good — or at least innocent. When such an act, deserving in itself of approval, turns out disastrously, like Antigone's celebration of her brother's funeral rites, there is bound to follow a strong feeling of amazement and dismay. The conscience is deeply shocked; and there arises that peculiar sense of vertiginous insecurity which I have called for convenience the tragic qualm.

In this connection it is worthy of remark that in Greek you are always pretty sure what the protagonist is going to do. He seldom or never disappoints you; whereas in Shakespeare the protagonist's behaviour is always more or less doubtful until it is settled forever by the inertia of the action. That Orestes will kill his mother, is certain from the first; he has come to do so and do so he will — he acts consistently in the spirit of his intention: what is uncertain is the consequence of his doing so. Whether Hamlet will kill the king or not, is always pretty much a matter of conjecture before he has done so. In fact that is just the question. In the one case it is Hamlet's character which is on trial; in the other it is Orestes' act.

From this shift of dramatic emphasis has resulted a difference in the treatment of character which is no less significant of the romantic tragedy as compared with the Greek. While the Greek protagonist is calculated solely with reference to the action, whose moral character is reflected upon him; the Shakespearean has developed a character of his own which is partly implicated in the action but is also partly independent of it and uncommitted to it. The former is an agency, not an end in himself. It is not he to whom the action is indebted for its main interest and its peculiar effects, but contrariwise. In consequence, he exists only in and for the play; or what amounts to the same thing, there is no more of him than is necessary to motive the drama, with which he is virtually coterminous. On this account he has simplicity, breadth, and integrity — he possesses a general, abstract, and typical value

— to which his modern rival can make no pretension. He represents the fates and liabilities of human life rather than the varieties and variations of human nature.

The Shakespearean character, on the other hand, as a personality more or less inviolable and sentimentally superior to the mere circumstances of his lot, appears to live with a larger life than that of the action, with which his character is only partially identified. Whoever dreams of measuring Hamlet or Othello or Lear — or even Macbeth for that matter — solely by what he does? Such is the variety, richness, and complexity — such is the ethical interest of his character that it is impossible to confound him with his fate, even while one bewails the pity of it. In retaining his apartness and distinction he preserves a kind of saving grace or eminence in his downfall which makes it dramatically endurable. He remains uncompromised because he seems so much more important than the catastrophe, or indeed, than the whole play itself. He stretches away, as it were, indefinitely beyond the boundaries of the drama in which he figures — often meanly enough in comparison with the impression of his psychological significance. There is hardly one of all the company who does not occasionally let slip some evidence to a trait of character which is not involved in the piece or required by it — some hint or reminiscence as though of a previous state of existence. Indeed, so complex is their consciousness that it occasionally splits up or divides against itself to the detriment of the dramatic action. It is as much Hamlet's dissension with himself as anything else which embarrasses the tragedy. For these reasons it is possible to talk — yes, and to dispute so much about any of Shakespeare's main personages: there appears to be so much more of them than the action is adequate to account for that the remainder, the extra-mural portion, is an inexhaustible subject of speculation and conjecture. Hence the fascination of what may be called the private character of his *dramatis personæ,* which manifests itself in innumerable odd ways — in biographies of his heroines' girlhood, in discussions of Hamlet's whereabouts and occupations before the curtain went up, even in reference to Lear's and Cordelia's compensations in another world.

That the stage has gained in a way by this treatment of character is undeniable. But what it has gained in one way it has lost in another. Though it has gained in curiousness, in variety, or what we like to call human interest; it has as surely lost in dramatic and literary consistency. That the characters should outgrow the action and cease to be solely the creatures and servants of the drama, is impossible without impairing the accurate adjustment of parts and functions, the nice application of means to ends upon which depends the perfection of art in general and of dramatic art in particular — without introducing an element of excess or superfluity, a principle of disorder which tends to warp and sprain the play. The fact is that the Shakespearean *dramatis personæ* are too big for the mimic world which they feign to inhabit; they are themselves realities masquerading in a world of fiction; they belong, not to the stage, but to existence. Dare

I say so — they are too natural, particularly the women? I confess that to me at least it seems at times a little incongruous, even a little grotesque to watch these intensely animated characters, complex with all the complexity of life, gesticulating, grimacing, frowning, smiling, running the gamut of a thousand expressions and inflections, bustling about with all the irresponsible vivacity of nature, " in a fiction, in a dream of passion," amid a factitious and highly artificial scene clapped together transparently enough out of a few bits of painted canvas, a rickety slide or two, and a set of flimsy hangings, the whole bounded by an arc of garish footlights and a row of staring spectators. On the contrary, the Greek actor in his buskins, his mask, his robe and trappings, with his restrained gestures and intonations, may seem a singular figure when deprived of his appropriate accompaniments. But put him in his place, in the midst of a scene and an action carefully insulated, to say the least, from actuality; and he ceases to be grotesque or incongruous: he and his surroundings are of a sort.

In one particular, however — in the nature of the actions imitated and in the fidelity of the imitation it must be acknowledged that Greek tragedy bears no little likeness to the Elizabethan — quite enough, indeed, to justify the numerous parallels that have been drawn between them and even to support the contention that Shakespeare's is the likest of all tragedy to the Athenian. Nor is the similarity so very extraordinary after all. There is naturally a kind of family resemblance among all the members of a *genre*. From this particular point of view life is bound to present pretty much the same aspect whoever views it. The frightful rivalry and competition, the monstrous waste of life, the atrocious expense of suffering, which are the very conditions of existence on the planet — from such sources all tragedy indifferently must draw its materials, which are much more elemental and simple than the comparatively artificial and complex interests of comedy. But it is true that the Greeks and Shakespeare are alike in looking at these things far more piercingly and nakedly than the poets of any other nation. They see the facts more nearly and distinctly through fewer veils and conventions. And there is, in consequence, a kind of unflinching realism about their representation of the tragic data which carries them a long way in company. Parricide, matricide, suicide, infanticide, rape, incest, insanity, sacrilege — these formed the stock in trade of the one as of the other. But such a likeness is more or less superficial, touching the matter rather than the spirit. It is the resolution, the accommodation between experience and conscience, which is vital. And here, it must be acknowledged, the Athenian takes leave of the Elizabethan. While the latter was content to exhibit " the weary weight of all this unintelligible world " with hardly more than a sentimental palliative for its atrocities, the former boldly attacked the problem involved in the frustration of human happiness, and by reconciling the discrepancy at its root, succeeded in allaying the spectators' apprehensions for the miscarriage of justice, at the same time relieving and relaxing the passions excited by such a spectacle in a manner to suggest the Aristotelian metaphor of a moral catharsis.

Specifically, his problem, as he saw the riddle of the universe reflected in the legendary and heroic mischances with which he worked, was this: why should an act which is performed with virtuous or blameless intent and which is to all appearance good and meritorious in itself, work irreparable mischief for its author. In order to answer this question he undertook to show, or rather to convey the impression, that such an act, whatever its motives, was in reality committed in violation of moral law and that so far from being innocent or even indifferent, it was, as a matter of fact, subversive of order and discipline. In other words, it was not merely inexpedient but wicked and on that account properly liable to disaster; while its perpetrator himself was not merely unlucky or unhandy, but criminal as well and therefore obnoxious to correction and punishment.

To take Sophocles, the maturest and clearest expression of Greek tragedy, as an example — his whole theatre seems to presuppose some universal and abstract principle of law and order, ὥστ᾽ ἄγραπτα κἀσφαλῆ θεῶν νόμιμα presiding over existence—a kind of moral police, to put it crudely — which provided automatically and of itself for the regulation of human affairs and for the execution and removal of disturbers, who, if suffered with impunity, would unsettle the equilibrium of earthly things. Any deed, done in contravention of this principle or law, however innocent might be its motives, was essentially criminal, as involving in fact a breach of the moral peace. Ignorance itself, like rectitude of intention, constituted no defense, though dramatically they both served to recommend the offender to the sympathies of the beholders — in short, to qualify him a tragic character; for otherwise his fate would have no particular interest — it would be a clear case of retribution, raising no doubt and occasioning no qualm. As for the remoter mystery between the law and the culprit's conscience — with this Sophocles has little or nothing to do; he is content to leave such matters, as too high for him, between the knees of the gods. Only once, in *Œdipus Coloneus*, he attempts something like a vindication of their purposes. But as a general thing, what he is concerned for — and in this particular his preoccupation is sufficiently unlike ours to make its appreciation difficult — is to demonstrate the moral consistency of life as against a purely casual or mechanical coincidence and to assign to men's actions specifically human and intelligible values of good and evil in place of the neutral and noncommital attributions of right and wrong to their good or ill success —

> ὧν νόμοι πρόκεινται
> ὑψίποδες, οὐρανίαν
> δι᾽ αἰθέρα τεκνωθέντες ὧν Ὄλυμπος
> πατὴρ μόνος, οὐδέ νιν
> θνατὰ φύσις ἀνέρων
> ἔτικτεν, οὐδὲ μήποτε λάθα κατακοιμάσῃ,
> μέγας ἐν τούτοις θεός, οὐδὲ γηράσκει.

Nor was this interpretation due to a confusion of nomenclature, as has often been assumed. Sophocles was no dupe of a vocabulary. Rather, if there were such a confusion of vocabulary at all, it was a concomitant result, with this interpretation, of the spirit of those who used the language. The conviction of the correlation of misery with wickedness, of prosperity with righteousness, together with what we should call the indifference to motives, which inspired the solution of Greek tragedy, was not confined to Sophocles and his fellow playwrights. It suffused the consciousness of the Greeks. The happy man was the good man; or as we say, for the idea is not without modern echoes, he was the man who had done well. In fact, so thoroughly was the identification ingrained in the popular mind, that there was a general prejudice against misfortune as in itself an impairment of character. But while the Greek temper was consistently moral, it was consistently intellectual too. Not only were the unhappy obviously wrong; but since no one acted ill knowingly, all wrong doing was finally a form of ignorance or misjudgment — that is, an error of some sort. Ignorance too was criminal. And while this conception of conduct was not pushed relentlessly to its logical conclusion — for Aristotle seems to discriminate in debarring from tragedy what can be only the man of evil impulses — yet it did tend to turn the Greek's attention from the motive-grubbing with which we are familiar and fix it upon the act and its consequences, which as a matter of fact furnish the only practical means of estimating the moral significance of character.

As a matter of curiosity, suppose we spend a few minutes in pushing Sophocles' conception to its logical conclusion. We must then arrive at some such conception as the following. In case there are acts which tend to violate or do actually violate the moral order, there must be a cosmic will or intention, since a moral order implies a corresponding scheme or plan. But what is this moral sense or purpose, this cosmic will? It can not be necessity, for that frequently resists or contravenes the moral order, if actuality is to be taken as the index of necessity. Nor can it be a mere ascription or attribution on the part of our own moral character, for that would have no power to enforce its decrees. Nor can it be identified with the will of Zeus — certainly not the Æschylean Zeus, nor even of an educated and properly advised Zeus such as is anticipated in the *Prometheus Bound*. Is it, then, simply inherent in the constitution of things? And if so, wholly material after all? For how did the universe get to be a moral affair? And here, I suppose, we reach the term of speculation. The cosmos was to Sophocles a moral cosmos, however it came to be so, just as ours is a mechanical one though we can not explain how or why, and in fact, consider the query impertinent — partly, no doubt, because we can not answer it. The force, however, which insures and sustains this moral order of Sophocles' is fate. In the dramatic economy of the tragedian it is fate which puts the moral order through.

III

WITH these general considerations in mind it is
possible to dispose more or less systematically and
intelligibly of several details which are usually
handled in a rather empirical and disjointed fashion as notations of fact rather than as consequences
of a principle.

In the first place, it ought to be clear from this
point of view why Greek tragedy should manifest
itself so frequently under a sort of typic form which
has been described as a conflict of duties. In the
light of the recent discussion it is obvious that
through some such opposition as this the particular
problem with which this tragedy has to do, is at once
set out in the strongest possible light and receives
the most satisfactory and convincing solution. A
protagonist, acting, as in the *Antigone,* with complete faith in the sacredness of his undertaking
only to discover in the end that so far from acquit-
ting himself of his obligations he has actually incurred the penalty of an offense as serious to all
intents and purposes as the debt which he has
endeavoured to meet — such a character affords in
his own person the most striking contrast between
anticipation and fulfilment and at the same time
suggests the most reasonable explanation of his disgrace. As his motives are the highest conceivable
on the one part, so is the tragic anomaly of his fate
the most shocking and bewildering; and as his trans-
gression is patent and undeniable on the other part,
so is the rehabilitation of the moral order equally

certain and reassuring. In such wise the double requirement of Greek tragedy with respect to qualm and catharsis finds complete and ready satisfaction.

In this respect nothing could be more striking than the contrast with modern or Shakespearean tragedy. It is almost an unexceptional rule that the Greek protagonist ruins himself in the discharge of what he believes to be a duty — and not always an agreeable one at that; whereas the modern protagonist falls in the indulgence of his own desires. To the one fatality appears in the guise of an obligation; to the other in that of a temptation. Œdipus, Antigone, Orestes — it is not so much that they are following their own inclinations — or even what seems to them individually to be right and just, but what the audience too would unanimously recognize as such. And it is precisely this — the conviction of guilt, brought home to protagonist and audience under such circumstances, which makes the qualm of Greek tragedy. Indeed, I sometimes wonder whether tragedy in the highest sense can exist without such conviction of guilt, notwithstanding that it is, on the contrary, the conviction of innocence in like circumstances which makes the poignancy of modern tragedy. But not to quarrel over degrees and to accept the facts as they are, the difference is real and significant. If the Greek protagonist is tragic by the conviction of guilt, where the modern is tragic by the conviction of innocence, it is that the former is led, by his devotion to what he thinks a just obligation or claim against his conscience, to incur the violation of some other engagement equally sacred and binding.

At the same time, simple as the matter seems. when viewed in its proper connection, it is to this very source that much of the misunderstanding of Greek tragedy must be referred. Not infrequently has it happened that one of these obligations or the other has lost its authority for the modern conscience with a resultant falsification of feeling for the situation. In a humanitarian age it is not surprising that Prometheus' offense against the celestial ordinance should appear a trifle as compared with his services to mankind and that he himself should have come to be a purely sympathetic and romantic character, such as Shelley has done his best to familiarize us with. With a weakening of the ancient civic sense, too, something of the same sort has happened to Antigone. But nevertheless it was originally this strict antinomy of approximately equal duties which afforded Greek tragedy one of the fairest opportunities for the production of its own peculiar effects, not the least notable of which was the characteristic duplicity of feeling it aroused for the protagonist.

This impression, composed of the two emotions, pity and horror, by which Aristotle defines tragedy — just these two and no others — is to be accounted for in the same way and by the same order of considerations as before. Not that Greek tragedy might not produce other emotions too — as a matter of of fact Aristotle himself has arranged for others; but such others are adscititious and incidental. Pity and horror alone are inherent in the idea of the species and essential to its formula. Since the action of the protagonist itself bears a double face or interpretation, in qualm and catharsis, the emotions of the audience are twofold also. In as far as it is well intended and directed to an end commendable enough in itself, it arouses pity for its devoted author upon whose head it recoils with such fatal effect; while in as far as it is mischievous in fact, as it violates the celestial canon and jeopardizes the established order, it must needs arouse an equal horror for the rash and impious agitator who has ventured to trouble the tranquillity of men and gods. For the blind and passive sufferer of a fate so dismaying as that required to produce the tragic qualm, pity is the only possible emotion; as is horror for the malefactor convicted of a felony sufficiently monstrous to justify the judgment which overtakes him and so to work the revulsion of feeling necessary to the catharsis.

I do not wish to insist upon the moral import of tragedy unduly: I know how reproachful such remarks must seem to my own generation. At the same time I can not leave this topic without a protest. While I do not think that tragedy ought to preach a sermon or read a lesson, it does seem to me that nothing can be more preposterous than the contention that Aristotle, in defining the *genre* by the emotions of pity and horror, meant to imply that its being is exclusively æsthetic, in the modern acceptation of the term, and devoid entirely of moral purpose or concern. As though pity and horror were necessarily immoral or amoral emotions! As though it were not a kind of misnomer to speak of them as æsthetic emotions at all! That there are emotions which are exclusively æsthetic

even in the straightened significance now given to
the word, I have no doubt. But no one whose judgment has not been warped by the perversions of a
latter-day criticism would dream of classing pity
and horror among them. For what is there so likely
to move the latter as the spectacle of blind and infatuate iniquity; so likely to move the former as the
spectacle of sudden and staggering adversity? The
conflict of good and evil, I believe, is still, for all
our sophistication, the surest and deepest of all
emotional appeals. And in view of the facts I can
conceive nothing more impudent than the pretension to range Aristotle among the partisans of
such a doctrine as *l'art pour l'art,* because he has
formulated tragedy in terms of the very emotions
which are most closely identified with our moral
perceptions.

At the same time, pertinent as is his notation of
that drama with which he was acquainted, it is a
mistake to assume that his definition is true for
tragedy in general or romantic tragedy in particular.
Since neither problem nor solution is identical, as
I have tried to show, it follows that the characteristic sentiment of the latter will be differently constituted with respect to its emotional notes. I
do not mean to deny that pity and horror are in
some sense elicited by every tragedy. They are
both present to some extent and in some manner
from the very nature of the *genre.* The apparent
moral obliquity of the catastrophe, which is the
motive of the qualm — itself, as I have tried to
show, a constant factor — is bound to raise a kind
of horror, as also a kind of pity for the luckless

actor. But these feelings are quite different in timbre from the passions to which the Greek play is conditioned by its peculiar interpretation of tragic actuality. They have not the same purity or the same consistency; they are not in a fixed and definite ratio decisive of the character of the drama; they are variable and indeterminate. As a rule, the modern protagonist is either a pathetic character, like Othello, or an antipathetic one, like Macbeth. Otherwise, in default of a solution authoritatively moral, we should be unable to bear his fate, to which we are reconciled, as I have already suggested, in the one case by an impression of his sentimental superiority to his situation, in the other case by a conviction of the poetical justice of his downfall. The active principle in the first case is sympathy; in the second, disapprobation. But sympathy is not identical with pity, or disapprobation with horror. And even when our feelings for the modern hero are mixed, these are, on the whole, the sentiments between which we are divided. What pity and horror we feel are caught up and engaged with these more or less loosely.

For an exhaustive discussion of the subject, however, this is hardly the place. All I wish to do here, is to point out that these two passions, pity and horror, are critical of Greek tragedy alone; and though they may enter into the general description of any tragedy, yet it is misleading to use them as a universal definition of the whole *genre* without reference to specific versions of the tragic paradox and specific expedients for its accommodation. For as opinion changes with regard to the tragical contin-

gencies of life — what they are and how humanity is
to be reconciled to their existence; so must the
feelings and sentiments voiced by the drama change
also, and along with them the attitude toward the
tragic character, whose qualifications will obviously
be controlled by these very conditions. So it is
with the modern protagonist. And it is by the
same reasoning that Aristotle's discrimination
against certain types as compared with certain
others, is to be explained and justified.

The main difficulty with Aristotle's doctrine of
characters seems due to the fact that it makes no
provision for the prevailing pathetic or prevailing
antipathetic protagonist of later tragedy — in particular, and the saying has been thought a hard one,
it disqualifies Macbeth and Richard III. But the
fact is that such a type is not Greek; it does not
conform to the double *rôle* for which the Greek
protagonist was cast. While it is possible, of course,
to rationalize the ruin of a thorough-paced villain
by the law which he has violated, yet his downfall
causes no dismay and inflicts no pang; it is just what
ought to happen. Hence it offers no moral problem;
in the eyes of the Greek there was nothing tragic
about it. It might be calamitous for the villain;
but objectively, for the audience it was a source of
unalloyed satisfaction, just as his career was an
occasion of unmigitated disgust. On the other
hand, the virtuous or pathetic character is unfitted
to the part for a contrary reason. While the sight
of such a person suffering an untoward fate, may
indeed appear sufficiently enigmatical to trouble
the spectator and awaken his suspicions, yet the

very nature of the case precludes the possibility of a moral settlement. In the adversity of the just there is neither reason nor consistency. As Aristotle says, it is simply shocking. And the difference of our own feeling in this respect serves to measure the interval between the two tragedies. On this account the only possible protagonist for the Athenian was the sort that we have had in mind all along — the fallible character, neither wholly good nor wholly bad, but liable to error. As such he is subject to pity by his infirmity and to horror by his iniquity — he is amenable equally to the requirements of problem and solution.

In addition to these features of Greek tragedy, which may be regarded as primary inasmuch as they derive immediately from its postulates and are necessary corollaries of its definition, there are others mentioned by Aristotle as incidental and ancillary. Their presence is the test of a complex, as distinguished from a simple action, which hinges solely upon a *metabasis* or reverse of fortune, while the former may also include a peripeteia, an agnition, and a sensation ($\pi \acute{a} \theta o s$).[1] As a matter of fact, then, these secondary characters are merely special devices for reinforcing the emotional impression of qualm and catharsis, which, as he observes, is more impressive when the incidents of the drama occur

---

[1] Though Aristotle fails to mention $\pi \acute{a} \theta o s$ with $\pi \epsilon \rho \iota \pi \acute{\epsilon} \tau \epsilon \iota a$ and $\grave{a} \nu a \gamma \nu \acute{\omega} \rho \iota \sigma \iota s$ as one of the differentiæ of complex tragedy, he discusses it immediately in connection with these other two as a third part of the $\mu \hat{v} \theta o s$. At the same time the *Prometheus Bound* is opened by a $\pi \acute{a} \theta o s$, if indeed the whole play is not one prolonged $\pi \acute{a} \theta o s$. Since the whole distinction is of no great importance in this connection, there is no particular use in discussing here.

contrary to expectation, and still more so when they occur by reason of one another.[1] So a peripeteia is defined as an effect by which an antecedent produces, not the consequence expected, but one entirely unlooked for and yet necessary and intelligible. In much the same way an agnition is the recognition by a character of some person or object of whose identity he was at first unaware. As such an effect is likely to cause a revulsion of feeling and a change of intention on the part of the character concerned, it frequently though not invariably involves a peripeteia. A sensation, as I have ventured to translate the term $\pi\acute{\alpha}\theta os$, is a particularly harrowing incident, which instead of being reported by messenger or otherwise, is enacted under the eyes of the spectators. As conducive of surprise and suspense, intensity and immediacy, these effects may be looked upon as elements of plot in the present connotation of the word. To be sure, they want the elaboration of the modern intrigue, where the dramatic action has come to be developed chiefly in the sense of the " interesting " as the *dramatis personæ* chiefly in the sense of the " characteristic." But though they have remained subject to the primary uses of tragedy in the enforcement of problem and solution, yet their very presence should be a warning against

[1] $\delta\iota\acute{\alpha}\lambda\lambda\eta\lambda\alpha$. Hardly by cause and effect in the modern connotation, as the case of Mitys' statue at Argos proves. The connection in Aristotle's mind, I venture to think, was moral, not physical. Of course I do not mean to imply that Aristotle was without the notion of causal sequence and that he may not have had it in the corner of his eye in this case. But I conceive that his idea of cause in this instance would have included that of reason also; it would have involved an answer to the question why as well as to the question how.

a not uncommon manner of speaking as though Greek tragedy were deficient somehow in dramatic action and were largely an affair of declamation and recitation.

Such an insinuation is founded only in a serious confusion. It is not unusual nowadays to talk as though a lively and bustling stage or a picturesque and striking tableau were all-sufficient evidences of dramatic quality. But if movement and stir, spectacle and panorama were indeed dramatic, then would vaudeville be justified of its triumph. Under the circumstances it is hardly otiose to remark that for genuine drama it is hardly enough to set the characters' legs in motion; their passions must be aroused as well. It is not so much motion as emotion that makes drama. Mrs. Siddons is said to have had a way of pronouncing Lear's curse, while holding her arms rigidly at her sides, with an effect that was terrible beyond gesticulation. Only as the outward act gives rise to feeling or expresses it, does the act itself become dramatic. It is not mere action but significant action that counts. Nothing could be busier than a scene of Victor Hugo's. It is full of sound and fury, commotion and vociferation; and yet when you come to look inside for the internal drama which all this outward show and circumstance should body forth, what hollowness and vacuity you find! While as for the vaunted violences of the romantic stage they too miss the mark as often as not. Critics have wasted their ingenuity in trying to defend the sanguinary ending of *King Lear*. In spite of the spiritual interest and importance of the murder which closes *Othello*, it is a fair question whether Shakespeare has not overreached himself in strangling Desdemona in public. In all such cases the mind is so shaken or distracted by the physical act as to be incapable of attending to its ethical import. The impression, so far from being enhanced, is blunted by the theatrical exaggeration.

On the other hand, such a poem as Goethe's *Iphigenie* goes to the opposite extreme. Admirable as it is in its own way, it is lacking both in dramatic action and in theatrical activity. It has nobility; but it is the nobility of reflection, not of passion. No wonder that Goethe himself could never see it performed with patience. And yet tragedy, while representing passion, does not present it for its own sake. Tragedy implies an aim, an end or purpose to be accomplished — a labour, πόνος, an exertion. There is a fatal necessity constraining the *dramatis personæ* to act and causing an interplay of motives, a fluctuation of emotion. To use the phraseology of the day, a play is not static but dynamic. It involves will, volition; it is not a mere state of feeling or even a succession of such states — but rather an agitation of spirit. Hence the necessity of a *metabasis*, as Aristotle calls it, or reverse of fortune. And it is just the point of drama that this revulsion of feeling should be capable of visible translation. Of all modern dramatists it is Shakespeare who combines most effectively this dramatic movement with theatrical activity. It is another and not the least of his many superiorities that he should so often succeed at once in setting up a genuine dramatic action in the souls of his people and in expressing so perfectly that inner revolution by an outward and physical animation. In Racine's tragedy, perfect in its kind as it is, there is always, it must be acknowledged, a disposition to repress the latter element in accordance with the proprieties and to rely too exclusively upon recitation alone to carry the dramatic action. As a matter of fact Corneille's most admired effects are usually an affair of eloquence, even oratory.

In this respect too much altogether has been made of the so-called statuesqueness and plasticity of Greek tragedy. As long as the performance was supposed to be confined to an impossibly high and shallow stage, along which the actors were silhouetted like the figures in a bas-relief, such a conception was perhaps unavoidable. But with the orchestra as the site of the action it is no longer necessary or plausible. That Greek acting had little of the minute realism which characterizes ours, is undoubtedly true. But that it was prevailingly declamation and recitation, that it wanted stage-effect, the text of *Electra* should be sufficient to disprove, to say nothing of Aristotle's commentary. Indeed, on the strength of the devices that I have been speaking of — peripeteia, agnition, and pathos — M. Lemaître goes so far as to rebuke Aristotle for his sensationalism. Very well. But what what does M. Lemaître expect? What is tragedy if it is not sensational? And while Greek acting lacked realism, there must have been a breadth, a massiveness, a gravity about it more suitable to the desperate purposes of tragedy, for that dark and sinister background, than our painstaking pastiche of common reality, of the speaking voice and the daily face.

IV

FROM this sort of criticism there is danger of carrying away a false and one-sided idea of the subject. In the end Greek tragedy does leave an impression of dignity, repose, and serenity, more or less suggestive, perhaps, of the epithet statuesque. But the satisfaction resides, as I have already indicated, in its treatment, not in its subject-matter. In the latter aspect it is, if anything, more terrible, monstrous, and revolting than our Elizabethan tragedy of blood. In the German *Sturm und Drang* itself there is nothing to exceed the story of the Atreides, upon which the *Oresteia* and the two *Electras* are based. The reproaches that Voltaire addressed to *Hamlet* might just as well have been addressed to the *Œdipus*. The mere repetition of such names is enough to show how elemental is the the substance of Greek tragedy and how helplessly its composure depends, not upon this crude and sanguinary material, but upon the spirit with which it was animated and the ideas with which it was informed. As mere stuff its superiority over the *Nibelungen Lied* and *Beowulf* is not great. As drama its superiority consists in the profound moral significance with which the Greek had imbued it. And in this case the merit belongs to the race as well as the dramatist, for whose hand it was partly prepared before he touched it. It was the genius of the people which had fitted these sinister old legends for tragic treatment by deepening their content and suggestion. In themselves they are like windows opening upon a remote and savage antiquity, through which it is still possible to catch a glimpse of wild irrational powers moving obscurely in the gloom, of the fitful workings of casualty and chance — perfidies of nature and miscarriages of reason. Consider only the labyrinth of *Œdipus* or the ambages of *Ion*.

These were the subjects that gave the Greek his opportunity. He was grappling with tremendous problems, he was struggling for a foothold on the brink of unreason, he was confronting the irresponsible demonic forces of creation, he was wrestling for the secrets of destiny. And the ground-work of his tragedy was vast, portentous, and preternatural.

And yet out of all this confusion and anarchy there seemed to be something slowly shaping — an event, an issue, a fate — directing itself more or less vaguely, in the midst of uncertainty and dread, to some far off and indistinguishable end. Careless of guilt and innocence, heedlessness and premeditation, it spared one and spoiled another indifferently; it required the child of its parents and the mother of her son; it snared alike the crafty and the unwary, the pious and the scoffer. Unprognosticable, it did not want for records: whatever came to pass, bore witness to its passage; in particular, its trail lay over certain great houses and illustrious families. Capricious as its dealings with the individual might seem, it was impossible in the long run to deny them a kind of coherence or rough and ready logic. Was it possible to go still farther: in spite of misleading appearances and occasional inconsistencies could they be reconciled on the whole with the ideal of an absolute and impartial justice?

Such was the problem which the dramatists inherited. In the case of Æschylus, however, it is evident that this attempt at the moralization of fate has by no means met with perfect success. In what remains of the Promethean trilogy, which is with the *Oresteia* the most significant in this respect of all his extant work, the result looks very much like a compromise. The atmosphere of *Prometheus Bound* is, it must be confessed, a pretty uncertain medium for the conveyance of clear ideas. It is the day after the deluge, and the air is still thick and troubled. Even Æschylus himself is shaken. It would be hard to say how much of the modern feeling of security is due to a belief in the uniformity of nature, how much to a faith in the beneficence of an over-ruling providence. The latter serves to guarantee the moral order in as far as it has not become a matter of total indifference to us, for we seem to have given up any very serious thought of the establishment of such an order in the world at large; while the former acts as a warranty for the physical order with whose ascendency we seem to have made up our minds to rest content. But however this may be and whatever their relative proportions, take away these two convictions and our world would fall to pieces. And yet Æschylus had neither of them. He had no sense of the mechanical concatenation of nature and he had no surety for his gods. Divinity, as his religion and traditions represented it, might be poetic; it was anything but moral. In a word, it was a divinity quite in the present æsthetic taste — an artistic being without moral irrelevances, which would heartily have applauded the programme *l'art pour l'art*, but would hardly have made a reliable guardian of manners. In default, then, of a deity to whom the regulation of such matters might safely be entrusted, Æschylus could only fall back upon fate itself as above and beyond the gods — or else let the moral order go by the board, and with it the only law and security for existence of which he had any conception.   But if Zeus' treatment of Prometheus was shocking, was it not equally shocking of fate to permit, to say nothing of ordaining, such an atrocity?   What possible justice was there in condemning Prometheus to torture for his benefits to humanity in defiance of a tyrant, usurper, and parricide, whose highest title to consideration would seem to consist in the fact that he was able to command the services of Kratos and Bia?

That this question, which is obviously the question raised by the drama, is answered in a thoroughly decisive and satisfactory manner, it would be idle to maintain in the face of all the conflicting interpretations of which the play has been the subject. At the same time, I believe that even as far as it goes, the drama does answer the question partially, and answers it in accordance with the general principles of Attic tragedy.   That Æschylus sympathized with Prometheus, is pretty clear.   No doubt the audience sympathized with him too.   But notwithstanding the representations of modern criticism I venture to think that he was not to the Greek the purely sympathetic character which he has become for the modern. As far as bare intention goes, he was properly an object of pity in his distress, after the usual fashion of the tragedy in which he figured. At the same time his sacrilege, which has lost its sting for us, must have made him for the Greeks an object of horror equally. Either so; or the feelings by which Aristotle defines the impression of his tragedy, must be so indefinite and diffused as to make his statement altogether pointless — an *aperçu* rather than a definition. That Æschylus makes no attempt to gloze his protagonist's fault, ought to be decisive. Unmistakably as he sympathizes with Prometheus, it is significant that he carefully refrains from justifying him. On the contrary, he appears on one occasion at least to have put an admission of guilt into his mouth — ἥμαρτον, οὐκ ἀρνήσομαι. Nor does it matter particularly how ἥμαρτον be translated in this connection; to err or even mistake in these matters was for the Greek, as I have pointed out, none the less a sin. In so far, then, Æschylus keeps the idea unobscured. Prometheus suffers; but then Prometheus has violated the law for Titan as for man, and to that extent his punishment is just.

And yet while this is true, it must be conceded in excuse of another range of interpretation that Æschylus shows a little reluctance to *trancher* the question. It is as though the matter were not quite clear in his own mind. While he refrains from justifying Prometheus, it is equally significant that he does not exert himself to justify Zeus either. Rather he represents him as himself obnoxious to justice — wherein, to be sure, he seems to have followed his traditions. For his own part, however, he is by no means sure that the law of Zeus is a moral law; while as for his act itself he evidently regards it as abhorrent in its extremity and depicts it as an act of violence — a $\pi\acute{a}\theta os$ in the technically Aristotelian sense. Hence his reserves. He will not gainsay the offense, but his heart is divided. If both are liable — for does not fate impend upon Zeus also? — then he seems to feel as though the fault of the god excused or minimized that of the Titan. There is something wrong somewhere — with the institution of Zeus, perhaps. Of one thing alone he is perfectly certain — that order is better than chaos. The rule of Zeus may be arbitrary, it may rest on force; and yet it is a rule. It may not be thoroughly equitable as yet, as an institution it may need rectification; but it is better than confusion, it is the one means to security and stability. He who resists and defies it, is guilty of an attempt to subvert the provisional moral government in the interests of anarchy. There is no help for it: he is an agitator, a disturber of the peace; he must be quelled.

Prometheus, then, is the revolutionary. He is the first of mutineers, and to this fact he owes his fortune as the great romantic and humanitarian symbol. He belongs to the race of dissidents, nonconformists, insurgents, or whatever name they may be called, who revolt against a necessary discipline, traditional or established, in the name of a lawless and indeterminate ideal. No wonder that he received an apotheosis in the age which promoted revolution to the rank of a political institution. He is one of that dangerous class of reformers who refuse to proceed by due process of law, who are impatient of its restraints and delays, and would suddenly take the execution of justice into their own hasty hands. Like them he obeys no higher principle than his own sympathies; he will justify the means by the end and shelter in the day of judgment under the fairness of his intentions. He is the classical embodiment of individual justice; he does what seems good in his own eyes. That he would do right, is sentimentally a migitating circumstance; his crime is that he would do right wilfully and after his own mind. That he happens to right a wrong, to anticipate a reform — that he is the noblest of rebels, makes the demoralization of his example no less — rather the greater. Nor does it affect the issue particularly that his rebellion is directed against a tentative and imperfect administration. What administration is otherwise?

The illustration may seem far fetched; but I never read the *Prometheus* that I am not reminded of a *pensée* of Pascal's:

" It is proper to observe right; it is necessary to observe might. Right without might is powerless; might without right is tyrannical. Right without might is disputed, because there are always the wicked; might without right is reviled. It is necessary, therefore, to unite right and might, and for that purpose to make right mighty or might right.

" But right is subject to dispute; might is easily recognizable and is indisputable. Hence it is impossible to annex might to right, because might has contradicted and asserted that she alone is right. And so, since it is impossible to make right mighty, we have made might right."

Not that this conception answers exactly to Æschylus' whole thought. What Pascal regards as a permanent state of affairs, Æschylus contemplates as a transient condition. But Pascal's notion is true enough for the moment marked by the *Prometheus Bound,* " might till right is ready." In order that justice may be ultimately ensured, it is necessary first to found a power capable of maintaining some sort of order and discipline, from which by a process of gradual correction and improvement may be developed a more and more perfect justice, in which the rights of humanity itself shall receive their proper recognition. Such is apparently the condition on which Zeus is suffered to reign; he too must adjust himself to a higher principle than his own conveniency. For the correction and perfection, as for the maintenance, of that moral order to which the obedience of inferior beings is due, Zeus himself is answerable to the fate which palpably overhangs him throughout the tragedy. He must reconcile himself with Prometheus, he must find a *modus vivendi* with the champion of mankind, which has its rightful place also in the universal polity — before his sovereignty is confirmed. If the conclusion of the trilogy were in evidence, it is probably with this accommodation that it would deal. The first necessity, however, is to create the idea of justice and to establish it. And if Zeus is justly on probation for his management, Prometheus is no less justly in duress for rebelling, in the hot-headed old Titanic fashion, against the sole authority by which this result may be accomplished and its fruits secured. Before the advent of justice the world must be broken of Titanism.

Such, it seems to me, is the sense of the drama; and the *Oresteia* tends, I think, to confirm this conclusion. The theme is the same in both instances. In the latter case, however, where we have the whole story, there is less danger of mistaking its purport. The only difficulty is that just as the modern reader's impression of the *Prometheus* is falsified by a failure to feel the horror of Prometheus' sacrilege, so here his judgment of the *Oresteia* is liable to be warped inversely by an inability to feel the pity of Orestes' murderous legacy. What requires emotional correction with respect to the tragic passions at present, is not the odium but the pathos of the action. There is nothing equivocal about Orestes' guilt: matricide is as abhorrent to-day as it ever was. But private vengeance is no longer recognized as a duty; there is nothing that is sacred, little that is sympathetic, about it. In the mind of the Greeks, however, who appreciated the obligation of the latter as fully as the abomination of the former, the situation inspired the usual tragic duplicity of feeling. They were of a temper to be touched by the dutifulness of Agamemnon's avenger and to be horrified at the impiety of Clytemnestra's executioner. Otherwise, I am at a loss to account for my sentiments in reading the trilogy; for I must confess that my wishes are for the success of Orestes and his sister, much as I may reprobate the deed by which it is assured. Nor is this the sentiment of the situation as such; it is not in the *Electra* of Euripides. The Æschylean Orestes, though a criminal in act, is no epileptic monster like the Euripidean: albeit he does not lend himself so readily to humanitarian attitudinizing, there is as much to be said for him as for Prometheus. And curiously enough, it is Euripides who finally says it, though not much to his advantage, in vilifying Apollo as the instigator of his crime. As for Æschylus, however, he accuses Apollo no more than he does Zeus — for one thing which romantic criticism has overlooked is the fact that if Zeus is to blame for Prometheus' plight, Apollo is equally to blame for Orestes' and with less excuse because without provocation. At best the circumstances are different, the responsibility is the same. It is fair, therefore, to argue that Æschylus' idea must have been alike in both cases. But if anything is clear, it is that the author of the *Oresteia* is no romanticist; he is not disintegrating the moral edifice but cementing it; he is not relaxing discipline but tightening it. It is not at Apollo's expense that he claims the audience's pity for Orestes, whose saving virtue, as compared with Prometheus, is his submission to authority. What is impossible and intolerable in his situation is the fault of an imperfect and makeshift institution, the *lex talionis,* whose whole enormity is finally demonstrated in the fatal dilemna of this last sad inheritor of a bloody old tradition. The impulsive movements of private retaliation must give way to the deliberate decisions of an impartial and dispassionate court. And though it would be an insult to justice, were the perpetrator of what is after all a monstrous crime, allowed to go scot free, yet it is only equity that he whose sufferings have been the occasion of reform, should benefit by the amendment to whose adoption he has at least contributed.

In these pieces at which I have glanced as those most critically interested in the method and conception of Attic tragedy, Æschylus is concerned mainly for the reconciliation of might and right through the medium of divine legislation — what we should call nowadays in secular terms the evolution of justice. The subject corresponds with his place in the history of tragic ideas and responds to the conscious craving for a definite moral constitution. His problem is one of institutional morality — if such a phrase is permissible in such a connection; its solution is an affair of moral statesmanship and administration. Personally I do not believe that a more tremendous tragedy than *Agamemnon* has ever been written: I do not know of any tragic impression more awe-inspiring than that produced by Cassandra arrested by the spirit of prophecy at the door of the Atreides' palace. For this reason I hesitate to call the problems of private morality deeper and necessarily more tragic, after the current manner of speaking. But at all events they are different; and it is these problems, raised by spontaneous impulses and by promptings of conscience hopelessly at odds with the determinations of life and society, which are Sophocles' peculiarly.

In *Prometheus* and the *Oresteia* the tragic schism is wholly external; it is due to a maladjustment which may be corrected without permanent harm to the persons involved. But every anomaly felt as tragic is not to be explained or reconciled so happily. There are instances in which it is inherent and fatal; in which it involves an organic lesion. It is so with Œdipus; not only is his crime his own but the responsibility is his also. Unlike the Æschylean Orestes he acts by and for himself and at his own peril. To be sure, it may be said that like Prometheus he acts in behalf of others and in the interests of the general, whether or not by prescription. But there is a difference. It is not without intention that Sophocles has centered the drama, not upon that portion of his protagonist's career which has been mazed and darkened by celestial counsels, but rather upon that portion in which he, the child of fate — παῖς τύχης, as he calls himself with cruelly unconscious irony — has the temerity to act by his own lights with infatuate confidence in the clarity of his own vision — he, the puppet of destiny, blindfold from birth, who has never taken a step with a full sense of the conditions and consequences of his action. It is this pretender to clairvoyance, this dabbler in enigmas, the reader of the riddling Sphinx whom Sophocles represents as pretending lightheartedly to unravel the mystery of his own being. He is a great criminal, to be sure; but he has become so inadvertently and as a result of such a skein of fatality that it is doubtful whether his lot would not be wholly pitiful (as, indeed, many have found it, *le grand Corneille* among them, who have failed to attend strictly to the action) if it were not for the pertinacity with which he is seen to pursue destruction in insensate conceit of his own sufficiency. And to the same effect the length of time which is supposed to have elapsed since his crimes — so long have they lain concealed that they would seem entitled to a measure of immunity, as by a kind of unwritten statute of limitations, were it not for the fact that he himself is the one who finally unearths them. Had he been brought to account by another, it would have appeared little better than a divine inequity. I do not believe that anyone can read the tragedy intelligently without being sensible of presumption, of gross moral impropriety in the bias whereby Œdipus is impelled to seek for himself the solution of his own problematic existence. It is no correction of institutions that will mend his case — nothing but a reformation of the entire character.

With all this I am puzzled to understand why the *Œdipus* has never received the same sort of philosophical rating as the *Prometheus*. Its significance is, if anything, more profound and is certainly much more general. It is the very type of life universal. While lending itself with equal readiness to " symbolic " interpretation, it has never been surpassed as a figure of human responsibility in particular. We are all of us without exception in Œdipus' case — rounded like him with ignorance and mystery, and yet obliged to act incessantly and at our own hazard, so that our every step seems a presumption deserving of disaster and our every judgment an arrogance inviting rebuke and humiliation. Of all Greek tragedy the *Œdipus Tyrannus* seems to me not only the most characteristic of the genius which produced it but also most applicable to our hapless human lot.

At the same time I must confess to a particular affection for the *Electra*. Perhaps it is the situations that especially please me — Orestes at the gate of the palace overhearing his sister's lamentation; Electra herself with the funeral urn in her hands; the recognition with its sudden revulsion of feeling. In the face of the impending abomination there is something singularly affecting in the attachment of these two ill-starred children of a murdered father — the dependence of the one, the assurance of the other. But however this may be, the important matter for the inherence of Sophoclean tragedy is the shift of the traditional center of interest from Orestes himself to his sister. However it may be with him, she at least is under no divine compulsion. Her only abettor is her conscience. She acts of her own accord and by the exigency of her own nature.

But after all the clearest illustration of Sophocles' conception of the tragic as something intimate and essential is to be found in neither of these pieces but in the *Antigone*. Ethic I was about to call it. And for that matter what is the source of tragedy in the *Antigone* but the collision of an ethic with a moral principle — of the fatal propensities of character with the prescriptions of social or civil expediency or necessity? It is the usual Sophoclean theme, the theme of *Œdipus* and *Electra;* but it comes out here more distinctly than elsewhere on account of what appears to us the superior sanctity of the former, the individual principle — or rather, probably, on account of the comparative insignificance of the latter. And yet in view of the Greek's devotion to his city — a devotion for which, narrow, short-sighted, and suicidal though we esteem it, he showed himself willing again and again to sacrifice every advantage and undergo every hardship, I can not make so light of Antigone's contempt of what to her countrymen was patriotism as do many critics for whose opinions I usually feel the greatest deference. What else was her conduct in Greek eyes than treasonable? And little as we are at a point of view to appreciate this sentiment (though this is by no means the only instance on record of sectional or parochial animosity or of the obloquy incurred by non-adherents of local or party politics) I still believe that Antigone's disloyalty to the polity — or what was bound to seem such in the heat of a great public excitement — must have been a scandal to a Greek audience, which was, on the other hand, in no less favourable disposition of spirit, in comparison with us, to sympathize with her religious scruples as distinct from the purely personal pathos of her condition and being. And so it is, I believe, that Sophocles intended her to appear — like other tragic protagonists, as an object of horror no less than of pity; otherwise, there would be something gratuitous in the extraordinary severity which characterizes his chief magistrate, by her attitude to whom, as the representative of the government, Antigone's faithlessness to the commonwealth is dramatically measured. To be sure, such asperity is natural enough to a person or a people in the reaction succeeding immediately upon a tremendous crisis. But if that were all, if the point were merely psychological, Sophocles would hardly have been so careful to restore the equilibrium by meting out a final judgment to Creon for exceeding the just measure, There is no doubt, it seems to me, about his intention; he will not countenance contempt of the supreme impersonal law on the part of an individual whatever his or her title on other grounds to admiration or respect; for " value dwells not in particular will."

But at the same time, while *Antigone* fits the framework of its *genre* and is no exception to the general definition of Greek tragedy, I am well aware that for us to-day, whose ideas of religious and civic duty are so different, such an interpretation must seem far-fetched and forced. Indeed, there is no tragedy, I fancy, even of the Greeks, with respect to whose moral bases we are at such a disadvantage. The burial motive is as remote from our instinct as the cult of the city; we are as unfitted to respond to the one as to the other. It is the person of the heroine almost exclusively that appeals to us. Elementally, she is not the representative of any special duty or set of duties — though if she were not sustained by a sense of duty, she would not be the noble and touching figure she is. For our emotions it is not the mere political and social crux which makes the play — this is but the vehicle; it is the case of conscience. What renders the tragedy peculiarly affecting among the tragedies of Sophocles, what gives it its specific flavour is not merely the bare dilemma — the consciousness of rectitude which can neither surrender its convictions without shame nor persist in them without ruin, but the nature of the protagonist — her sex and youth, her ill-omened birth and her attachment to the son of her executioner. No wonder that she has become for the modern one of the great sympathetic characters of literature, like Cordelia, and her tragedy a sentimental one.

On the other hand, while Sophocles holds the scales even — while he gives the ethical and the moral elements alike their due — to the heroine's womanliness its meed of compassionate admiration as to the tyrant's arrogance its fitting correction, at the same time that he asserts the existence of a higher authority than the judgment of particulars — yet for all this, which escapes us more or less but was clear enough to the Greeks, I would not assert that he himself had in mind any such fleshless formula as that which I have applied to his work. All I mean, is that he conceived in a certain way and to a certain effect, which I have tried to analyse — roughly and bunglingly enough, I dare say. No doubt he worked by touch, not by measure. He was not likely to stop to anatomize an effective subject if it yielded the proper emotions on inspection. But that in spite of the modern perplexity of its theme and the spontaneity of its creation the *Antigone* does take down regularly, I have tried to show. Generically and schematically it is, like the other works of its author, the tragedy of the individual will.

In general terms, it is from the same source, the conflict of the ethic with the moral, that Euripides derives his drama. But unlike his predecessors he fails to sustain the supremacy or even the importance of the latter principle, and failing to do so, misses the distinctive double note of Greek tragedy. His favourite procedure is to represent morality as a hollow convention or tradition with little or no title to reverence or credit. As a result his characters are either interesting sinners like Medea and

Phædra or superstitious bigots and credulous gulls like Orestes and Menelaus. They are seldom or never actuated by conscience or conviction, a sense of duty or obligation, but impulse or appetite, desire or caprice. Like Racine's heroes and heroines, they are creatures of passion, not of resolution — they suffer their destiny rather than incur it. Of the same order too are the motives of his divinities like the Aphrodite in *Hippolytus* or the Apollo in *Ion*.

Particularly *Ion* — what can be said of its purport? What system can possibly make moral sense of such a skein of divine knavery and deceit? In these respects the play is so illustrative of the Euripidean skepsis as to merit a brief analysis. If the prologue as spoken by Hermes contains the data of the piece — and I can see no justification on this occasion for traversing Euripides' usual practice — then, we must take it for settled that Ion is the son of Apollo and Creusa.[1] After an indefinite interval of neglect, during which Creusa has married Xuthus, and her child, miraculously rescued from exposure and carried to Delphi, has been brought up in the service of the temple, Phœbus, desirous at last of establishing his son advantageously, plots to fob off the youth upon Xuthus as an illegimate son of the latter. This fraud he has no great difficulty in perpetrating with the aid of his oracle, assisted to some extent by Xuthus' credulity. The scheme is in a fair way to succeed but for Creusa's ignorance of the boy's identity. And this is a weak joint in

[1] But compare the interesting introduction to Verrall's edition of the play, to which I am not a little indebted.

the structure of the drama; for it would seem
natural that Phœbus should contrive some means of
advising Creusa beforehand of his amiable intentions. As a matter of fact, however, Creusa, revolted
by her husband's attempt to smuggle his suppositi-
tious child into the family, conspires with her servant
against Ion's life but to such ill effect that she
is in imminent danger of losing her own. In the
pinch there seems no way of saving her but to declare
the truth. Hence the production by the priestess
of the cradle and the so-called " proofs." However,
it may be with the cold-blooded critic, this evidence
is sufficient to convince Creusa that Ion, the youth
whom she has plotted to kill, is indeed her child;
while for the audience the evidence is confirmed, we
must believe, by the testimony of Athena, who by
way of saving Apollo's face, appears as the *dea ex
machina,* in Euripides' habitual manner, to close the
play. The piece terminates, then, with the triumphal
accomplishment of the celestial rascality. Xuthus
has already been brought to acknowledge the boy as
the fruit of his own amour; and now Creusa accepts
him for her part by a similar motive, though on
better grounds. The principals are in accord; and
Ion's fortune is assured. As to the possibility that
Xuthus may learn of the deception on some future
occasion, that contingency lies without the boundaries of the play and need not be discussed.

Upon the ethics of the characters, divine and
human, concerned in this travesty of providence,
comment is superfluous. They are all unscrupulous
equally. If anything, indignation sways slightly to
the advantage of Xuthus as the party actually

abused. Nevertheless he himself is quite unable to appear in court with clean hands. The only case deserving of commiseration is Ion's. He has no first-hand information of any sort concerning his birth or the manner of it; he knows only the two contradictory accounts of his parentage — the one sponsored by the oracle to the effect that his father is Xuthus, the other by Athena to the effect that his father is Apollo and his mother Creusa. It is all very well for the audience to credit the latter report; they have a confidential source of information in the prologue. It is very well for Creusa too to do so, if she will; she knows the circumstances of her son's birth and exposure. It is very well even for Xuthus to think as he does at his own peril; he knows at least his past and its opportunities. For all of these parties to the transaction there is some possibility of comfort in their faith. But what can be the state of Ion's mind? Obviously, one of the divine communications must be a lie — either the oracle of Apollo or the messenger of Apollo is false. And if one is false, which? And if either is false, what is the security for the other? Why not both, then, since they speak for the same principal? And in that case, how about the priestess with her cradle and her " proofs " ? Ion may like to take his mother's word. But faith and security are dead forever. From the happy, confident and confiding ministrant of the god, serving the temple and scattering the intrusions of the birds with playful threats and mimic violence, he is doomed logically to an anxious and troubled future; and he passes sullenly into the great doubt that has been prepared for him.

Such is the characteristic moral ambiguity or obliquity of the Euripidean *dénouement*.

And the illustration is a fair one. As Euripides' tragedy is destitute of a principle of any kind it has no minatory or exemplary force to speak of. If it is moral at all, it is so, not in the Æschylean or Sophoclean, but in the modern, the humanitarian, manner. In this one sense, since his drama — with the exception of a few artless and appealing but hardly tragic figures, like Ion, who are usually the dupes or victims of the plausible and unscrupulous knaves about them — since his drama is a marvellous illustration of the vices, frailties, and weaknesses, the " humanity " of mortals, its author is not undeserving of the epithet with which he has been graced by a late romantic admirer, " Euripides the human " — an attribution with whose sentiment a majority of Athenian critics would probably have concurred.

In these respects Euripides is not very unlike Ibsen. Like the latter he too is unmistakably decadent and obsessed by the nightmare of ugliness. It is not so much, perhaps, that he dotes upon the sordid, the base, and the malodorous — though at times he displays no little complacency in their depiction — as that they haunt and fascinate him; they block up his view till he can see little or nothing else. As far as he is concerned, the heroic has ceased to exist; Helen is a baggage, Agamemnon a politician, Menelaus a cuckold, Ulysses a trickster, Orestes an epileptic. For the tragic emotion of horror he substitutes disgust; for the moral qualm of his predecessors a shrinking of the flesh, a sense of physical repugnance and nausea. His most distinctive dramatic effect results from a certain uncanniness of character and motive. He is temperamentally ambiguous, equivocal, evasive, shifty. He is prone to blink the issue, to refuse to look the tragic fact square in the face. His instinct is to deny it, if possible, to juggle it away by some trick of theatrical legerdemain; at all events to deprive it of moral relevance and competency.

It is evident, for instance, that he can see no sense, no reason of any kind in the sacrifice of Iphigenia. It is merely odious to him as it was to Racine centuries later. And yet what becomes of the tragedy without it? There is no apparent violation of justice, nothing to raise a doubt or suggest a suspicion; there is no qualm, no agony of question, no mystery at once terrible and revelatory. It is all perfectly simple, open, and morally intelligible. The interest centers exclusively upon the *dramatis personæ* and their conflicting emotions. It is distinctively a modern, a psychological play. As contrasted with the Æschylean and Sophoclean tragedy of principle, it is concerned solely with character and its expression.

In the *Electra,* on the other hand, the absence of a clear moral issue has resulted in what is mainly a drama of incident. Orestes is nothing more or less than a monster for his pains, Apollo a scoundrel for instigating him to an unnatural murder; that is all there is to it. Aside from the morbid psychology incidental to the situation attention has nothing to perch upon except the stratagem and imposture by which Ægisthus and Clytemnestra are disposed of. The tragic problem has vanished completely; there is nothing left but a particularly harrowing and truculent melodrama.

As a result of his inability to make anything out of his fables and his impatience with the interpretations of others, Euripides is reduced, in the article of theme, to the secondary *rôle* of critic. This is his fundamental weakness as a playwright. It shows itself in the loose construction, the faulty economy, the feeble effect of his individual dramas taken each as a whole, to say nothing of his faultfinding digressions on the management of his predecessors. In particular, since he sees no sense in his action as such and has no inkling of its final cause or rationale, it is only with the greatest difficulty that he can bring a play to a close at all — only by some conventional or arbitrary expedient, a dramatic *cliché* or theatrical miracle. As a matter of fact, his pieces seldom conclude; they terminate. Hence his abuse of the *deus ex machina,* which in contradicting or interrupting the logic of events, is to all intents and purposes a nullity, as in *Iphigenia at Aulis,* or else is effective only in dispelling the illusion, as in *Orestes.*

The effect of all this activity was inevitably to discredit and invalidate the value of the symbols with which Euripides himself was obliged to work. In transforming in this way the old mythology into a new psychology, his treatment of his matter resulted in dissolving its moral ideas and in emptying it of its moral content. But inasmuch as he had nothing else to build upon, he virtually knocked the ground from under his own feet and was obliged to search his materials for other means of defraying the expenses of a public performance. It is for this reason that in turning his attention from the sense of the transaction as a whole, he comes to make so much of its constituent moments. Unable to comp ehend the ebb and flow of the tides, he can only admire the ebulliency and agitation of their surface. In this manner he becomes the dramatist of passion. This is his merit and distinction. For this kind of thing he was eminently fitted. Before he created them, such figures as Phædra and Medea had never been dreamed of; and in some respects they have never been surpassed from that day to this. And yet this limitation — for limitation it is to see nothing but the passions to which an action gives rise and to miss its moral import as a whole — results in laying the principal dramatic stress upon sentiment; it makes the pathetic the sole effect of tragedy.

Even in the *Hippolytus,* which comes closest to the standard of his predecessors, the interest centers in the hero's character even more than in his behaviour. In a way it is almost a temperamental problem which is propounded — and solved — in the sense of Greek virtue. But the fact that it is solved at all, is the important matter in this connection, since it is the solution that gives tragedy its moral significance. Hippolytus is responsible for his own predicament. Attractive as his youthful person may be and praiseworthy as is his attachment to Artemis in itself, he is still the victim of his own immoderation. Nevertheless, there is a modern tinge to the story. Hippolytus is an appealing, a

" sympathetic " hero in a manner in which neither
Agamemnon nor Œdipus nor Orestes nor any of his
predecessors, with the possible exception of Antigone and Prometheus, were appealing.   Further,
the duty that he follows is but his own inclination
in disguise.   So warmly has he made himself a party
to the traditional feud between the two goddesses
that he can not refrain from taunting Aphrodite
as a fly-by-night.   Nor is Artemis' threat to have
her revenge on Aphrodite at some future time by
the slaying of Adonis or otherwise, particularly
reassuring for the permanent establishment of righteousness.

> Ἐγὼ γὰρ αὖθις ἄλλον ἐξ ἐμῆς χερὸς
> ὃς ἂν μάλισθ' οἱ φίλτατος κυρῇ βροτῶν
> τόξοις αφύκτοις τοῖσδε τιμωρήσομαι.

Indeed, there is in the play not a little of the divine
wantonness for which its author was in the habit of
disparaging his deities.   It too is marked by the
Euripidean rictus.

And the *Bacchæ*, if it is anything like Euripides'
last word, only confirms, with something of the
solemnity of a testament, the melancholy story
which the *Hippolytus* would appear to have
interrupted but half-heartedly and for a moment.
If the play has any sense, it can mean nothing but
a divorce between divinity and justice, which Æschylus and Sophocles had done their best to reconcile.   It is nothing short of a repudiation of an over-
ruling providence.   The gods are gods, he seems to
say, they do as they list; there is but scant virtue

in them.   In short, as I, Euripides, have always contended, the order of the universe is not moral but emotional.   Such is, to be sure, Euripides' one wailing refrain; but in the *Bacchæ* he seems at last to acquiesce, and not without complacency in a conscienceless fatality.

It is so that Euripides, the most imitated as the most consonant of classic dramatists with later tastes, serves as a kind of transition between the serious drama of ancient and modern times.   In his case interest had already begun to shift from moral to psychological problems, from the quality of actions to the characters of men and the activities of nature.   It as though he had undertaken to forecast the terminals toward which the modern drama would move in its evolution, even to the amorphous and indiscriminate *drame* into which tragedy proper has finally degenerated, not to speak of the Shakespearean tragedy of character, which he may have influenced in a measure through Seneca, and the Racinean tragedy of passion of which he was obviously the direct and immediate inspiration, while the deformation of his tragedy as a *genre* was eviently in the direction of late or modern comedy.

CORNEILLE: THE NEO-CLASSIC
TRAGEDY AND THE GREEK

I

IT is not solely the fault of our critics that we have no such criticism as the French; it is also the fault of our literature. To write a history of English literature like M. Lanson's history of French literature is, even on that small scale, impossible from the nature of the subject. To be sure, there is no such general interest in the former as in the latter. The historian or the critic who undertakes French letters finds an opinion already formed, a canon already established. His meal is at least partly ground for him; he has only to make his dough. But this is not all the difference. English literature, unlike the French, does not constitute a coherent body of thought, a consistent "criticism of life," with a fairly continuous growth or evolution; and a similar treatment of it, as a branch of intellectual development, is therefore out of the question. In fact, our literature is not so largely an affair of definition; not only is it poorer in ideas, it is also patterned less closely in accordance with theory. In all English there is no example of the *genre tranché*, such as Sainte-Beuve loved; hardly of a conscious school or formula, or even of a preconceived purpose. It is individual, capricious, empiric, indiscriminate. The writer himself seems hardly conscious of his own inclination, but follows instinctively the line of least resistance. Not only is the Shakespearean comedy utterly promiscuous, compounded of many simples, a thing without prescription; it is also more or less a thing apart, without a history, itself a "sport" like the genius which produced it. To the student of English, for whom such work has become standard, it is something of a surprise to read Corneille with Voltaire's commentary at hand and observe the nicety with which the critic pretends to discriminate among his author's ingredients, not merely as they are good or bad, but as they are agreeable or otherwise with the literary type before him. It is a revelation of the comparative precision and purity of the ideas in accordance with which French literature was, and in spite of the confusions of the *romanticists* still is, to some extent, written and judged.

But at the same time, definite as are the lines on which French literature moves, the symmetry of the French classic at all events, and of the classic French drama in particular, is likely to appear rather rigid and formal to the student of English. And yet there is one side by which Corneille and even Racine may appeal to him. With an instinct of definiteness and regularity which is peculiarly French, their work combines singularly enough something of that promiscuity, of that anomalousness, which he is used to in English, though with a difference. For it is not the mere adaptation of a foreign or an ancient model which is characteristic of that particular literature.

Indeed, if it were nothing else than an imitation of the pure classic, like Milton's *Samson Agonistes,* the neo-classic drama would be of comparatively little interest. As a matter of fact, however, it was an attempt to interpret one life in terms evolved by another. Naturally the new wine tended to dilate, even to disrupt, the old bottles, while conforming to their general outline. But since a literary form is not merely a vehicle of thought but an outgrowth of it; the attempt, such as it was in other respects, necessarily involved, in their application to new uses, a criticism of the terms themselves and of the ancient ideas implicit in them. And it is this fusion, or rather this collision of two cultures in the one set of expressions, with all its complicated discrepancies and contradictions, which constitutes the peculiarity of the neo-classic tragedy. In fact, so peculiar is it that the reader who approaches it from the side of an integral tradition, however heterogeneous the latter may be, hardly knows what to make of it at first, and will never, the chances are, acquire a genuine taste for it.

While in Racine's case it is the product as a whole which the foreigner finds disconcerting, yet in Corneille's the feeling of individual incongruities is perhaps the more noticeable. To the English reader in particular, if I am successful in recalling an original impression, Corneille presents at first sight a sufficiently curious spectacle. As a great spontaneous genius—for such, however outlandish to us in manner, he certainly was—capable both of the happiest turns and the flattest lapses, he finds his nearest English counterpart in Shakespeare, though in the

ethic appreciation of character and in the phantasma-
goric sense of life he was so far inferior. For this
reason it is unsafe to judge Corneille before one has
taken his range. He is not a poet to be measured by
any one piece, even by that perfectly unique masterpiece of irony and statescraft, *Nicomède*; for he never
succeeded in attaining a level and keeping it. There
are always times when his hand is out. He has his
ups and downs at every period, in nearly every play.
His development is not rectilinear and continuous,
but radial and spasmodic. And it is necessary, in order to know him, not merely to establish the *loci* of
his career chronologically, but also to ascertain his
high-water marks and plot his curve from one to another—the intrigue of *le Menteur*, the rhetoric of
Pompée, the romance of *le Cid*, and so on. In some
such manner alone one comes to understand the
elevation to which his spirit rose from time to
time. And though it ebbs as often as it touches such
an extreme, yet, together with a sense of the instability of his genius, one gains also a sense of its variety and compass, for it recedes merely to flow again
in some new direction.

As a bold and vigorous temperament, on the other
hand, a Norman, with a taste for the romantic and
sensational, for intrigue and adventure, but constrained and embarrassed by the timidity of a conventional and imitative society and age, he approaches
most nearly to Dryden, though he lacked the latter's
easy adaptability and his thoroughly English
common-sense and humour. But for all that there are
about the author of *Tyrannick Love* a stiffness, not

so much of temper as of craft, an awkwardness and also an imperturbable solemnity in the pursuit of the tragic which are very like the author of *Polyeucte*. Indeed, Dryden is probably, of all English dramatists, the one who resembles Corneille most, whether because he deliberately formed himself upon his illustrious contemporary or was naturally of a kindred spirit. At times when Dryden is at his best, his note is almost identical with certain of Corneille's.

> Que tout meure avec moi, madame: que m'importe
> Qui foule après ma mort la terre qui me porte?
> Sentiront-ils percer par un éclat nouveau,
> Ces illustres aieux la nuit de leur tombeau?
> Respireront-ils l'air où les feront revivre
> Ces neveux qui peut-être auront peine à les suivre,
> Peut-être ne feront que les déshonorer,
> Et n'en auront le sang que pour dégénérer?
> Quand nous avons perdu le jour qui nous éclaire,
> Cette sorte de vie est bien imaginaire,
> Et le moindre moment d'un bonheur souhaité
> Vaut mieux qu'une si froide et vaine éternité.
>
> *Surena*, i., 3.

> How vain is virtue, which directs our ways
> Through certain danger to uncertain praise!
> Barren and airy name! thee Fortune flies,
> With her lean train, the pious and the wise.
> Heaven takes thee at thy word, without regard,
> And lets thee poorly be thy own reward.
> The world is made for the bold impious man,
> Who stops at nothing, seizes all he can.
> Justice to merit does weak aid afford;
> She trusts her balance and neglects her sword.

Virtue is nice to take what's not her own;
And while she long consults the prize is gone.
                                   Aureng-Zebe, ii., 1.

La vie est peu de chose; et tôt ou tard qu'importe
Qu'un traître me l'arrache, ou que l'âge l'importe?
Nous mourons à toute heure; et dans le plus doux sort
Chaque instant de la vie est un pas vers la mort.
                                   Tite et Bérénice, v., 1.

Decidedly Corneille is the greater playwright. But it is impossible in his case as in Dryden's to overlook this significant sense of constraint, because it is a critical symptom of the *genre* as it was in that age. There are writers more artificial than Dryden and Corneille; but there are few, if any, who produce, with so strong an impression of power, the same peculiar effect of *gêne*. Racine is more artificial and conventional; but Racine has learned to move smoothly and elegantly within the bounds prescribed him. He is, to all appearance, happily unconscious of interference or obstruction. But in Corneille's case it is not so much that he is hindered in the satisfaction of his desires as that he is not quite sure what he wants himself—or ought to want. For this state of mind the *Examens* are conclusive. It is sufficient to quote from that of *Rodogune*:

On m'a souvent fait une question à la Cour, quel étoit celuy de mes poëmes que j'estimois le plus, et j'ay trouvé tous ceux qui me l'ont faite si prévenus en faveur de *Cinna* ou du *Cid* que je n'ay jamais osé declarer toute la tendresse que j'ay toujours euë pour celuy-cy, à qui j'aurois volontiers donné ma suffrage, si je n'avois craint de manquer en quelque sorte au respect que je devois à ceux que je voyois pancher d'un autre costé. Cette préférence est peut-estre en moy un effet de ces inclinations aveugles qu'ont beaucoup de péres pour quelques-uns de leurs enfans plus que pour les autres; peut-estre y entre-t-il un peu d'amour propre, en ce que cette tragédie me semble estre un peu plus a moy que celles qui l'ont précédée, à cause des incidens surprenans qui sont purement de mon invention, et n'avoient jamais été veus au theátre; et peut-estre enfin y a-t-il un peu de vray mérite, qui fait que cette inclination n'est pas tout-à-fait injuste.

It is instructive to compare this tentative judgment with Lessing's, who was an inveterate classicist after his kind and knew precisely what he was after.

Denn wozu alle diese Erdichtungen? Machen sie in der Geschichte, die er damit überladet, das geringste wahrscheinlicher? Sie sind nicht einmal für sich selbst wahrscheinlich. Corneille prahlte damit als mit sehr wunderbaren Anstrengungen der Erdichtungskraft; und er hätte doch wohl wissen sollen, dass nicht das blosse Erdichten, sondern das zweckmässige Erdichten einen schöpfrischen Geist beweise.

But it is only fair to remark, too, that his criticism, excellent as it is in method, as well as the usual present-day estimate, rests upon a misconception in assuming Cléopatre as the personage of the piece by whom it necessarily stands or falls. For the mistake there is the more excuse because Corneille himself speaks to the same effect. And yet it seems obvious enough that the interest does not centre in Cleopatre at all, but in Antiochus. Antiochus, not Cléopatre, is the genuinely Corneillean character. And the recognition of this fact requires some readjustment of criticism.

By the time Corneille had made *Nicomède* he had, to be sure, developed a kind of formula; his succeeding plays do follow essentially the same receipt. But it is in reality nothing more than a *procédé*, not a theorem, and it does not always work. All his life he remained virtually divided between impulse and authority, unable to choose definitely, but anxious to effect a reconciliation, between the old and the new, the medieval and the antique—to *accorder les règles anciennes avec les agrémens modernes*, in his own words—in short, between those two conceptions of literature and life which were brought into such violent confrontation by the renaissance and which have since come to be distinguished, rather vaguely though conveniently, as romantic and classic. Hence the curiously experimental character peculiar to his drama, which is in fact a compromise among the rival claimants to his regard and is consequently full of contradictions and inconsistencies.

II

To define broadly the difference between these two views of literature, it may be said, in very general terms, that the modern or romantic manner has made itself remarkable mainly for its research of actuality. The thrill and tingle of sensation, the smart of experience, the distraction of accident and circumstance, the harsh and stinging contact of things material—these are the effects it chiefly admires and imitates. The sole literary development of any importance since the Greeks has consisted almost wholly in devices for the more accurate registration of fact, whether of character or incident, until the

kaleidoscopic spectacle of nature and the parti-
colored phantasmagoria of human life have come to
constitute for modern literature and art the only
serious concern. To the Greek tragedian, on the contrary, art was the sole reality, not life; life itself was
merely phantasmal, a vain and misleading appearance.

'Ορῶ γὰρ ἡμᾶς ουδὲν ὄντας ἄλλο κλὴν
εἴσωλ', ὃσοικερ ζῶμεν, ἢ κούφην σκιάν.
                                        Ajax, 125–26.

That it was infinitely poignant, infinitely suggestive,
he saw; but he saw also that it was infinitely prolix,
irrelevant, and disconcerting, and that its poignancy,
no less than its suggestiveness, was the result, not of
its significance, but of its indefiniteness. On the
whole such a vision, by its very confusion and uncertainty, afflicted him, like a nightmare, with the nameless moral horror which still lurks upon the confines
of the *Prometheus Bound*—the horror of a man who
has just made good his escape from a world of chaos
and unreason. To his mind it was in no way desirable
that a poem should be *suggestive,* that it should produce a vague and tantalising sense of illimitable
possibility, but rather that is should be *expressive*—
that it should contain, not so much an exact reproduction of experience and of the emotions proper to
it, as some principle for its intelligible ordering and
interpretation. In short, the main affair was the general idea after which the play was cast. And it is for
this reason that Greek tragedy always produces a

profound conviction of design. It is not a free observation or impression of life, as we say nowadays,
giving rise to any number of inferences and suggestions. It is an arrangement, an adaptation, set, not
to catch an exact image of reality, but to mirror the
author's thought. It does not disturb or trouble or
distract by the flicker of its surface reflection or the
opacity of its intention, like *King Lear*; it settles and
confirms and tranquilises, like the *Œdipus*. And
finally it displaces every other possible interpretation, informing the consciousness with its own image
and idea to the exclusion of all others. It is whole and
single and complete, a closed system which neither
admits nor raises conjecture—at once a cosmos and
a revelation.

Even if the Greek had had the pretension to make
his drama a *pastiche* of life, as we do ours, it is doubtful whether he could ever have succeeded in doing so
on account of its peculiar construction. The chorus
alone would have been enough to destroy the acute
sense of actuality. To say nothing at present of the
temporal and spatial restrictions which it imposed
upon the action and which were enough in themselves to divide it from existence and give it an air of
intelligent fabrication—even then, if a bit of real life
could have been exposed there in the Greek orchestra, it would not have looked real with the chorus
between it and the spectators. The chorus itself
might be conceived as looking at life directly; but
in no case could the audience, viewing it through the
chorus, be conceived as getting it otherwise than as
refracted by the medium through which it passed,

like the report of a bystander. And such, in all probability, as De Quincey ingeniously suggests,[1] was in
effect its artistic force. It framed off the representation, setting it apart, if not altogether insulating it,
from actual existence, re-enforcing its idealistic character and at the same time rationalising what we are
prone to consider its artificiality. For, whether the
chorus were technically spectator or actor, it is clear
enough in any case that Greek tragedy is, by its very
interposition, separated from experience by at least
one more remove than modern tragedy; and represents, therefore, an additional mental distillation or
rectification of fact.

Of course it would be absurd to say that modern
literature engages in its productions no ultimate significance at all. If it did not—if it merely imposed
upon the phenomena of experience the more or less
arbitrary form of some *genre,* as naturalism tries to
do—it would, like naturalism, be hardly felt as literature at all. In a comparison of Shakespeare's four
tragedies, *Hamlet, Othello, King Lear,* and *Macbeth,*
it is curious to observe that the last is dramatically
superior to the others, and is at the same time the
clearest, the most intelligible in design, and reveals
most distinctly the presence of a controlling purpose,
the imprint of a definite idea. There is little or no more
difficulty about the meaning of *Macbeth* as a whole

[1] De Quincey, *The Theory of Greek Tragedy. Cf.* Brunetière, *L'Evolution d'un genre, Études critiques sur l'histoire
de la littérature française,* vii. "Nous n'avons plus sous les
yeaux les événements eux-mêmes, mais le reflet des
événements dans l'imagination du poète."

than about that of the *Ajax*—a circumstance, perhaps, which gives it its deceptive air of similarity to the Greek. On the contrary, *King Lear,* which is the least subservient to such control—for how can any vital congruity be established between the last act and the acts preceding?—is dramatically the least effective and produces what effect it does produce, like life itself, scatteringly and piecemeal, with a final sense of mystification, bewilderment, and agitation. For it must be constantly remembered, in judging of these matters, that a piece which requires for its significance the perception of some wider principle of order than the piece itself declares, is precisely a fragment of life, not a work of art. And it is vicious criticism, for instance, to say of *King Lear* that it is not in itself inconsistent with the Christian conception of a beneficient overruling Providence or to refer to its unreason as a case carried up to some higher court for revision.[2] A play is significant in itself or not at all. To Sophocles any mere concatenation of circumstances, such as composes *King Lear,* no matter how close the mechanical articulation or the causal connection, would not constitute a drama unless it yielded a consistent idea.

It is not, then, that romantic literature is entirely lacking in that purposefulness which discerns a leading idea amid the ferment of existence and organises its material accordingly; it is rather that in modern

[2] Compare A. C. Bradley, *Shakespearean Tragedy*, lect. viii. This, moreover, is a fallacy which tends to vitiate Freytag's treatment of the tragic.

literature such ideas have come to play a part subordinate to the registration of discrete impressions.
And yet this is not the whole story either. Not only
has the influence of ideas decreased, their character
has also changed. A literature will always reflect the
sense of its makers. If they are concerned mainly
with their kind, and with the world which they inhabit only as the theatre of human action, then will
their interpretation, as well as their vision of life, be
in the main a moral one. But, on the other hand, if
they are interested in the universe chiefly for its own
sake, as a curious spectacle in which man figures like
any other object only that he is locomotory, then
will every fact have a value in and for itself irrespective of any ultimate significance; while those who
consider curiously will find, no doubt, the meaning of
the whole to consist in some idea or expression or
formula about the relation of the various parts which
appear in themselves so very interesting and important. And their exposition of life, like their conception of it, will be mainly materialistic or, in modern
language, scientific. Now some such change as this it
is which has, to all appearance, taken place. Whereas
the Greek had little or no mechanical sense of fact,
the modern has been more and more inclining, in accordance with the latter view, to consider nature itself as of superlative importance, and consciousness
as but a small and even subordinate part of it. Hence
that growing curiosity about things as things and
that supreme confidence in the illusion of physical
law and order which are reflected by his literature, on the one hand in the promiscuous repro-

duction of every sort of sensation and impression, and on the other hand in the suggestion of some out-lying mechanical nexus as an all-sufficient principle of literary order. In this sense, however, the world made no appeal to the Greek dramatist. As a mechanical contrivance it left him cold—if such, indeed, it really be. At all events, it had not for him this particularly dreary illusion which has come to form its main significance for us. For this very reason he was able, with far less interest than we take in nature, to see and describe objects much more clearly than we are able to do. He perceived them more nearly as they are—at least in their relation to human life, with which he was himself preoccupied. For his illusion was essentially a moral one. Never would he have fallen into such fatal confusion as did Renan in alleging the unchastity of nature as a criterion of conduct. He was more likely, in the inverse sense, to prescribe to nature from his own conscience. Indeed his religion, which Symonds calls at once a religion and a poetry, was an attempt to animate the physical universe with human passions, while his tragedy itself was an attempt to moralise that religion and through it nature as a whole. Whence its superiority; for the moral illusion is, after all, that which stands the best chance of not being altogether false, and even if false, is still the most ennobling and sustaining. And this is just the character of a great literature everywhere, a profound conviction of the unreality of those things which have been misnamed reality and the substitution for them of some high and abiding form of thought.

From our point of view, however, this moral is, it must be added, of a peculiar sort. The Greek, unlike the modern tragedian, made no effort to deduce his *action* from character. In this respect his drama is not moral, at least not ethical at all. The essential matter for him was not the manner in which personality is manifested in conduct. His first interest was in the action itself. The persons were of subordinate importance and derived their character, as well as their significance, from the action. Aristotle is explicit on this point. What principally preoccupied the dramatist was the attempt to justify the quality of good or evil with respect to these actions as they tended to promote human happiness or the reverse. Were they productive of misery, he had to demonstrate their deviation from abstract right and justice, and contrariwise. And so it is that in vindication of the moral law the protagonist is always disposed of in accordance with the quality attached to his acts, for, says Aristotle, "Men are so and so by their characters, but happy or the reverse by their actions." It is for this reason that the Greek tragedies had such an exemplary force. Since the *action* is not the outcome of a unique character, but is only illustrated in the characters, its like might occur to one person as well as to another. Hence they touched the audience with an immediacy of pity and horror to which the romantic tragedy of character can make no pretension. Hamlet's and Othello's fate can befall only a Hamlet or an Othello; Œdipus' and Orestes' might befall any one. Of course we are bound to assume nowadays that nobody but Œdipus could have behaved like Œdipus. But not so the Greek; at all events that was not what he undertook to show— the exclusively Orestean nature of Orestes' deeds. His dramatic *motif* affirmed only that the deeds were evil and brought unhappiness, and were therefore to be abhorred on the ground not merely of expediency but of principle, while the character of Œdipus or Orestes himself, who shared the obloquy of the action, was revealed only in so far as it served to support this conclusion. By the moral idea of Greek tragedy, then, it is necessary to understand, not exactly an idea about human character and conduct in general, as Matthew Arnold uses the term in his discussions of poetry, but rather an idea about the quality of human actions, without particular reference to character, in conformity with some abstract principle of right and wrong.

To relieve this difference it is hardly necessary to do more than compare the impressions to which such plays as *Prometheus Bound, Œdipus Tyrannus,* and *Iphigenia at Aulis* probably did once and certainly do now give rise. While we, untroubled for the moral consistency of our world, shudder at a suggestion of material confusion physical, social, or industrial, the great and haunting terror for the Greek, the nameless apprehension that lurked upon his life, stealing into consciousness at moments of depression and pervading the whole fabric of his tragic literature, was the dread of moral disorder. The horror of *Prometheus,* for instance, which has become for us, as far as the drama retains any meaning at all, a vague horror of chaos, of a world deranged or a lapse

of "law," was undoubtedly to Æschylus exclusively
moral. It was the horror of a profound and serious
mind beginning to take account of its religious conceptions, its ideas of man and God, of guilt and responsibility, as contrasted with the horror of a
present-day mind, accustomed to regard the stability
of things as dependent upon the uniformity of nature
rather than upon the integrity of the human spirit.
To such a mind as was that of Æschylus, the story
of Prometheus was a mystery, full of "labyrinths
and meanders," unreasonable, monstrous, abhorrent,
to be harmonised with the conscience at any cost.
For with characteristic frankness the ancient dramatist recognised a set of "phenomena" whose significance we have now with characteristic casuistry jug-
gled away. I mean that kind of case in which we
have made a distinction as between moral and
physical consequences. That there are occasions in
this world when a man is obliged to settle for debts
which he has neither incurred himself nor consented
to, and to expiate such consequences as he has never
forseen, is undeniable. To our minds such cases,
though they continue to form the basis of modern
tragedy, are generally meaningless, because we deny
the victims' responsibility. We are content with the
air of baffling and inscrutable mystery which they
diffuse about our tragedy,

> dont les sombres pensées
> Sont d'un nuage épais toujours embarrassées,

and which indeed constitutes its prevailing tone. But
not so the Greek. With his moral prepossessions, with

his tendency to see the moral everywhere, he was not willing to let such transactions pass as irrelevant or meaningless or only mechanically significant. They must, he felt, if the moral consistency of the world was to be preserved, possess a moral import. And in such case it was necessary to impute a moral accountability to their principals. Accordingly he never thought of denying Prometheus' and Œdipus' responsibility. "Ημαρτον, οὐκ ἀρνήσομαι," says Prometheus himself. Guilty without intention, even contrary *to* intention, they may have been; but as human beings they were liable for the consequences of their activity. And while they were objects of pity on the one count, they were as surely objects of horror on the other. Hence the curious duplicity of feeling peculiar to classic tragedy, which instinctively strikes us, through our conventional admiration of antiquity, as gruesome and even shocking. And indeed to us, in whose minds the moral illusion is so greatly weakened, it seems no doubt a hard saying that man is answerable for what he does as well as for what he intends. We think to enjoy the privilege of action without assuming the responsibility; and when anything goes wrong, we have a convenient little way of shrugging our shoulders and leaving it with circumstance or providence. It is not so, however, that life would look to a consciousness thoroughly and consistently moral. Such a consciousness would find no satisfaction, either, in a physiological interpretation of what was and still is to some extent felt as the fatal obligation of blood, implicating the descendant in the vices and virtues of his ancestors and making the child responsible, like Iphigenia, for the parent; for to such a consciousness the human creature would appear, by the same illusion of moral order, accountable for what it is as for what it does. Nor is it wholly otiose in this connection to refer to the exemplary "statue of Mitys at Argos, which killed his murderer by falling upon him while he was watching a spectacle"—a kind of incident which appears to Aristotle highly commendable for plots, "since such a thing seems not to happen at random"; while to the modern critic it looks altogether accidental and quite unfit for tragedy, because where Aristotle was ready to divine a judgment, and supply a moral connection, we can detect only a bare mechanical sequence without any retributive force whatever. And so it is for this reason, because we have shifted the centre of gravity from man to nature, from the moral to the physical, that so much of modern tragedy is essentially fortuitous or unintelligible, or what comes to the same thing, is spiritually irrelevant, a tragedy

Of accidental judgments, casual slaughters,

and that the classical tragedy has generally turned to nonsense in the hands of its adapters.

To Corneille, for instance, Œdipus is merely a blameless unfortunate. "[Il] me semble ne faire aucune faute," he says, "bien qu'il tue son père, parce qu'il ne le connoit pas et qu'il ne fait que disputer le chemin en homme de cœur contre un inconnu qui l'attaque avec avantage." Hence his desperate and grotesque exertions to put Œdipus obviously in the wrong, as he succeeds in doing finally in a manner undreamed of by Sophocles, by hatching up a love affair between Dirce and that universal lover Theseus, and making of Œdipus a commonplace and silly intermeddler. In like manner he professes himself unable to comprehend Sophocles' motive in prolonging the action of *Ajax* so far beyond the death of the protagonist; though with the assistance of Aristotle's commentary it ought to be clear enough that the quality of the action, the idea of the drama, remains undefined until the disposition of Ajax's body is finally settled. Indeed, Aristotle's whole teaching with regard to the characters and the "purgation of the passions" appears to him so dark, devious, and dangerous that, once having made it respectful obeisance as to a Gessler's hat, he prudently takes another road for the future. Nor can Racine, who in imitating Euripides comes perhaps the nearest to imitating antiquity, see much more sense in Iphigenia, but attempts, with the aid of the unhappy and officious Eriphile to substitute a shabby and conventional poetic justice for the profound naturalism of the original fable. "Quelle apparence que j'eusse souillé la scene par le meutre d'une personne aussi aimable et aussi vertuese qu'il failloit représenter Iphigenie?" Even Euripides, who is himself, on one side of his literary being, nothing more than an adapter of Greek tragedy, has so little appreciation of the morality of his predecessors that he tries to evade it, whenever he can, by some puerile *ex machina* interference or some decadent falsification of motives. On the one hand the *dénouement* of his *Iphigenia in Aulis* is in flat contradiction with the *morale* of the remainder of the piece. The sacrifice is accomplished at Iphigenia's exit; the effect is produced already, and the effort to arrest it later is absurdity. On the other hand, his Orestes is no longer the pathetic and terrible figure of tradition and tragedy, Electra's brother, Clytemnestra's son. He is a contemptible, whining, besotted, epileptic parricide, at the mercy of a faithless and uxorious poltroon—a thoroughly Ibsenesque situation. He is already near the bottom; he has one step farther to fall into Racine's semi-comic dupe of a vain and jealous coquette. While as for Seneca's, Dryden and Lee's, and Voltaire's parodies, what can be said of them, save only that such is the power of the tremendous old story that it is still capable of stirring obscurely the depths of our nature in spite of these marplots, whenever they will let the son of Laius himself upon the stage? Even Boileau, the last great arbiter of things classical, how unequal does even he show himself to the greatness of his theme!

> Aussi pour nous charmer, la tragedie en pleurs
> D'Oedipe tout sanglant fit parler les douleurs,
> D'Oreste parricide exprima les alarmes,
> Et, pour nous divertir, nous arracha les larmes.

It is not unlikely that in trying to make this point at all, I have overemphasised it. Such matters do not bear forcing. But I have done all I set out to do if I have made it clear that Greek tragedy did not pretend to represent actuality or any such physical or mechanical system as seems to us to be implied by actuality. On the contrary, it undertook to represent a series of sensations (the action) which should produce upon the spectators a deceptive effect of reality, but should, in fact, differ from it altogether in being informed with a moral idea, such idea constituting the writer's sense of the transaction. It is on this account that a Greek play seems to us so set and rigid. It is indeed in durance—in durance to a principle more or less abstract.

III

And yet, in spite of all his fumbling, something of this constraint, of this ideal purposefulness of classic tragedy Corneille felt, and not only felt but also succeeded in imitating and in fastening so unshakably upon the neo-classic drama that it is conceptually more nearly akin to the Greek than is that of any other nation, though neither he himself nor his immediate successors had fully measured the spirit that they were imitating. But while he often missed the idea of the Greek, he was very susceptible to its form. And it is undoubtedly true that the depth and seriousness of Greek tragedy, if not actually due to this cause, was at all events greatly intensified by its concision, which was, in turn, more or less accidental and a result of its peculiar manner of development. There was no room in Greek drama for a distracting play of circumstance. Its very limitations, as is not unusual in art, made its strength. The chorus, which anchored it so firmly to a given ground and held it so closely to a brief moment of time, prevented it from straying away in search of incident or from dissipating its substance in irrelevant sentiment. It could not become epic, on the one hand, a mere scenic chronicle of events, or lyric, on the other, an excited outburst of purely individual feeling. It was forced to remain a *genre tranché*. In its brief compass it could deal only with the moral issue or upshot of an action as denoted in character.

Something of this focalisation, then, it is certain that Corneille saw and aimed at in adopting the "unities," which represented to him, as to the critics of his day, the structural merits of classicism. With regard to two of these unities, those of time and place, it is fitting that a word should be said. They have been so abused and decried in the course of a long and violent reaction that they have finally come to appear something monstrous and abhorrent, a damning evidence of literary servility and fatuity. That they sometimes put Corneille and his followers to strange shifts can not be gainsaid. But the fault was not so much theirs as the dramatists', who were frequently unwilling to accept a stuff, or unable to cast it into a shape conformable with their own theories.

It has been generally assumed that the unities of time and place were only devices for securing verisimilitude. And inasmuch as it is indifferently easy for their enemies to show that they contribute nothing to the probability of drama, but quite the contrary, and as their friends with singular blindness have insisted upon defending them on grounds so obviously false and untenable, the romanticists have leaped to the conclusion that they are altogether vain and inadmissible on any grounds. The fact is, however, that to Corneille, as to all the neo-classicists, whether they were conscious of it or not, the unities of time and place were, in actual practice, nothing more than a convention to secure dramatic relevancy and concentration. In this respect they were quite successful and were used by Shakespeare in *Othello* and by Æschylus in *Agamemmon* and the *Eumenides*, to mention but a few instances, although it was Corneille who first reduced them to a regular theatrical *procédé* in taking them up into his drama and reinforcing them in his *Examens* and *Discours* with an ample apologetic criticism. With this assistance it is by no means difficult to follow the steps by which the convention was developed or to define the exact shape which it finally took to his imagination.

In the *Cid* he is as yet rather embarrassed. He acknowledges as much in the *Examen*: that he has managed matters rather clumsily and that he did not then see his way clear to the manner in which the unity of time might be made a practicable working stage device. Indeed it is doubtful whether he had as yet divined the ideal to which such a unity would contribute. But it did not take him long to perceive that the reckoning of dramatic time is at best a very uncertain process; and consequently, when events are sown thickly together, without any reference to their duration, the impression produced is as likely to be that of a day as of any other period. In other words, he understood what dramatists have always understood and critics have often forgotten, that a

play is meant to be acted and seen, not pored over
and anatomised, and that dramatic effect is largely
an affair of hints, suggestions, and intimations, to
which the audience pays small attention at the moment but which produce their result insensibly and
in the mass. And therefore it is no very difficult matter to crowd the stage with incidents in a manner
quite impossible to the reason, and yet to give the
impression that they are confined to twenty-four
hours in the naturalest way in the world. In short, it
is an affair of plausibility, not of probability. And
this is virtually Corneille's discovery—a discovery
which made the unity of time possible as a condition
of French tragedy.

Il est si malaisé qu'il se rencontre, dans l'histoire ny dans
l'imagination des hommes, quantité de ces événemens illustres
et dignes de la tragédie, dont les délibérations et leurs effets
puissent arriver en un mesme lieu et en un mesme jour sans
faire un peu de violence à l'ordre commun des choses, que je ne
puis croire cette sorte de violence tout à fait condamnable,
pourveu qu'elle n'aille pas jusqu'à l'impossible. Il est de beaux
sujets où on ne la peut éviter, et un autheur scrupuleux
se priveroit d'une belle occasion, et le public de beaucoup
de satisfaction, s'il n'osoit s'enhardir à les mettre sur le
théâtre, de peur de se voir forcé à les faire aller plus viste
que le vray-semblance ne le permet. Je luy donneroit, en ce
cas, un conseil que peut-estre il trouveroit salutaire: c'est de
ne marquer aucun temps préfix dans son poëme, ny aucun
lieu determiné où il pose ses acteurs. L'imagination de l'auditeur auroit plus de liberté de se laisser aller au courant de
l'action si elle n'étoit point fixée par ces marques, et il
pourroit ne s'appercevoir de cette précipitation, si elles ne

l'en faisoient souvenir et n'y appliquoient son esprit malgré
luy.

As for the unity of place he would treat that in
general like the unity of time; he would, that is, allow himself, to begin with, as much latitude as he
could plausibly neutralise in the final effect produced
upon the audience. Between the treatment of time
and place in drama, however, there is unfortunately
one serious difference. In the case of the former there
is nothing in the nature of a play that need remind
the spectators of the duration of the action as such;
whereas the *mise en scène,* the scenery and stage-
setting, forces the latter consideration immediately
upon the attention of the audience. The only way out
of the difficulty would seem to consist in making
the setting as non-committal as possible and in particular in avoiding all changes of scenery, whether the
action shifts its ground or not, just as all indications
of time were previously avoided.

Je tiens donc qu'il faut chercher cette unité exacte autant
qu'il est possible; mais comme elle ne s'accommode pas
avec toute sorte de sujets, j'accorderois tresvolontiers que
ce qu'on feroit passer en une seule ville auroit l'unité de lieu.
Ce n'est pas que je volusse que le théatre representast
cette ville toute entiére (cela seroit un peu trop vaste), mais
seulement deux ou trois lieux particuliers enfermez dans
l'enclos de ses murailles. . . . Pour rectifier en quelque façon
cette duplicité de lieu quand elle est inévitable, je voudrois
qu'on fist deux choses: l'une que jamais on ne changeast
dans le mesme acte, mais seulement de l'un à l'autre, comme
il se fait dans les trois prémiers de *Cinna*; l'autre, que ces

deux lieux n'eussent point besoin de diverses décorations, et qu'aucun des deux ne fust jamais nommé, mais seulement le lieu général où tous les deux sont compris, comme Paris, Rome, Lyon, Constantinople, etc. Cela aideroit à tromper l'auditeur, qui, ne voyant rien qui luy marquast la diversité des lieux, ne s'en appercevroit pas, à moins d'une reflexion malicieuse et critique, dont il y en a peu qui soient capable, la pluspart s'attachant avec chaleur à l'action qu'ils voyent representer.

That is to say, if the stage represent no place in particular, or represent a place with no particular character, there will be no remarkable incongruity in seeing any or all of the characters appear in such a scene, for it is obviously the kind of place in which any one might appear, though there is, to be sure, no particular reason that any one in particular should appear there. Such a place would naturally be a room,—an out-door scene would be too characteristic and peculiar for the purpose; and it would be a public room of some sort, or certain of the characters might seem out of place or suggest awkward doubts of their motives. So in the *Examen* of *Polyeucte*:

L'autre scrupule regarde l'unité du lieu, qui est assez exacte, puisque tout s'y passe dans une salle ou antichambre commune aux apartemens de Félix et sa fille. Il semble que la bien-séance y soit un peu forcée pour conserver cette unité au second acte, en ce que Pauline vient jusque dans cette antichambre pour trouver Sévére, dont elle devroit attendre la visite dans son cabinet. A quoy je répons qu'elle a eu deux raisons de venir au devant de luy: l'une pour faire plus d'honneur à un homme dont son père redoutoit l'indignation, et qu'il luy avoit commandé d'adoucir en sa faveur; l'autre, pour rompre plus aisément la conversation avec luy, en se retirant dans ce cabinet, s'il ne vouloit pas la quitter à son priére et se délivrer par cette retraite d'un entretien dangereux pour celle, ce qu'elle n'eust pû faire si elle eust receu sa visite dans son apartement.

This is the second stage. The apologetic ingenuity is misplaced and weakens the case by continuing to rest it on the mistaken principle of verisimilitude. He should have claimed at the very outset the immunity of convention—just as he goes on to do a little later when he comes to understand the real strength of his position and pushes his idea to a logical conclusion.

In order that a play may go on it is necessary that the characters meet. Now, inasmuch as the characters are represented by the actors, these characters will appear to meet whenever the actors do. But the actors meet on the stage, and the stage is decorated to represent a scene. The difference between the stage and a scene, however, consists in this, that the one belongs to the theatrical reality, the other to the dramatic fiction; so that the scenery transforms the stage into an imaginary realm supposedly within the bounds of the play. Of course this is just the difficulty. But it may be obviated by letting the decoration represent a public room, as before, but one which all the characters are free to enter under any circumstances, avowedly on some more or less probable pretext, but in reality and by tacit agreement for the sake of carrying on the piece.

Mais, comme les personnes qui ont des intérests opposez ne peuvent pas vray-semblablement expliquer leurs secrets

en mesme place, et qu'ils sont quelquefois introduits dans
le mesme acte, avec liaison de scénes qui emportent néces-
sairement cette unité, il faut trouver un moyen qui la rende
compatible avec cette contradiction qu'y forme la vraysemblance rigoureuse. . . . Les jurisconsultes admettent des
fictions de droit, et je voudrois, à leur example, introduire
des fictions de théatre pour établir un lieu théatral qui ne
seroit ny l'apartement de Cléopatre, ny celuy de Rodogune
dans la piéce qui porte ce tître, ny celuy de Phocas, de
Léontine, ou de Pulchérie dans *Héraclius*, mais une salle sur
laquelle ouvrent ces divers apartemens, à qui j'attribuërois
deux priviléges: l'un, que chacun de ceux qui y parleroient
fust présumé y parler avec le mesme secret que s'il étoit
dans sa chambre; l'autre, qu'au lieu que dans l'ordre commun il est quelquefois de la bienséance que ceux qui occu-
pent le théatre aillent trouver ceux qui sont dans leur cabinet
pour parler à eux, ceux-cy pûssent les venir trouver sur le
théatre sans choquer cette bienséance, afin de conserver
l'unité de lieu et la liaison des scénes.

It is easy enough to say that this is conventional
and artificial; but that once said, the worst is over.
To be sure, in such a practice time and place were
abstract. But the statement means nothing more than
that they belonged to the play, not to reality; that
they pertained to the idea of the *genre*, not to the
idea of nature—which is no more than to say that
a play is a play. Or, to put it in other words, the
drama happened on the stage for as long as it was
acting—surely no very grave fault in a stage play,
since everybody knows that it never happened elsewhere or at any other time. Schlegel himself states
the principle clearly enough in his *Dramatische*

Kunst und Litteratur, though he misapplies it mischievously:

> Der Begriff der Taüschung hat in der Kunsttheorie grosse Irrungen angerichtet. Man hat oft darunter den unwilkürlich gewordenen Irrthum verstanden, als ob das Dargestellte wirklich sey. . . . Nein, die theatralische Taüschung wie jede poetische ist eine wache Traümerey, des man sich freywillig hingiebt. Um sie hervorzubringen, müssen Dichter und Schauspieler die Gemüther lebhaft hinreissen, die berechneten Wahrscheinlichkeiten helfen nicht im mindesten dazu.

Exactly: the illusion of art—and the wonder is that any one should forget it—is wholly specious.

Such was the spirit of Corneille's teaching. And judiciously managed in accordance with this spirit, as Racine finally caught the trick of managing them, the unities of time and place are in themselves no more shocking than the gross conventions of the Elizabethan stage, for which we show ourselves so tender because they happen to be in our way—a placard doing duty for a scene or a lantern for the moon or other such like clumsy makeshifts as Shakespeare has himself ridiculed in the *Midsummer Night's Dream*. But, to push the case at once to an extreme, is the fact that the action of *Bérénice*, after the fashion of *Polyeucte*, passes willy-nilly in an antechamber contiguous to the apartments of Titus and Bérénice any more offensive to "verisimilitude" than the chasm between the third and fourth acts of the *Winter's Tale*? The fact is that Corneille and Racine may be right as well as Shakespeare. For as long as the main business of drama is accomplished, what difference does it make about such matters as these? Given the type of tragedy, it is of very small moment, after all, where *Bérénice* takes place, provided only the display of emotion for whose sake the piece exists be adequately carried off. In the whole range of neo-classic tragedy, it is safe to say, there is no more audacious violation of probability, no more purely artificial device, than the "double time," so called, which gives rapidity and intensity to *Othello*. If it is improbable that Titus and Bérénice should in reality open their hearts so freely as they do in the place assigned them, it is physically impossible, not to say absolutely inconceivable, that Desdemona should deceive her husband in the time at her disposal. If Othello could have told the hours, the murder would never have been committed. And what is so singular, in the light of that romantic criticism which is continually reproaching Racine with Shakespeare, is the fact that the Shakespearean contrivance is in this case of exactly the same character as that by virtue of which Corneille begins by cramming the events of the *Cid* into a single day—what else is it than a unity of time?—only more daring. Nor does Æschylus do otherwise in making the return of Agamemnon succeed immediately upon the fall of Troy; it is but one time and one scene. Beside such examples the procedures of Racine and Corneille, which we are invited to reprobate as unnatural, are marvels of verisimilitude and credibility. So true is it that Shakespeare himself, or any other playwright for that matter, had no slightest compunction in using a bold and literally impossible artifice when it suited his purpose. What cared he, or Æschylus, in such a case for a timorous probability as long as he secured the dramatic intensity which the play demanded? Indeed, as Shakespeare proves—even to the satisfaction of the romanticists, I hope—such artifices are as likely to help as hinder; it all lies in their appropriateness. So the bare stage was an advantage to the romantic drama, whose strength consisted in reproducing, by a variety of incident, a sense of the bewildering *wirr-warr* of existence. And equally was the rigidity of the performance an advantage to Greek tragedy, whose strength consisted in the illustration of moral ideas. The only question, then, is not whether such a device is conventional and artificial, but is it in harmony with the spirit of the drama to which it is applied and does it assist the impression which that drama aims to produce? Only, if there is to be a convention, let it be as simple and elementary as possible. A monologue, for instance, is better than a "confidant" male or female, a direct explanatory address to the audience in the Greek manner than such an exposition as introduces Voltaire's *Oedipe* or Corneille's *Medée*.

> J'aimerois mieux encore qu'il declinast son nom,
> Et dit: "Je suis Oreste," ou bien "Agamemnon."

But while the neo-classicists were by no means blameless in these respects, yet the unities of time and place did, on the whole, agree so thoroughly with the general intent of their tragedy that it remains, with all its faults, the strongest structurally and the

most effectual in design—that is, the most respon-
sive to ideas—of any modern tragedy: so false is the
whole romantic working-hypothesis that lawlessness
is strength.

IV

And yet there were dangers which neither Corneille
nor his successors escaped in attempting to reproduce the formal austerity of Greek tragedy. For if
the unities of time and place have their conveniency,
they have their liabilities, too; and it would have
been well if their employers had always remembered
that, while they were favourable to a strictly ideal
design, they were altogether incompatible with
breadth and variety of action or theatrical exuberance
of any kind. Racine puts the matter very clearly in
the preface to *Bérénice*.

Mais ce qui m'en plût davantage, c'est que je le [le sujet]
trouvai extrêmement simple. [And he continues:] Il n'y
a que le vraysemblance qui touche dans le tragédie, et quelle
vraysemblance y a-t-il qu'il arrive en un jour une multitude
de choses qui pourroient à peine arriver en plusieurs se-
maines? Il y en a qui pensent que cette simplicité est une
marque de peu d'invention. Ils ne songent pas qu'au contraire
toute l'invention consiste à faire quelque chose de rien, et
que tout ce grand nombre d'incidents a toujours esté le
refuge des poëtes qui ne sentoient dans leur genie ni assez
d'abondance ni assez de force pour attacher durant cinq
actes leurs spectateurs par *une action simple, soutenuë de la
violence des passions, de la beauté des sentimens, et de
l'élegance de l'expression.*

This is undoubtedly the formula of such a type of drama, not on account of *"vraysemblance,"* wherewith we still love to delude ourselves, but on account of artistic consistency, which would preclude the use of a form for any other purpose than that for which it is fitted. And to this law, the law of congruous simplicity, Racine conforms pretty faithfully. Both Corneille and Voltaire, however, are grave offenders; and though Corneille's superiority as a dramatist is so great that he carries it off very much better than Voltaire, yet even his plays do not escape the sort of grotesqueness which arises from the application of a simple and severe method to a luxurious and diversified material. No one has ever felt the effect of the inconsistency more keenly, though he seems to have no suspicion of the cause of it. Hear him discoursing of the four last scenes of the first act of the *Cid;* it is one of the curiosities of literature:

Le Comte et D. Diégue se querellent au sortir du palais: cela peut passer dans une rue; mais après la soufflet receu, D. Diégue ne peut pas demeurer dans cette rue à faire ses plaintes, attendant que son fils survienne, qu'il ne soit tout aussitot environné de peuple et ne recoive l'offre de quelques amis. . . . En l'état où elles [les scènes] sont icy, on peut dire qu'il faut quelquefois aider au théatre, et suppléer favorablement ce qui ne s'y peut representer. . . . Ainsi, par une fiction de théatre, on peut s'imaginer que D. Diégue et le Comte, sortant du palais du Roy, avancent toujours en se querellant et sont arrivez devant le maison de ce prémier, lors qu'il reçoit le soufflet, qui l'oblige à y entrer pour y chercher du secours.

And all this in spite of the fact that the Count and Don Diégue move not at all and that the scenery never changes. It was this sort of thing which provoked Dryden to remark facetiously that in regular French drama "the street, the window, the houses, the closet, are made to walk about, and the persons to stand still." But the cream of Cornielle's commentary remains:

Si cette fiction poétique ne vous satisfait point, laissons le [D. Diégue] dans la place publique, et disons que le concours de peuple autour de luy, aprés cette offense, et les offres que luy font les prémiers amis qui s'y rencontrent, sont des circonstances que le roman ne doit pas oublier, mais que, ces menuës actions ne servant de rien à la principale, il n'est pas besoin que le poëte s'en embarasse sur la scéne.

Such is the desperate plight to which Corneille is reduced in his first masterpiece in order to give a kind of plausibility to its successive scenes. And though it must be remembered that the *Cid* is one of his freer plays, and that his comments with respect to it are intended to be apologetic rather than exemplary, yet the case, while an extreme, is withal a fair one. In almost every instance Corneille's intrigue is too complicated for his form. His *Rodogune*, for instance, on which he prided himself particularly, is on this account curious rather than impressive; and the "inventiveness" of the fifth act, which Voltaire pretended to admire and tried to imitate, with even worse effect, is, under the circumstances, a blemish rather than a beauty. Indeed, he as much as confesses

the fault himself, and even prides himself upon it
with an ingenious and amusing vainglory quite his
own. Of *Heraclius* he remarks justly enough:

> . . . Le poëme est si embarrassé qu'il demande une mar-
> veilleuse attention. J'ay veu de fort bons esprits, et des per-
> sonnes des plus qualifiées de la Cour, se plaindre de ce que
> sa représentation fatiguoit autant l'esprit qu'une étude
> sérieuse. Elle n'a pas laissé de plaire, mais je croy qu'il l'a
> fallu voir plus d'une fois pour en remporter une entiére
> intelligence.

In short, Corneille is romantic by his plot and
classic by his design. And it is to this fundamental
incongruity between the form and the *fond* of his
drama that his difficulties with the unities and his
frequent apologies are due.

Nor is the tendency to stuff the action the only lee
shore upon which neo-classicism drifted in attempting
to lay its course by Aristotle and the Greek tragedians. It was all very well to attempt to bring the
French drama out of the maelstrom of romanticism
and to devote it to the service of ideas, provided the
dramatist had any ideas to devote it to. But inasmuch
as the unities rigidly limited the amount of incident,
reducing the action almost to the dimensions of a
situation as compared with that of the romantic
drama, this very limitation was liable, in default of
any serious or worthy purpose, to leave the writer,
like Benvenuto Cellini, without sufficient materials
for his casting, and oblige him to an unnatural pro-
longation of the action, particularly as the modern
taste demanded a larger play than the ancient. In
short, in assuming the restrictions which would as-

sist in the expression of a genuine idea, the dramatist, in the absence of such an idea or in case of its inadequacy, ran the risk of falling into a sort of casuistical extenuation of what motives, emotions, and the like the situation afforded him, eking them out as best he could with aphorisms, *sententiæ*, gnomic utterances, commonplaces, and what not, which lent an air of factitious moral reflection to his drama. To read Corneille in one mood it would seem as though the *Cid* must have attracted him, as it might have attracted Dryden, for the equivocalness of the situations; for there is nothing more common in literature than the acquirement of a taste for what was originally a defect and the gradual erection of a failing into a merit and a subject of imitation. Certainly in such speeches as Chiméne's,

> Pour conserver ma gloire et finir mon ennuy,
> Le poursuivre, le prendre, et mourir après luy.
> > *Le Cid*, iii., 3.

the dramatist is swimming triumphantly in some supersensible medium, equally remote from the idealised atmosphere of the Greek and the romantic æther of Shakespeare—the kind of medium which characterises such plays as the *Conquest of Granada* or *Aureng-Zebe*. So too in *Horace*—to set aside pieces like *Heraclius* in which the *equivoque* is inherent in the material—the permutations and combinations of relationship and of feeling between Camille, Sabine, Horace, and Curiace are figured out, not only with amazing thoroughness and ingenuity, but also with

something of that forced and factitious wit which is
nowadays associated with the name of Cowley. Nor,
in fact, is Corneille, like Cowley, without a weakness
for quibbles even in the most inappropriate places.
While the elder Horace is bewailing what he supposes to be the cowardice of his surviving son fleeing
before the Curiaces, he has still levity enough to ex-
cogitate his little witticism.

> N'eust-il que d'un moment reculé sa defaite,
> Rome eust été du moins un peu plus tard sujette.
>> *Horace*, iii., 6.

But the fourth and fifth scenes of this same act, the
third, are the triumph of that sort of emotional emulation or competition of sensibility which makes this
literature look at times like a mere work of ingenuity—an attempt to see how many changes might
be rung upon a given theme.[3]

Nor for all his tact is Racine by any means innocent of the same vice. The passage in which Aricie
undertakes to explain her love for Hippolytus, though
well known, is too good an example to remain un-
quoted:

> J'aime, je l'avoûray, cet orgueil genereux
> Qui jamais n'a fleché sous le joug amoureux.
> Phedre en vain s'honoroit des soupirs de Thesée:
> Pour moy, je suis plus fière, et fuis la gloire aisée

[3] For some suggestive remarks on the character and result
of Corneille's dramatic casuistry, consult Brunetière's *Études
critiques sur l'historie de la Littérature française,* vi., Corneille, sec. ii.

D'arracher un hommage à mille autres offert,
Et d'entrer dans un cœur de toutes parts ouvert.
Mais de faire flechir un courage inflexible,
De porter la douleur dans une ame insensible,
D'enchaîner un captif de ses fers étonné,
Contre un joug qui luy plaist vainement mutiné :
C'est la ce que je veux, c'est la ce qui m'irrite,
Hercule à desarmer coûtoit moins qu'Hippolyte,
Et, vaincu plus souvent, et plûtost surmonté,
Preparoit moins de gloire aux yeux qui l'ont donté.

Phedre, ii., 1.

This is not to exhibit human character or passion, to say nothing of human action; it is merely to force an opportunity, to exploit a situation. And, though it is necessary to forgive much to an episode which serves as an occasion to Phedre's magnificent outburst of jealousy in the closing scene of the fourth act, the weakness of such a passage is unmistakable.

With Racine and Corneille the drama is indeed something more than this. With Voltaire, however, it is just about this and little more. It is very much with respect to action what a pun is with respect to language, a play upon incidents, a dramatic quibble—a fact which may account for the inveteracy with which he praises *Horace* in and out of season.

Chere Obeide!

exclaims the condemned lover in the *Scythes*,

Prends ce fer, ne crains rien; que ton bras homicide
Frappe un cœur à toi seule en tout temps reservé;
On y verra ton nom; c'est la qu'il est gravé.

Les Scythes, v.,5.

Even Goethe himself, when he attempts to be classical, does not escape. His *Iphigenie* is neither the expression of characters in action nor the notation of a transaction by means of characters. It contains neither actions nor passions. It is rather the protraction of a situation in "sentences"; and however noble and elevated those sentences, it has very much the same air of research which has perhaps done more than anything else to give this whole literature the name of "artificial."

And yet this subtilisation of motives, particularly those of a paradoxical or antithetical sort, conveys a suggestive and instructive lesson; because the weakness would seem to be, not merely coincident with a certain school or period, but inevitable whenever the modern attempts to revive the spirit of antiquity, as though to us its singleness of eye, its grave and congruous simplicity were forever impossible—this curious dialectic and a peculiar sort of flatness or tepidity which is the natural counterpart of such an ingenuity and which is so familiar to every reader of French poetry. Without going outside the language compare, for example, this morsel of Corneille's *Suite du Menteur*, which Voltaire singles out for special praise, with a brief passage from a writer who, himself an admirer of the ancients, was yet quite untouched by the classical literary affectation, the artistry, of the renaissance—I mean Montaigne:

Quand les ordres du Ciel nous ont fait l'un pour l'autre,
Lyse, c'est un accord bien tost fait que le nostre.
Sa main entre les cœurs, par un secret pouvoir,
Séme l'intelligence avant que de se voir;

Il prépare si bien l'amant et la maîtresse
Que leur âme au seul nom s'emeut et s'intéresse :
On s'estime, on se cherche, on s'aime en un moment ;
Tout ce qu'on s'entredit persuade aisément,
Et, sans s'inquiéter d'aucunes peurs frivoles,
Le foy semble courir au devant des paroles.
La langue en peu de mots en explique beaucoup ;
Les yeux, plus éloquens, font tout voir tout d'un coup ;
Et, de quoy qu'à l'envy tous les deux nous s'instruisent,
Le cœur en entend plus que tous les deux n'en disent.

La Suite du Menteur, iv., 1

It is on a somewhat similar subject, his friendship
for de la Boetie, that Montaigne speaks in the following terms:

Si l'on me presse de dire pourquoy je l'aymois, je sens
que cela ne se peut exprimer : il y a, ce semble, au delà
de tout mon discours et de ce que j'en puis dire, ne sçay
quelle force divine et fatale, mediatrice de cette union. Ce
n'est pas une particuliere consideration, ny deux, ny trois,
ny quatre, ny mille ; c'est je ne sçay quelle quinte essence
de tout ce meslange, qui, ayant saisi toute ma volonté,
l'amena se plonger et se perdre dans la sienne. Je dis perdre,
à la verité, ne luy reservant rien qui luy fust propre ny qui
fust sien.

It seems, indeed, as though there were but a single
moment in the world's history when men could be
unaffectedly simple without shallowness or banality;
and, that moment passed, they must needs be intricate or nothing.

Les grandes choses [says Sainte-Beuve], et qui sont simples à la fois, ont été dites de bonne heure: les anciens moralistes et poëtes ont dessiné et saisi la nature humaine dans ses principaux et larges traits; il semble qu'ils n'aient laissé aux modernes que la découverte des détails et la grâce des raffinements.

And so, if the inference is correct, it evidently indicates a source of weakness as dangerous to modern classicism as is the risk of distraction and confusion to romanticism.

> L'esclave imitateur nâit et s'évanouit;
> La nuit vient, le corps reste, et son ombre s'enfuit.

RACINE

I

WHEN Racine began his career as a dramatist, he found the general definition of French tragedy already formulated by Corneille. However the latter had come by his conception — whether freely and of his own instance, or in yielding to the pressure of official criticism, or what is even more likely, in attempting to effect a compromise between these two influences — the upshot of his labour was, to all intents and purposes, the doctrine of the three unities. All that remained for Racine was to adapt himself to these prescriptions. Nor should the difficulty of the task be underrated. It was one which Corneille himself had failed to accomplish. Classic by method and finally, perhaps, by conviction, he was incurably romantic by temperament and inspiration and was never wholly successful in conceiving an action thoroughly agreeable with his own formulæ. There is something bungling and unhandy in his efforts to cage a broad and rambing plot within the narrow limits required by his theory; something cramped and ungraceful about the result. In a word, it would hardly be unjust to say, whatever praise he may deserve for its discovery, that he never understood the practical working of his own invention; he never altogether grasped the principles of congruous simplicity characteristic of the classic drama.

To illustrate this statement I need only refer to *Rodogune*. The *Cid* would be an even better example, though scarcely so fair an one, since it was written while Corneille was still serving his apprenticeship. But to the citation of *Rodogune* for such a purpose it is impossible to take exception since Corneille himself expresses a decided preference for it over all his preceding performances including both the *Cid* and *Cinna*. And the significant matter is the reason he assigns for his favouritism. Abstractly, the frame work is of the utmost severity, such as is ideally prescribed by the unities of time and place, as Corneille insists that he is practising them. But what he congratulates himself upon is anything but the harmonious accommodation of material to plan. Rather, he justifies his fondness for the play by " the surprising incidents," which, he assures us, are purely of his own " invention " and " have never before been seen on the stage." To be sure, he acknowledges that his " tenderness " for this particular drama may be in the nature of a parental partiality — it contains so much of himself; but the very fact that he feels it at all, is pretty good evidence that he never quite realized the obligations which his own profession of the unities imposed upon him, particularly with reference to the selection of congruous subject-matter. And to this charge he pleads guilty in so many words in the *Discours de la Tragédie:*

" It is so unlikely that there should occur, either in imagination or history, a quantity of transactions illustrious and worthy of tragedy, whose deliberations and effects can possibly be made to happen in one place and in one day without doing some little violence to the common order of things, that I can not believe this sort of violence altogether reprehensible, provided it does not become quite impossible. There are admirable subjects where it is impossible to avoid some such violence; and a scrupulous author would deprive himself of an excellent chance of glory and the public of a good deal of satisfaction, if he were too timid to stage subjects of this sort for fear of being forced to make them pass more quickly than probability permits. In such a case I should advise him to prefix no time to his piece or any determinate place for the action. The imagination of the audience will be freer to follow the current of the action, if it is not fixed by these marks, and it will never perceive the precipitancy of events unless it is reminded and made to take notice of them expressly."

Here, then, is his confession. Do the best you can to crowd the incidents of your play into the compass of a single day and dodge circumspectly anything that may call the attention of the audience to the passage of dramatic time in the hope that they may not notice the imposture. Every Corneillean tragedy conforms more or less closely to this general rule. I can not think of one in which there is not some embarrassment in supposing that the whole action elapses within twenty-four hours.

On this account it is not quite fair to represent Racine as merely taking over Corneille's model. To the formal theory and criticism of French tragedy, it may be, he contributed little. But if drama is a craft in any sense of the word, then the man who took up tragedy at the point to which Corneille had brought it and carried it on to the point where Racine left it, can hardly be said to have added little or nothing to it. And the misconception arises, I believe, from a persistent confusion with regard to one of the unities — to wit, the unity of action.

However it may be with the unities of time and place, we are commonly assured that all drama, the romantic not excepted, has one unity in common, the unity of action; for such unity, it is speciously added, is indispensable to a dramatic work of any kind. That the statement is true in one sense, may be granted; most statements are so in some sense or other. But that the romantic drama possesses unity of action in the same sense as the classic drama — or even anything that would have been recognized as a unity by Aristotle — such a position can hardly be maintained with any great show of plausibility. Indeed, so great is the difference in kind that the use of the same term with reference to the two dramas is misleading and bewildering in the extreme. As well say that romantic tragedy possesses unity of time and place because each individual scene is within itself continuous and stationary.

The fact is that the romantic and the classic actions are conceived in two quite different manners and produce two quite distinct impressions. While the latter, as everybody acknowledges, is concerned only for the upshot or issue of a certain business or transaction; the former is concerned equally for its inception and development — for the soil in which the tragic seed is planted and the climate in which it is ripened even more than for the fruit which it finally bears. It is as though the romantic playwright were absorbed in demonstrating how such a result was brought about by successive steps; while the classic playwright is interested only in the nature and symptoms of the disease itself. Scrupulous as is Sophocles in general, he is, to all appearance, quite indifferent to the antecedent improbabilities of his *Œdipus Tyrannus;* evidently he recognizes no obligation to account for his tragic consequences. In the romantic action this tragic matter is anatomized or parcelled out into its various constituent incidents, circumstances, and details, the which are all set forth severally and serially in such a manner that the spectator gains his notion of the tragedy as a whole by a retrospective and discursive act of the imagination. In the classic form the tragic affair is caught at its culmination or crisis in such a way that it is made to yield all it contains of human significance and purport. The former is historical, the latter moral. The one views its subject as a process or a becoming; the other as a state or a being. If I were not afraid of being misleading in my turn, I should insist upon this distinction and assert for the sake of contrast that in the matter of procedure the one is dynamic or kinetic, the other static — not that nothing happens in the latter but that what does happen, happens inside the situation. At all events, as far as names are concerned, the romantic drama, from the point of view of method, may safely be described as analytic, the classic as synthetic.

That these two ways of handling plot are, in reality, so diverse as to merit different names, and that the unities of time and place are thoroughly incompatible with the romantic conception, no modern reader with a sense for Shakespeare and Sophocles can deny, when actually put to it. On the very surface of things it is impossible to think of a moral fatality of tragic magnitude historically, as originating, developing, and terminating all in the course of a single day — even a more or less elastic stage day — or to treat it historically, as confined to such a period: the preparation alone would be prohibitive. In *Othello* Shakespeare has indeed tried something of the sort; but even here he has taken pains to truncate his action uncommonly, beginning much farther in than is usual with him. And still in this case the result, as far as it is not purely romantic, is Corneillean — the action, where it is not extended, is merely compressed and makes no pretense to the congruous simplicity demanded by the unities. In a word, it is still analytic, no matter what artifice has been used to make it appear foreshortened. And it is just Racine's distinction to have recognized this fact—— of the essential incompatibilty of such an action with the unities of time and place, a fact to which Corneille was totally blind — and to have succeeded in working out a genuine unity of action in the strict sense of the word — a synthetic action, that is, — which would be comformable with the other unities — though, indeed, it is a distinction that is usually overlooked or misesteemed.

As a matter of fact, the notorious rivalry between the two great poets, amounting to little less than open hostility, ought to be quite enough in itself to discredit the commonplace that Racine was a mere successor or continuator to Corneille. In reality, Racine, while accepting Corneille's definition of the drama in general terms, censures expressly his management of at least two unities, those of time and action, with severity. As Corneille was in the habit of handling it, the unity of time was by his own confession nothing but a barefaced trick or deception — barefaced to the reader, however it might appear to the spectator. It consisted, as he himself explains, in ignoring the actual duration of events in favour of an hypothetical stage-day of twenty-four hours or thereabouts. Upon his choice and organization of material it exerted little or no influence. For the playwright who is embarrassed by the extent of his subject or by a plethora of incident he has no better advice, as has been seen, than to refrain from mentioning the topic on the off chance that the audience may fail to notice the congestion of the action. In short, for all his floundering Corneille never succeeded in imagining, much less in defining, a unity of action commensurate with his ideal unities of time and place. The nearest he comes to doing so is in his " unity of peril " ; and how unsatisfactory that was he was himself the first to acknowledge. To all intents and purposes his action remains of the same dimensions as that of the Spanish *commedia;* it is as diffuse and protracted, as wanting in concision and concentration: — his efforts are directed solely toward disguising its character. Apparently it never occurred to him that the solution of the whole problem consisted in such an *ordonnance* of his plot that the unities of time and place should be involved in the nature of the action itself and should result from it, instead of being imposed upon it as a durance or constraint. As a matter of fact, the unities of time and place, as far as they are valid at all, are only functions of the unity of action.

At all events, it is directly against this method of dramatic composition that Racine directs his satire in replying to the detractors of his *Britannicus*:

"What can be done," he asks, "to satisfy such rigorous judges" as these umbrageous Corneilleans? And he answers:

"Nothing is easier in defiance of good sense. All you have to do is to abandon naturalness for extravagance. Instead of *a simple action* [italics mine] made up of a modest amount of material, which takes place in a single day and advances gradually to a conclusion sustained only by the interests, sentiments, and passions of the characters, you must cram this same action with a great quantity of incidents which could not possibly come to pass in less than a month, with a vast amount of stage clap-trap the more amazing the more unlikely it is, with a multitude of declamations wherein the actors are made to say just the contrary of what they should."

And to the same effect in a familiar passage of the preface to *Bérénice* he insists upon this pertinent simplicity of action:

"Nothing matters much in tragedy save likelihood; and what is the likelihood that there should happen in a single day a multitude of things which could hardly happen in several weeks? Some there are who think

that this simplicity is a sign of small invention.   They
fail to notice that on the contrary all invention consists
in making something out of nothing and that all this
great mass of incident has ever been the recourse of those
poets who have felt their genius too frail and scanty
to hold their audience for five acts by *a simple action*
[italics mine, again] supported by the violence of the
passions, the beauty of the sentiments, and the elegance
of the expression."

As compared with Corneille's confessed weakness
for " surprising incidents," the like of which had
never before been seen on the stage, these expressions would seem to be sufficiently explicit.   It is
not the multitude or variety of incident which is
to furnish forth the perfect tragedy; it is passion,
sentiment, expression, which, so far from disagree-
ing with simplicity of action, in reality concur with
it; for here as everywhere it is upon this significant
simplicity of action that the whole weight and force
of Racine's authority is brought to bear.

As for the unity of place — it is in itself a minor
matter anyway.   That is to say, the unity of place
offers no such difficulty in the problem of verisimilitude as does the unity of time.   There is no prohibitive improbability that an action of any extent, provided it be confined to the linear dimension,
should not occur in a single place.   One may be
born, wed, and die in the same room, as far as that
goes — though it is impossible to imagine all these
events as taking place on the same day.   It is for
this reason, perhaps, that Racine nominally conforms to Corneille's receipt in setting all his dramas
for a single room or apartment — with the excep-

tion of *Phèdre,* which is set, in accordance with an earlier recommendation of the same authority, for a single " site." Nevertheless his own practice implies a kind of criticism of Corneille's. With the latter the single room or cabinet which served as the local habitation of his drama was a stage fiction no less truly than his dramatic day. Conventionally — though as a matter of fact it often shifts from one spot to another — it was feigned to adjoin the apartments of the principal characters and to represent a kind of indifferent or neutral ground where all parties to the action were equally at home, and where etiquette and precedence were suspended in the article of entrances and exits. Actually, it was a mere theatrical spot, non-committally furnished and decorated, where the actors met regardless of verisimilitude, whenever the playwright needed them, for the purpose of carrying on the play. In the hands of Racine, however, this convention becomes more or less of a dramatic reality. There is some difficulty, to be sure. in actualizing the " locations " of *Phèdre;* but as a general thing, his action does take place in the chamber where it is cast, whether the harem of a sultan or the anteroom of an emperor, the appearance of his characters in that particular spot is reasonable, and a violation of etiquette, if there is one, is always excused by the logic of the situation.

Now, all this was possible — Racine was able to make the unities of time and place a dramatic reality instead of a theatrical fiction by means of his own contribution to French tragedy — a contribution which I have spoken of, properly or not, as the discovery of a genuine unity of action. But no matter for the name; his originality consisted in seeing — what is fairly obvious at present but what at the time escaped the eye of the *grand Corneille* — that a drama as a whole is determined by the plot and that in order to have a certain kind of tragedy it is necessary to begin with a certain kind of action. Unlike Corneille he was sufficiently in sympathy with the Greek spirit to perceive the artificiality of the Corneillean tragedy with its arbitrary limitations of the plot as contrasted with the intimate connection between the action and what virtually amounted to the unities of time and place in the best Athenian tragedy, and to recognize that the success of the same unities in French and the perfection of the type to which they belonged hinged likewise upon the conception of an action which should reduce the dimensions of tragedy to the proportions of a *crise* or paroxysm. As Lemaître points out, he begins *Britannicus* twenty-four hours before Nero's first crime; *Bérénice* twenty-four hours before the heroine leaves Rome; and *Andromaque* twenty-four hours before Pyrrhus decides in favour of his captive. Only so was it possible to confine the drama to a single room or even site and to a single revolution of the sun. Tragedies do occur in rooms and they occur of a sudden, no doubt; but they are tragedies of emotion, not of incident. They are affective tragedies — tragedies in which much is felt and something is said, but in which comparatively little is done. They are tragedies in which the characters suffer their fate — in a single word, they are tragedies of passion and the characters are patients.

And this is, I fancy, the explanation of that Christian passivity ascribed to Racine's drama and referred by Sainte-Beuve to his Jansenist education. While Corneille, it has been pointed out, remains a pagan to the end, Racine manifests, as the saying is, a genius naturally Christian. As compared with the softness and infirmity of Racine's characters, there is about Corneille's something a little extravagant and demonic, even Titanic —

> " Qu'il joigne à ses efforts le secours des enfers,
>   Je suis maistre de moy comme de l'univers." [1]

It is as though the former were concerned to point in them the moral of original sin and efficient grace. In themselves they are powerless for virtue — puppets of temptation like Phèdre, recipients of evil suggestion, *possedés* — without force or initiation of their own. That such is the effect of his drama I have said myself; nor would I deny that his schooling at Port-Royal may have inclined his mind to such an interpretation of life and humanity. But I would insist that such an interpretation conforms also to the formal obligations of his tragedy and is not so very different after all from the tragic vision of the Greeks. Whether they were naturally Jansenist is a question I should hardly care to raise. But granted Racine's problem, he could scarcely have found another solution of it so happy as that afforded him by this tragedy of pathos and infirmity.

Nor is it without significance that so many of his

[1] In quoting Corneille and Racine I use the spelling and accentuation of Fournel's edition (*Librairie des Bibliophiles*) based on the last editions published during the authors' lives.

dramas bear the names of women — *Andromaque, Bérénice, Iphigénie, Phèdre,* to say nothing of *Esther* and *Athalie,* which lie outside of my *cadre,* as do also *Alexandre* and *Les Frères Ennemis.* Of the exceptions — in *Mithridate* alone does an heroic figure dominate the stage, though even he is in his period of *défaillance* and eclipse. As for *Bajazet* it had much better been called after Roxane; while *Britannicus,* too, is something of a misnomer for a play that centers upon the adolescent Nero. The truth is that as a tragedy of passion the nature of Racine's drama —like the depravity of Nero himself with its long suppression and gestation, its violent spasm and its quick collapse — is essentially feminine.

Obviously, such a drama is not without its incidental technical advantages over and above its simplifications of the unities. Its preparation, for instance, is immaterial and subjective: it is all internal and mental, dependent upon the state of mind of the characters; and hence it requires little exposition save what is involved in the psychology of the situation itself and developed *pari passu* with the progress of the play. On the contrary, it is noteworthy that one of the best evidences to the artificiality of Corneille's dramatic construction is furnished by the inherent difficulty of his exposition — he complains of it himself — which makes pretty nearly every one of his entrances into the matter a *tour de force.* At the same time the Racinean outbreak or *dénouement* has the corresponding merit of being as sudden and violent, like an explosion or convulsion of nature. All that is necessary is to apply a match to the train — to invent the one little contingency capable of precipitating the catastrophe. Consider how simple is the machinery of *Andromaque* in comparison with that of *Lear* or *Hamlet;* it is a mere release or trigger. There is no difficulty in imagining such a tragedy as occurring in a single day and in a single chamber wherever the combustible happens to be stored. And it was to his conception of a tragedy of this sort — as an eruption of the most vehement of human passions — that Racine, I repeat, owed his invention of a modern action perfectly in keeping with the unities of time and place.

In this connection it would be unpardonable to omit a reference to what is after all the great superiority of the classic drama. The supreme merit of the simplified or synthetic plot which is the determining feature of that drama, whether in the hands of the Greeks or of Racine, consists in the fact that it allows the dramatist time and opportunity for the conception and development of a definite and deliberate theme. " Le premier mérite d'une œuvre dramatique," declares Vinet, " c'est qu'une idée s'en dégage nettement et vivement, c'est qu'on puisse, comme un discours oratoire, la réduire à une proposition." The great weakness of the romantic drama has always and everywhere been its lack of theme. And particularly is this statement true of the Spanish *commedia* as practised by Calderon, Lope de Vega, and Tirso de Molina. With the exception of a play or two like *La Vida es Sueño,* Spanish tragedy is almost themeless — unless for the tiresome *pundonor*, and that is a motive rather than a theme. Or if a romantic tragedy has happened to catch a momentary glimpse of something that might have served it for a theme, the pressure of incident has been so irresistible as to jostle it out of sight forthwith.   In the best of instances it remains rudimentary and inchoate, hardly rising above the suggestion of a motive.   There is no place or leisure for it in the serried procession of events, marching hurriedly by numerous degrees from a distant inception to a remote issue.   The interest is distributed so impartially over the series that little or no attention is left with which to exhaust the sense of a single situation.   As far as I can remember, there is nothing in romantic tragedy, for example, to parallel the discussion over the corpse of Ajax — the soliloquies of Hamlet, perhaps, excepted; and even they seem strangely clouded in comparison.   As for Corneille, he does marvellously well in this respect for all his disadvantages, as witness *Pompée* and *Cinna*.   But naturally enough, under the circumstances, it is in Racine, whose characters of passion have little more to do than just to exhaust the sense of their situation, that the theme attains its fullest development.   And it is one of his aptitudes that this treatment should suit so well with the particular passion that he picked as the lever of his tragedy.

That, as compared with the Greeks, his conception of passion was limited must be conceded, —

" C'est Venus toute entiere à sa proye attachée."

It would be idle to deny that his exclusive preoccupation with one master passion — this virtual identication, for dramatic purposes, of passion with sexual desire, gives his drama as a whole an air of one-sidedness. But whether the theater be dedicated to Cypris or Dionysus makes little difference; the point is that though the Greeks used other motives, they reached the same destination by the same route. Their action is viewed in the same manner, synthetically, as a spasm or fit of emotion; it is by madness, fatuity, or some other brief and violent distraction that the Greek *dénouement* is brought to pass. With them the tragic motive is a passion too — a something suffered or endured, —

$$\epsilon \pi \epsilon \grave{\iota} \; \tau \acute{a} \; \gamma' \acute{\epsilon} \rho \gamma a \; \mu o \upsilon$$
$$\pi \epsilon \pi o \nu \theta \acute{o} \tau' \; \acute{\epsilon} \sigma \tau \grave{\iota} \; \mu \hat{a} \lambda \lambda o \nu \; \acute{\eta} \; \delta \epsilon \delta \rho a \kappa \acute{o} \tau a.$$

And like Racine again they were obliged to think of their hero's fatality as a kind of distemper or malady. It was not at random that Boileau with Racine in mind enjoined the tragic poet,

" Et que l'amour, souvent de remors combattu,
Paroisse une foiblesse et non une vertu."

Such a treatment is involved in the notion of the type, as the Greeks with their usual penetration had not failed to discern.

Ibsen, too, in reviving the type — the synthetic, as perhaps I may now be permitted to call it from my description of the action — has been forced to adopt the same dramatic tactics. Like Racine's his is, in its own way, the tragedy of an apartment and an obsession. Upon differences of tone and atmosphere it is needless to dwell; one has only to recall those ill-ventilated, stove-choked rooms of his, with their frost-blistered windows over-looking the snow-bound and sea-haunted moors and firths of the inclement north. But to all intents and purposes the mechanism is of the same sort — for all its moral confusion the action is subject to the same simplification and the motive is conceived as an infirmity.

To return to Racine, one-sided as his partiality for love may seem in the bulk, it still gives his single pieces a wonderful intensity and power; for after all there is no other human passion quite so impetuous and headlong. And what it lacks of itself in virulence it acquires by association with its accomplice passion, jealousy. Hence his constant employment of this second and subordinate motive as a prick or goad to the former. The perfection of his drama, therefore, consists in the complication of these two motives — love and jealousy. Hence while *Bérénice* serves well enough as a kind of outline of his tragedy, its fulfilment is represented by *Phèdre*.

To take *Bérénice*, for all its slenderness, as an example of his bare idea, is, I suppose, fair enough, since he himself in the preface seems to offer it as such. In the words of Vinet, whose comments on all this literature are uncommonly pertinent, " *Bérénice* n'est pas le chef-d'œuvre de Racine; mais c'est ce qu'il a fait de plus racinien." That the plot is meagre to the point of emaciation, may be granted; but for that reason the scheme itself is only the more salient. It consists obviously, in the author's own words, of " a simple action " — hardly more, to be exact, than a situation. It is a posture and a precarious one, terminating in a single expressive gesture of renunciation and regret:

" ' Tout est prest. On m'attend. Ne suivez point mes pas.
Pour la derniere fois, adieu, Seigneur.'

' Helas! ' "

The development, then, will consist of three parts: first an explanation or " exposition " of the relations of the parties in confrontation; second, a demonstration of the emotional tensions and their potency; and third, an exhibition of their release and an indication of the outcome. All that is necessary for a representation of this sort is that the personages should meet and speak together; and this they may do as well in one room as in the universe at large. As a matter of fact, I am not sure that the impression is not intensified by the sense of confinement and constraint so produced, as it might be with an explosion in a narrow space, and as it is also to my mind by the absence of blood-letting at the close. " It is unnecessary," says Racine, " that a tragedy should be glutted with blood and death. It is enough that the action should be noble, the actors heroic, the passions excited; and that the entire piece should be redolent of that majestic grief which makes the pleasure of tragedy." And there is, indeed, about the play a sort of appalling tightness or constriction — binding the characters like a fatal ligature — to which an act of violence would be a relaxation and to which the piece is indebted for its individuality as compared with the other dramas of Racine. It may not rise to the highest effect of which tragedy is capable; but at

its acme, when Bérénice fancies that Titus is slip-
ping from her, it does rise to a very high pitch of
poetry:

" Pour jamais! Ah! Seigneur, songez-vous en vous-même
  Combien ce mot cruel est affreux quand on aime?
  Dans un mois, dans un an, comment souffrirons-nous,
  Seigneur, que tant de mers me separent de vous,
  Que le jour recommence et que le jour finisse
  Sans que jamais Titus puisse voir Berenice,
  Sans que de tout le jour je puisse voir Titus."

Nevertheless, its merits and demerits aside, I
am proposing *Bérénice* only as an illustration of the
author's bare idea. For the elaboration of the sketch
it is necessary to turn to *Phèdre*. If one were
considering the " art " of *Phèdre* without reference
to any particular thesis, it would be difficult to know
where to begin or end. Certainly, one could hardly
refrain from expatiating upon the delicacy and
firmness of drawing in the characterization of the
heroine,

     " La fille de Minos et de Pasiphaé; "

the subtlety with which from the first she insinuates
herself, with all the morbid fascination of her moral
distemper and personal disorder, into the blood and
senses of the audience. The *début* of all Racine's
heroines is tremendously effective — Monime's is a
good instance; but Phèdre's is, in especial, insidious:

" N'allons point plus avant, demeurons, chere Œnone.
  Je ne me soûtiens plus, ma force m'abandonne;
  Mes yeux sont éblouïs du jour que je revoy,
  Et mes genoux tremblans se dérobent sous moy . . .

Que ces vains ornemens, que ces voiles me pesent!
Quelle importune main, en formant tous ces nœuds,
A pris soin sur mon front d'assembler mes cheveux?
Tout m'afflige et me nuit, et conspire à me nuire . . .
Noble et brillant auteur d'une triste famille,
Toy dont ma mere osoit se vanter d'estre fille,
Qui peut-estre rougis du trouble où tu me vois,
Soleil, je te viens voir pour la derniere fois! "

Nor would a critic at large be likely to overlook
the knowingness of Hippolyte's " psychology " or
the propriety of his preferences — only a novice in
love would have had eyes for Aricie when Phèdre
was by — nor would begrudge a word or two for
Aricie herself, " la belle raisonneuse " of the salons,
who takes love to be some kind of syllogism. But
such matters and others like them deserve more than
passing mention; and in view of my immediate
subject I can dwell only upon what is indicative of
Racine's fundamental reduction of the tragic motive
to a passion in the primary sense of the word. From
this point of view it is Phèdre's passivity, her incapa-
bility of self-determination that is significant both
for this one play and for Racine's entire theatre
in general. It is this impotence which has won her
the doubtful distinction, already mentioned, of being
cited as an illustration of Augustinian theology.
But, however that may be, the characteristic trait
of Racinean tragedy is unmistakable in this, its
extreme instance. Phèdre is not merely a sufferer
and a patient; hers is the debility of innate depravity, and invalided and graceless as she is, her hapless
soul is the prey of the whole passionate intrigue

to which she is exposed. Hence her drama is the pendant and complement to that of the more limited and stubborn Bérénice, whose Hebraism stands her in good stead at her hour of trial.

In harmony with this difference of character the motive of *Bérénice* is simple and uncomplicated; it is the Racinean interpretation, sponsored by Boileau, of love as a passion or infirmity. By this one malady alone all the characters in common are afflicted; Antiochus himself is no more than a backing or foil to Titus and Bérénice. The intensity of interest is due, not to a conflict or conspiracy of passions, but to the strangulation of this one passion by circumstances. The play consists wholly of the fluctuations of this same passion between hope and disappointment and its final settlement upon resignation. In *Phèdre*, on the other hand, this single passion, while it is still agitated by its fluctuations and before it has settled down either to resignation or to despair, is exasperated by the goadings of jealousy — a motive virtually absent from *Bérénice*, if we except a brief impersonal resentment at the meddling of circumstances, for jealousy as such is not in Bérénice's character or in Titus' situation — there is too much of the prude in the former, too much of the *grand seigneur* in the latter; while Antiochus is too tame to be subject to it. But in *Phèdre*, if love is the emotional protagonist of the drama, jealousy is the deuteragonist. Nor is this all; there is a tritagonist also. In Phèdre's situation love is not merely an infirmity, it is a crime and an impiety. And in the devastation of her ineffectual spirit the outrages of love and jealousy are fatally abetted by

remorse.   Such is the complicity of passions
which instigates the emotional transport of the
tragedy — one of the finest I believe in dramatic
literature, as Phèdre is baited alternately by the
taunts of one and another.

" PHEDRE

" ' Ils s'aiment!   Par quel charme ont-ils trompé mes
    yeux?
  Comment se sont-ils veus? depuis quand? dans quels
    lieux?
  Tu le sçavois: pourquoy me lassois-tu seduire?
  De leur furtive ardeur ne pouvois-tu m'instuire?
  Les a-t-on veû souvent se parler, se chercher?
  Dans le fond des forests alloient-ils se cacher?
  Helas! ils se voyoient avec pleine license:
  Le Ciel de leurs soûpirs approuvoit l'innocence;
  Ils suivoient sans remords leur penchant amoureux;
  Tous les jours se levoient clairs et sereins pour eux!
  Et moy, triste rebut de la nature entiere,
  Je me cachois au jour, je fuyois la lumiere . . .'

" ŒNONE

" ' Quel fruit recevront-ils de leurs vaines amours?
  Ils ne se verront plus.'

" PHEDRE

                " ' Ils s'aimeront toûjours. . . .
  Miserable!   Et je vis! et jet soûtiens le veue
  De ce sacré Soleil dont je suis descenduë!
  J'ay pour ayeul la pere et le maistre des dieux;
  Le ciel, tout l'univers est plein de mes ayeux:
  Où me cacher?   Fuyons dans la nuit infernale.
  Mais que dis-je?   Mon pere y tient l'urne fatale;
  Le Sort, dit-on, l'a mise en ses severes mains.
  Minos juge aux enfers tous les pâles humains.' "

This is the kind of thing that Racine is really capable of: it is not only great tragedy, it is great
poetry; and it needs no commentary of mine by
way of reinforcement.

In conclusion, I would not be understood to
imply that Racine's entire drama squares in every
respect with the lines of *Bérénice* and *Phèdre*. Of
these two plays the one is too schematic, the other
too consummate to be thoroughly representative.
One does not repeat a *Phèdre* or a *Bérénice* —
though for quite different reasons. But for all that,
they define the type. They exhibit — all the more distinctly, if anything, for being exceptional in detail —
the characteristic originality which I have been trying to vindicate for their author. They declare
that simple or synthetic action, the discovery or
invention of which converted the serious drama of
Louis XIV from an artifice and made a modern
classic tragedy possible for once. And they reveal
the means whereby Racine accomplished this result
by treating the plot as a *crise* of passion — typically,
of love and jealousy — of which the characters were
patients or sufferers, so harmonizing his action with
the " unities " of time and place, which the criticism of the Academy and the example of Corneille
had fastened upon his stage.

To be sure, his technical procedure was not that
of the Greeks. The latter, by the force of circumstances of which the choric origin of their tragedy
was undoubtedly the most influential, had developed
out of the natural limitations of their action a congruous simplicity of treatment, from which the prag-
matic criticism of the Renaissance had formulated

the unities of time and place. Racine, in the presence of these canons, had found himself confronted with the problem of restoring, to a literature tumid with romantic elements, the simplicity in which it was wanting, by disengaging from the miscellaneous mass a unity of action to correspond with the conventions of his time. This was his contribution. And I have no hesitation in calling it original, and the drama to which he successfully appropriated it classic, though to that tragedy I shall have certain moral reservations to make a little later.

In the meanwhile, it will not be amiss to devote a few words to the subject of his versification — or more exactly, his dramatic style, for as a foreigner I do not feel myself competent to criticize the *facture* of his verses. And here, again, though his originality may not be so vital and important as in the case of his innovations upon the dramatic structure of his immediate predecessor, still it is not to be overlooked or neglected. Now, dramatic poetry, naturally, is confined to the business of drama. And drama, as far as it expresses itself in language — that is, as far as it is a matter of poetry at all — expresses itself in dialogue — or exceptionally, in soliloquy. But dialogue, while always seeking something of the illusion of speech, will draw its individuality from the situation which calls it forth. Typically, the Corneillean situation in its significant scenes was essentially a disputation, wherein each character represented his own thesis and strove to convince or argue down his respondent or respondents, as may be seen by the scenario of *Polyeucte*. Hence the characteristic temper of Corneille's dramatic style is orator-

ical and its most elevated note is that of eloquence.
As a matter of course, no tragedy in its serious moments — and Racine's is naturally no exception —
can afford to be less than eloquent at the least, or
it would sink to ordinary conversation and prose.
But the peculiarity of Corneille is that he is so
exclusively eloquent in his loftiest reaches, so seldom
or never anything else. His political orations are
concededly the best things he does. How greatly
they were admired, how compelling their vogue is
shown by the fact that Racine has executed one of
the most prominent scenes of his *Mithridate* in the
same taste. And while such passages are not those
that stick most tenaciously in my memory, even
those that do are in the same vein:

" La vie est peu de chose; et tôt ou tard qu'importe
  Qu'un traître me l'arrache, ou que l'âge l'importe?
  Nous mourons à toute heure; et dans le plus doux sort
  Chaque instant de la vie est un pas vers la mort."

Good lines; but their excellence is the excellence
of eloquence. Like all Corneille's best they are
perceptibly declamatory:

" NERINE

" ' Forcez l'aveuglement dont vous étes séduite,
  Pour voir en quel état le sort vous a réduite.
  Vostre païs vous hait, vostre époux est sans foy,
  Dans un si grand revers, que vous reste-t'il? '

" MEDÉE

" ' Moy.' "

Conceivably, however, there is room for something else even in the most serious drama, as we who are the heirs of Shakespeare need hardly be told. Not that Shakespeare himself despised the embellishments of elocution. Such commonplaces as Antony's harangue over the body of Cæsar and Portia's apostrophe to mercy witness clearly enough to the contrary. But then Shakespeare had no prejudices against doggerel or balderdash either. Everything was grist that came to his mill with the result that he had the widest range of expression that ever was, so that pretty nearly every variety of dramatic style may be illustrated by his example. And while Racine's scale is much more limited than his, as it is bound to be in many cases by the different logic of their *genres* so that comparison is illegitimate; still Racine's reach is much more comprehensive than Corneille's and demonstrates much more favourably, just as does the former's conception of the action, the possibilities of the types with which the two were dealing.

If now we place eloquence at one pole of the genuinely poetic tragedy, then at the other terminal we must obviously set up lyricism, a lyricism adapted — paradoxical as it may seem at first sight — to the uses of the drama and adjusted to the nature of the situation. The word *lyricism*, I should perhaps add, I use in its fundamental sense to denote the essential quality of lyric poetry and without recognition of the rather derogatory connotation it has acquired recently from reactionary French criticism. But lyric expression is the result of intense personal absorption; hence it would appear wholly incompatible with the gregariousness of drama, except for the more or less anomalous soliloquy. From the nature of the case, then, it can occur in nonchoric tragedy only at those rarer intervals when a character is rapt beyond the consciousness of his neighbours and his immediate surroundings either by recollection or by extreme excitement. And for the sake of clearness I will illustrate both of these cases by Shakespeare. Of the former variety Marcellus' speech in *Hamlet* after the disappearance of the ghost is a good instance:

" It faded on the crowing of the cock.
    Some say that ever 'gainst that season comes
    Wherein our Saviour's birth is celebrated,
    The bird of dawning singeth all night long:
    And then, they say, no spirit dares walk abroad;
    The nights are wholesome; then no planets strike,
    No fairy takes, nor witch hath power to charm,
    So hallow'd and so gracious is the time."

This is a lovely example of the dramatic lyricism of recollection. While the speech of Claudio, in *Measure for Measure,* on what he fancies to be the eve of his execution, though in another key altogether, is an equally good example of the dramatic lyricism of extreme excitement:

" Ay, but to die, and go we know not where;
    To lie in cold obstruction and to rot;
    This visible warm motion to become
    A kneaded clod; and the delighted spirit
    To bathe in fiery floods, or to reside
    In thrilling regions of thick-ribbed ice;

To be imprisoned in the viewless winds,
And blown with restless violence round about
The pendant world; or to be — worse than worst —
Of those that lawless and incertain thought
Imagine howling."

Such is a fair sample of the kind of lyricism produced and legitimatized dramatically by a sudden or violent excitement — in this case the dread of death.

Now, the characteristics of these two influences — of recollection and excitement both, the one induced by reaction, the other by shock — coalesce and run together inseparably in passion of the Racinean type — which with one and the same motion provokes the spirit of the patient and throws it back upon itself. Just as the expression of elevated ambition is naturally oratorical, that of love is naturally lyrical. For this reason the " lyric cry," which is almost wholly absent from Corneille, is audible again and again on the lips of Racine's characters, especially his heroines. It is possible that verses as picturesque as the following may be matched elsewhere in French tragedy of the time, though I do not happen to recall any:

" Et la Crete fumant du sang du Minotaure,"

or this:

" Ariane aux rochers constant ses injustices."

But in the passages that I have already quoted from *Bérénice* and *Phèdre* the novelty is undeniable:

" Ils suivoient sans remords leur penchant amoureux;
  Tous les jours se levoient, clairs et sereins pour eux!
  Et moy, triste rebut de la nature entiere,
  Je me cachois au jour, je fuyois la lumiere."

And it seems to me that there is a new note in
Monime's appeal to Xipharés at her *début* in the
second scene of *Mithridate:*

" Seigneur, je viens à vous. Car enfin aujourd'hui
  Si vous m'abandonnez, quel sera mon appuy?
  Sans parens, sans amis, desolée et craintive,
  Reine long-temps de nom, mais en effet captive,
  Et veuve maintenant sans avoir eû d'espoux,
  Seigneur, de mes malheurs ce sont là les plus doux."

It is not a purely lyric note, perhaps, and yet its
plaintive simplicity has very much the effect of
lyricism —at least of the applied lyricism of the
drama. But I can not hope to detect all Racine's
inflections, much less to illustrate them. I am satisfied to show that in introducing a certain lyric strain
into his tragedy he has provided it with something
of the dramatic relief of which the Greeks were
possessed by virtue of their chorus and of which
modern French tragedy was destitute until he
supplied it.

II

SUCH, it appears to me, are Racine's principal
services toward the revival of a classic tragedy in
modern times; — the discovery of a congruous simplicity of treatment by the segregation of a synthetic or unitary action, and what is less momentous,
the restoration of dramatic relief by the application

of lyricism to tragic dialogue. With these subsidies neo-classic tragedy reached its highest point of perfection. That it staggered presently and declined is no detraction to its momentary excellence; in that respect it was but equal in fate with its Attic prototype. As for its most powerful supporter, Racine, aside from his well-known intimacy with Euripides, it would be absurd, in view of the merits that I have just mentioned, to deny that his sense for Greek drama was finer than Corneille's, who, as a matter of fact, was never completely successful in shaking himself free of Spanish and romantic influence. And yet eager and sensitive though this taste of Racine's was, there are certain aspects of the Greek genius to which he is partially or wholly blind. That any one with even a tincture of the great Athenian tradition should find the invention of Eriphile or Aricie a happy one, seems incredible — though much may be forgiven Aricie as the mover of Phèdre's jealousy. In particular, however, he seems never to have fathomed the profound moral significance of the great Attic tragedians. Perhaps he was misled by his very devotion to Euripides, who is generally disdainful, if not oblivious, of the import of the material out of which Æschylus and Sophocles made so much. With Euripides, for example, Racine can see no sense in such a theme as the sacrifice of Iphigenia. " How shocking," he exclaims, " if I had stained the stage with the murder of a person so amiable and virtuous!" — a sentiment that corresponds perfectly with the opinion of Euripides' heroine,

μαίνεται δ' ὃς εὔχεται
θανεῖν. Κακῶς ζῆν κρεῖσσον ἢ καλῶς θανεῖν.

But even on those rare occasions when Euripides turns out to be a capable guide, Racine is not always equal to following him, as is conspicuously the case with *Hippolytus*.

In all Euripides' extant work, however, *Hippolytus* is exceptional in being conceived most nearly in the moral sense of his great predecessor, " the mellow glory of the Attic stage." To be sure, Racine owes a little something in this case to Seneca also; but his debt to the latter is merely that of one craftsman to another, and touches the *ordonnance* rather than the inspiration of the drama, which derives from Euripides direct. A comparison, therefore, of *Phèdre* and *Hippolytus* should be a fair test of the particulars in which Racine was insensible, as I have affirmed, to the deeper significance of the original classics. How thoroughly he — and not he alone but others before him — misunderstood the tragic logic of his original, he confesses naïvely in his preface:

" As regards Hippolytus," he says, " I had noticed among the ancients that Euripides was reproached with having represented him as a philosopher exempt from every imperfection — a circumstance which made the death of this young prince a subject of indignation rather than of pity. I have thought it necessary to give him some infirmity which would make him slightly culpable toward his father without impairing the magnanimity with which he spares the honour of Phèdre and allows himself to be abused without accusing her. I call an infirmity the passion which he suffers, in spite of himself, for Aricie, the daughter and sister of his father's mortal enemies."

Need I call attention, in passing, to the use of
the terms *infirmity* and *passion* as confirming in
themselves that view of the Racinean tragedy which
I have been developing, a view which in so far I
think to be consistent with the Greek? But this
matter apart, it is well nigh impossible to misinter-
pret Euripides' intention more egregiously than does
this quotation. Hippolytus, " a philosopher exempt
from every imperfection " ! His own maker would
never recognize him. For if one thing is certain, from
a study not merely of Greek tragedy but of Greek
thought in general, it is that Euripides and every
member of his audience must have recognized the
protagonist of *Hippolytus* as criminal — not in the
old elemental Æschylean sense, or yet in the majestic, civic Sophoclean wise, but criminal, nevertheless,
with respect to one of the most fundamental laws
for private man, τὰ περὶ ἀνθρώπους νόμιμα, one
grave enough to be inscribed above the temple of
the god at Delphi, the law of μηδὲν ἄγαν or temper-
ance, which seems almost to cover and include the
two other great maxims of Greek wisdom, γνῶθι
σαυτόν and κατ' ἄνθρωπον φρονεῖ, Know thyself
and Think as a mortal. A philosopher without
σωφροσύνη or prudence. What Greek would have
called such a mere mortal blameless?

Now, this difference of sentiment is decisive, not
only for the two plays under discussion, but also for
the ancient and modern point of view at large. And
the difference involves a double change of feeling —
one with regard to personal responsibility in general
and the other with regard to the virtue of temper-
ance more particularly. The fact is that the moderns

have pretty well lost the sense for the moral qualities of acts as such. Superficially, it seems curious that with our brutal Hegelian worship of the *fait accompli* it should be so. But this is the very point. If we are willing to forgive success its most heinous crimes, it is so because the deed itself appears to us without decisive moral character of its own. And if we are reluctant, on the contrary, to condemn the well-meaning mischief-maker, it is so for much the same reason. The attitude may be due wholly or in part to our sentimentality. Our interest has come to be ethic rather than moral; it has come to center in the characters, tempers, and dispositions of men and in conventions for accommodating and reconciling them, rather than in the great fundamental principles of humanity — the ἄγραπτα κἀσφαλῆ θεῶν νόμιμα. With this shift of attention to the ethic as distinguished from the moral our final verdict is swayed by the intention, for which alone we hold ourselves answerable, while we have ceased to acknowledge a like responsibility for our actions. With Pilate we wash our hands and protest the purity of our conscience. Our sympathies, like Racine's, are with the well intentioned; and we excuse the deed readily enough on the strength of the motive. Of course, this is nothing but casuistry pure and simple; it is nothing but a modern variation of the Jesuitical " direction of the intention," whereby a man might be absolved of the murder of his father provided only he killed him not with the idea of committing assassination but merely of securing his inheritance. But such is our modern emotional reaction; and it has already begun to affect our administration of justice so called, which a sane instinct of self-preservation has hitherto counselled us to leave intact. And since literature and especially tragedy is appreciated emotionally, it is in such manner that we apply ourselves nowadays to the appreciation of this kind of subject.

For the Greek, on the other hand, the act as such was neither indifferent nor negligible — on the contrary it had a distinct moral quality in itself. It was right or wrong, independently of intention, as it did good or harm — that is, as it respected or violated the institution of the supreme human polity, the ἄγραπτα νόμιμα; [1] and as such its initiator was responsible for it — he was wicked as it was evil, innocent as it was just. His intention was his own private affair — though it might serve to wheedle the pity of the spectators or bystanders or even the commiseration of the gods, as its theatrical representation did in the case of the spectators.

Now, in a good many cases, it must be acknowledged, there is a practical difficulty in deciding just what is the moral quality of an act as such, regardless of motive. But it seemed fairly safe to assume that those acts might be reckoned good which brought happiness in their train, and contrariwise. At least such a belief appears to be one of the natural tenets of conscience. To be happy is so evidently to have done well in life. In the words of Aristotle " Τὸ δ'εὖ ζῆν καὶ τὸ εὖ πράττειν ταὐτὸν ὑπολαμβάνουσι τῷ εὐδαιμονεῖν." Here

---

[1] For this conception of a moral constitution superior to the conventions of social ethics, an idea we appear to have lost, see Xenophon's *Memorabilia*, IV, iv.

is the whole story, with the exception of Plato's wise thinking. To be sure, the standard of happiness or well-being was likely to be low with the vulgar — hardly more than worldly prosperity, which is not much of a criterion either in ancient Attica or modern America. And perhaps, it was this baseness of ideal which led Euripides to criticize and even condemn the old moral standard altogether, with its identification of righteousness and well-being, of wickedness and adversity, which constitutes Sophocles' constant thesis — just as it was the general degeneracy of public opinion on the same subject which inspired Plato in his attempt to raise the ideal by disassociating happiness from all material accompaniments whatever and by confining it to the contemplation of the supreme good — an attempt which ultimately drove him to his doctrine of suprasensible ideas as the sole means of rescuing the eudæmonistic truism from the dissolving criticism of a Callicles or a Thrasymachus as well as of a Euripides.

In the *Hippolytus*, however, Euripides does for the nonce remain fairly loyal to the traditional belief in the moral quality of actions as a determinant of prosperity and misery. It is Hippolytus' conduct, not his motive, which renders him obnoxious to divine as well as to poetic justice. The offense which he has committed unthinkingly (with Racine we should probably acquit him of ill doing) consists in his exclusive and hence excessive cult of Artemis to the neglect and disparagement of Aphrodite. Not that his devotion to Artemis is blameworthy in itself; but Aphrodite has her claims also.

And it was the Greek notion, not that a man might acquire merit and plead exemption for the others by satisfying this or that claim, but that he should satisfy all claims in their due and proper proportion. In Æschylean and Sophoclean tragedy this conception is axiomatic. The tragedy arises from the protagonist's inability or unwillingness to satisfy all just claims — in the great tragedies from his inability to do so, as in *Electra, Antigone,* and *Œdipus*. Naturally, the more august the claims and the more conflicting and irreconcilable, the more stupendous the tragedy. While the lesser tragedies, if I may speak of degrees of tragedy, turn, not so much on the fatal contrarieties in the nature of things, like traps to break the soul, as on those inconsistencies of character in which the protagonist seems less unable than unwilling to pay all his debts, like Ajax by reason of hybris or like Hippolytus himself by reason of ἀκολασία or indiscipline. And if nowadays we fail to recognize Hippolytus' fault, it is because the obligation of sophrosyne or moderation has lost its authority either wholly or in part, just as is so often the case with one or another of the conflicting claims of Greek tragedy — the law of talion, for instance, which disputes with filial piety the *Electra* and the *Choephoræ*.

Nor is even the idea of sophrosyne an easy one for the modern; even Plato devotes an entire dialogue to the discussion of it — inconclusively, according to the critics. In this respect, however, I can not agree with them, since the positions which Plato preëmpts in the *Charmides* are those which he finally occupies in the *Republic*. The only reason for their temporary relinquishment in the former dialogue is the circumstance that the discussion has involved certain assumptions — principally that of the equivalence of happiness and meeting your obligations — which he will not at the time consent to have taken for granted, though he justifies them later. Hence it is that I can not look upon Plato's attempt at a definition as a failure. At least I can give no better account of the matter; and what that account implies is, in sum, that sophrosyne consists in taking one's own measure as a man and conforming to it — the virtue to know the measure and to be moderate. Wherefore my earlier remark that the maxim, μηδὲν ἄγαν, or Nothing too much, by which the Greek aphoristically translated the idea, virtually absorbs the other two gnomes in which Greek wisdom is epitomized, γνῶθι σαυτόν and κατ' ἄνθρωπον φρονεῖ — Know thyself and Think as a mortal. In short, sophrosyne was much as I have been expressing it, the recognition and satisfaction of all just claims. And this virtue, in which Hippolytus was so sadly to seek, was the polar virtue to the Greek. Mere mortification, asceticism, even the excess or exaggeration of a single duty he would not have understood as righteousness. Saintliness in the sense of austerity is an oriental, not a Greek, ideal. Such a character, if the latter could have comprehended it at all, would have struck him as unnatural, even monstrous. " Ὀύ γὰρ ἀνθρωπική ἐστιν ἡ τοιαυτήν ἀναισθησία," so says Aristotle. And he would have expected to see it draw the lightning, just as Euripides has represented it as doing. For it is this immoderation on the part of Hippolytus in slighting the natural human affinities or inclinations and in unsettling the balance of satisfactions by discharging one set of duties exclusively to the prejudice of all the others — it is this partiality which is adjudged a criminal arrogance or hybris. About his very chastity there is designedly something *farouche* and savage like that of his tutelary divinity, the harrier of Actæon. And it is this partiality which brings him within the scope of Phædra's baleful influence. In this way is vindicated the inflexible justice presiding over the great tragedy of the Greeks — for which reason I have said that however it may be with Euripides in general, *Hippolytus* at least is in the great tradition.

All this is so clear that the wonder is how Racine could have missed it. And yet little or nothing of it appears in his *Phèdre*. The compromise whereby he seeks to excuse his hero's entanglement in the coils of a penal process by endowing him with a fancy for Aricie, is too trifling to take seriously. It is Phèdre's passion that inflames the play; and any mere affection is bound to show pale and ineffectual in the blaze of such a conflagration. At best, Hippolytus' attachment for Aricie may be a motive as regards Phèdre, who is sensitive in just that particular spot; but it is no term in his own sequence of dramatic liabilities, his $\tau\grave{o}$ $\delta\iota$' $\check{\alpha}\lambda\lambda\eta\lambda\alpha$, as Aristotle would call it, for it does not appear that there is any mesh, in the ancient sense, between his fate and his tenderness for the daughter of a hostile house. This is not the issue; and he is never called to account on this score. On the contrary, so far has Racine missed the point, that this very senti-

ment for another woman — any woman would do
— which Racine imputes to him, does, as a matter
of fact, clear him altogether of the charge on which
he should by rights be sentenced and actually is
sentenced in the original version. The Hippolytus
of Racine has already paid his tribute to Venus and
no longer stands within her danger. Whether he is
guilty of filial impiety on the score of Aricie's an-
cestry and descent is another question than the one
Racine has discussed. His injection of such a motive into his preface is simply misleading. As things
are, the apprehension of Hippolytus by the fatal
snare is fortuitous and unintelligible.[1] In a word,
Hippolytus is not responsible for the plight in which
he finds himself. As a result, his tragedy is harrowing but not edifying. This is not to say that his
character or his conduct is without its interest or its
significance, but merely that the drama lacks the
severe determinism which Euripides has known how
to impart to this one subject at least.

But the *Phèdre,* it may be objected, is not Hippolytus' tragedy at all; and its author has given us
to understand as much by the change of title.
Granted. Racine's theater is for the most part a
tragédie des femmes; and it is not *Phèdre* which is
the exception. But this concession only makes the
predicament worse. With Phèdre in the leading
rôle it is without a problem, as with Hippolytus in
that part it is without a solution. I am still trying
to occupy the Greek point of view. That I myself
am no æsthete or æsthetician must be abundantly

---

[1] Compare Arnauld's ejaculation, "Mais pourquoi a-t-il fait
Hippolyte amoureaux?" Sainte-Beuve, *Port-Royal,* t. VI, p. 130.

evident by this time; a problem has no terrors for me — nor yet a thesis or a theme. I am even abandoned enough to believe that literature is all the better for something of the sort, provided it is humane and not economic or sociological or anthropological. And so I have the effrontery to repeat that with the substitution of Phèdre for Hippolytus in the principal part the play is destitute of problem, and being without a problem, is destitute of thesis likewise. To be sure, there is a kind of justice in Phèdre's fate; but it is that obvious, anticipated, matter-of-fact sort of justice to which the conscience does not have to be reconciled. Her guilt is as sensible as her sentence. She is a sinner — the fascinating and sympathetic sinner with whom a long course of modern literature has sufficiently familiarized us. Her seduction is undeniable. But she is plainly a dangerous woman, a *femme fatale;* and it is better that she should be put away. And in this decision we acquiesce without difficulty. There is no ambiguity in her lot, no misgiving in the minds of her judges.

The only compunction that her lot arouses has to do with the fate of her victim, Hippolytus; and to that problem, it has been seen, no solution is vouchsafed. In short, the logic of the tragedy is of a thoroughly modern type, of which *Macbeth* and *Richard III* are the readiest examples — the tragedy of wickedness or depravity. And like all tragedies of the type, it is a little awry. For what we fail to notice in our preoccupation with such protagonists is the circumstance that the merited visitation of their iniquities provides no satisfaction or

compensation for the sufferings of their victims —
the endless procession of Duncans, Banquos, and
Lady Macduffs. It is they who rise,

" With twenty mortal murthers on their crowns,"

in speechless expostulation with the ordering of their
destiny. What warrant can we produce for their
ills? Theirs is the tragedy — unrecognized and un-
riddled; for every tragedy is something of a mystery as of a sacrament. No, such tragedies are out
of focus somehow; and the Greek with his habitual
tact avoided them. It is not Phèdre's subtle and
pervasive corruption — that only proclaims her a
moral outlaw and debars her from tragic citizenship
altogether, as Aristotle explains clearly enough —
it is Hippolytus' waywardness which makes the
Greek subject:

Ουδείς μ᾽ἀρέσκει νυκτὶ θαυμαστὸς θεῶν.

To Euripides the woman is a malign influence, a
calamity to which Hippolytus' impudence exposes
him. And if in the case of Racine's heroine there
is a trail of fatality lying across her house, which
simulates the immanence of divinity after the Greek
fashion,

τὰ γὰρ ἐκ προτέρων ἀπλακήματά νιν
πρὸς τάσδ᾽ ἀπάγει,

it does little more, in reality, than give depth to the
tableau and perspective to the picture. It is physiological — an heredity, not a dispensation; a trans-

mitted taint rather than a suspended judgment
re-incurred for himself by every new successor to
the title. Its moral, as distinguished from its
æsthetic, effect would be, if anything, to raise a
doubt of her responsibilty and throw suspicion upon
the criminal rationale of her catastrophe. And while
it is hardly emphasized to that degree — being intended, I suppose, toward holding the sympathy of
the audience a little more surely — still in the upshot, the whole affair, with respect to Phèdre as
well as Hippolytus, comes in the modern version
to take on the appearance of an act of wantoness
on the part of Venus:

> " Puis que Venus le veut, de ce sang déplorable
>   Je peris la derniere et la plus miserable."

Not that Racine's drama has no sense; far from it.
But it is not the sense of the antique. And if I
am perchance singular in preferring the thorough
consequence and conclusiveness of the latter's dialectic; on the other hand, I believe that I am only
speaking in the spirit of my time when I add that
I prefer the former's interpretation of character for
its inherent momentousness and significance. In
spite of the dubiety and indecision of Racine's
Providence, I must confess that to me his Phèdre is
more appealing than Euripides', not only in her
reticences and indiscretions but in that by virtue
of which they subsist — her own being. For after
all, how much richer the character of the former
than that of the latter! And the change of taste
or sentiment, if I am right in my diagnosis, is far

from trivial; for it is inevitable that this enhancement of personality, which is at the bottom of it, should have exerted a tremendous influence upon the modern treatment, not only of character itself, but also of the issues and eventualities of the action.

In order to explain these consequences, however, I must refer hurriedly to the intellectual structure of tragedy as far as it furnishes a scaffolding for the problem which is the peculiar concern of the *genre*. Universally, tragedy would appear to include two components — the " fable," which represents the fact upon which it is founded, and the " art," whereby this raw material is fashioned into drama. As far as the subject-matter goes, the sentiment of tragedy seems to be aroused by the perception, in some event or other, of a dissidence between the demands of conscience and the data of experience — between our notion of justice or equity and our knowledge of actuality. Obviously, this dissidence must be a serious one — so serious, indeed, as to upset momentarily our feeling of moral security — to trouble and perplex and even confound for the time being our intelligence. This temporary sense of queasy and vertiginous insecurity I would call, with Aristotle's term *catharsis* in mind, the tragic qualm. From what precedes it is evident that the subject of tragedy involves a *contretemps* — or as Aristotle puts it for his own stage, a *metabasis* — and implies the agency of fortune. Any occurrence which meets these conditions, does in a measure inspire the onlooker with the crude sentiment, and in so far raises the question, of tragedy.

But such a state of consternation is intolerable —

especially if it is prevalent, as happens particularly whenever the tenure of life becomes generally precarious — in seasons of public insecurity, for example, in times of war or pestilence — conditions under which or the recollection of which tragedy is most likely to flourish. In the interests of sanity, then, it is necessary that the reason should be reconciled to existence and that the apprehensions to which it is subjected by the perfidies of nature should be composed and tranquillized. In other words, if the observer is to be brought to acquiesce in the shocking terminations of tragedy, he must be made to find in the apparent miscarriage of justice which the dramatist has chosen for his theme some solace of a sort for his own outraged sense of propriety. This is the " art " of tragedy. Without it there is only the representation of some harrowing and inscrutable casuality.

Now, as a matter of course, the gravest of such outrages occur in connection with the conflict of good and evil on those occasions when the latter seems to have won an unwarranted triumph over the former to the detriment of the personal happiness or well-being of its vanquished representatives. Hence tragedy has ever sought pretty much this one kind of subject. It has always been moral and eudæmonistic. And it has been greatest where its preoccupation with this topic has been most exclusive, as was the case with the Attic drama of the great epoch. Among moderns the New Englander has had something of the same conviction of moral immanence which inspired Æschylus and Sophocles. For him as for them the world was compact of good and evil; there was no room for moral indifference, no neutral zone in his universe — nothing but " the gods still sitting around him on their thrones, — they alone with him alone." But his end was not well-being but duty. And in this intent he was invulnerable to adversity, the stage-manager of the tragic scene. Nay, to the Puritan conscience with its suspicion of fortune and her works, the very name of tragedy was anathema.

To the Greek, however, with his moral and eudæmonistic leanings — nor should his intellectual and inquisitive temper be forgotten either — the problem presented itself in some such guise as this. Why did misery come to attach itself to a sort of action naturally calculated to ensure happiness? I say " why," not " how " advisedly; for unlike the modern, he was not to be fobbed off with anything less than a reason. In other words, with no discernible difference as between two acts — or at least, of two acts equally laudable as to purpose; why should the one promote disaster and disgrace, the other prosperity and repute? Or more narrowly still, why in this particular instance, say, should a certain design which might be predicted on general principle and analogy to further the advantage of its author — why should such a course of conduct, on the contrary, plunge its pursuer into an abyss of wretchedness and humiliation? How was such seeming perversity of circumstance to be explained? Such, I believe, was the riddle that Æschylus and Sophocles set themselves to read. And they solved it by the affirmation, tacit or explicit, of a cosmic law of righteousness, as a trangression of which they accounted every such outward act a crime, reckoning its frustration and disgrace a legitimate penalty of wrong-doing.

Nor was this notion of a supra-mundane policing of human activities singular to Æschylus and Sophocles. To be sure, it had its scoffers like Thrasymachus and Callicles, and its critics like Euripides. But it was so obviously a matter of course that the dramatist was safe in appealing to it as the basis of his solution and in deducing the necessary corollaries from it acceptably to his public. In this way, by the identification of adversity with guilt, he was in a position to explain the sufferings of his protagonist by holding him responsible for the misconduct (and notice how easily our own language falls in with the same kind of reasoning) of which they were supposed to be the consequences at the same time that he was able to soften the audience to the proper degree of indulgence for the sufferer by representing his trangression as uncalculated and involuntary. But though as the victim of a *contretemps,* he might well be regarded with a moderate pity, still as a trangressor and a source of impiety and pollution, he was an abomination and an object of horror. Hence the complementary emotions of pity and horror by which Aristotle defines tragedy in exponents of the action.

With the modern conceit of personality and its surpassing importance, however, such a resolution of the contrarieties of fortune becomes impossible. What is decisive in such an estimate of character is purity of motive, not precision of conduct. " Infirmity and misery do not, of necessity, imply guilt.

They approach, or recede from the shades of that dark alliance, in proportion to the probable motives and propects of the offender and to the palliations, known and secret, of the offense." Such, in the heart-felt words of De Quincey at the confessional, is approximately the modern and romantic doctrine of responsibilty. Consistently with such a view a formal contravention of prescription can not be pleaded in extenuation of that loss of happiness to which one is felt to be entitled by virtue of such merit as consists with good intentions. That good intentions alone are no guarantee of prosperity, however, is a depressing certainty of daily observation. With the moral negligibility of conduct the center of tragedy has begun to shift, and the old explanation is thrown out of focus. And yet the radical detestation of injustice persists unaltered — only it is now impossible to palliate the miscarriage by convicting the sufferer of involuntary culpability; he is exonerated by the sense of his personal worthiness. To all appearance, virtue has simply lost the *partie;* and there is nothing left for tragedy but to affix her signature to the humiliating admission.

And yet there does remain one way of escaping this recantation of our most earnest professions. While conceding, as now seems unavoidable, that there is but " one event to the righteous and the wicked," the dramatist may still claim a spiritual superiority for the former, not only in an equality of fortune, but also in an inequality of fortune which is all to the advantage of the latter. In other words, he may still solicit and win approval for a certain sort of character in the face of its material collapse.

In this manner it is possible to restore that confidence in the primacy of the individual conscience by which the modern sets such store. In spite of an ineptitude for affairs, an inadequacy to the situation which the ancient would have construed as the infatuation of guilt, Hamlet, Othello, and Lear are esteemed to have the nobler part for all their calamities, as contrasted with the wholly despicable conspiracy to which each falls a victim. And so this assertion of the sentimental preëminence of an approved character, irrespective of its ends and activities, has come — thanks to its conformity with our modern, and perhaps I should add our Christian, prepossession — to form the resolution of modern tragedy, of the neo-classic as well as the romantic.

That such a resolution is emotional rather than rational can not be disputed. All too obviously it supplies no genuine solution of the mystery of good and evil, happiness and misery which has vexed the heart of man for so many centuries. It is but a compromise at best; and as such it is an inherent defect of modern tragedy. Nevertheless there are two remarks to be made in extenuation. In the first place, the immediate appeal of tragedy is emotional any way; and such a reconciliation, though failing to satisfy mature reflection, does at least offer temporary alleviation of the heart-ache that accompanies the spectacle of such enormities as make the subject-matter of tragedy. While further, since it it is unreasonable to expect a thoroughly congruous art of an age without consistency, it is only by some such compromise that the dramatist can hope to mediate between the warring tendencies of our post-renaissance mood. In an order purely physical, for example, it is inconceivable that righteousness should influence our material well-being in one way or the other. Or else, if a man's fortunes are to be taken as the index of his deserts, as antiquity was prone to believe, then the protestations of his own conscience are unreliable as against the evidences of adversity. But either of these alternatives we are loath to embrace. The former implies an insensible determinism; the latter a moral causation. And in our reluctance we are driven to make the benefits and dignities of virtue, as of character, largely subjective and intimate — an affair of sentiment pretty exclusively.

As a result of this expedient of reconciling the heart, irrespective of the head, to the contingencies of the *dénouement* or catastrophe, there has ensued a momentous change of attitude toward the protagonist. I speak of the *dénouement* or catastrophe as a contingency deliberately; for in this light we are bound to consider it, *ex hypothesi*, on the strength of its hideous disproportion with the presumptive innocency of the victim. At least, since the " hero " is no longer to be held to strict accountability for his conduct to the extent of sharing impartially in the obloquy of his misdeeds, there is no choice save to call the catastrophe morally indifferent whatever his instrumentality in its production. As *Othello* and *Hamlet* are written, it is impossible to visit upon the heads of the titular characters the full measure of abhorrence proper to their infamies as such. Taken in themselves, the crazing of Ophelia by the

meditative Dane and the smothering of Desdemona
by the valiant Moor are not exploits particularly
creditable to their perpetrators. And yet in spite of
the egotistic squeamishness of the one and the jealous credulity of the other character, we are induced
to shift the blame from their shoulders to the in-
stigation of circumstance and the connivance of
opportunity — agencies admirably symbolized in the
Phèdre, for instance, by the person of the nurse.
Herein, obviously, consists the utility of the
" villain " ; he lets the " hero " out. For notice that
with this gentry Sophocles and Æschylus, whose
protagonists bear, like Œdipus, the opprobrium of
their own mischief, have no traffic. And though
there are foreshadowings of the villain, in the present acceptation of the word, in Euripides as a scape-
goat for some of the interesting adventuresses, like
Medea, for whom that author had such a particular
tenderness; yet the *rôle* owes its sinister prominence
to the exigencies of the sentimental reconciliation
and the modern tragedian's efforts to save his
hero's face at all odds — an effort in which he is
inevitably led to develop the ethical rather than the
moral possibilities of his action, treating it as revelatory of the complexity and richness of the protagonist's temperament, which to our notion constitutes its worth and value.

As a result of these conditions, then, the modern
protagonist or hero is invariably a " sympathetic "
character. If he were not — if he were to forfeit
the indulgence of the audience, he would lose what
standing he has and become identified with his own
performances. In that event, being as he is the

source of irreparable injury to others no less than
to himself, the illusion of his merits would vanish
and his tragedy would turn into the exceptional
type of which I have already spoken as the tragedy
of depravity or turpitude, exemplified by *Macbeth*
and *Richard III* and of which, as it is anomalous,
I need speak no further in this connection. Or else,
the audience, deprived of their faith in his innate
nobility, even if they succeeded by a miracle of
subtlety in retaining a purely intellectual confidence
in his own conscientiousness despite the damning
evidence of his own misdoing, would remain unrec-
onciled to the hardship of his lot, and the tragedy
itself as " art " would be a signal failure. There are
no two ways about it: while the Greek protagonist
might be represented as simply infatuate, the unavoidable outcome of the sentimental reconciliation
is the " sympathetic " protagonist.

I can not disguise that in all this there is more
than a trace of casuistry. But what then? Such
is modern sentiment, romantic even at its best and in
spite of itself; and since art must comply with the
convictions of its devotees, such is modern tragedy.
In contrast with the classic Greek it takes the hero
subjectively, as he is reflected in the mirror of self-
consciousness, and not objectively, as he would impress the dispassionate observer. It does not consider him an example but an exception, unique and
individual. It is less concerned to bring him to trial
as the citizen of a moral polity whose constitution
he is under suspicion of having violated than to
plead in his behalf the privilege of an unnaturalized
sojourner in a strange land with whose institutions,

customs, and manners he is unfamiliar and to whose jurisdiction he is not properly subject. So patently unadapted are Hamlet and Othello to their *milieu* that it is rather naïve to express surprise at the havoc they play with it. In this respect modern tragedy is uniformly confidential and biographical — not common and public, not historical. It embodies a distinct and hitherto unstudied variety of the " pathetic fallacy." Consistently, it has ceased little by little, notwithstanding its early deference for tradition, to draw its material from generally accessible and verifiable sources, and has taken more and more to substituting invention for interpretation. As far as the results go, it is not wholly inexcusable to distrust the sincerity, if not the legitimacy, of "private" tragedy altogether. For once the dramatist has begun to rid himself of fidelity to the record written or oral, there is nothing to prevent him from abusing his audience's sympathy " at discretion " to the confusion of all moral values whatsoever. Indeed, he is bound by the nature of the case to do a certain amount of violence to the judgment of his audience. Euripides himself has shown how the trick may be turned in his *Medea,* and Racine has not been slow to imitate him in *Phèdre.* I will not go so far as to say that Racine has passed the bounds permissible to his *genre,* but I can not deny that he has pushed our indulgence for his heroine to something of an extreme. And if the " sympathetic " hero is capable of such license while still subject to the authority of legend or notorious fable, what limit to his excesses when these last fetters are finally removed?

The answer, I suspect, is Ibsen. How many of the tremendous figures that dominated the Attic stage in the heyday of its splendour are " sympathetic " ? Not Orestes, nor Agamemnon, nor Œdipus Tyrannus, nor Electra, nor Clytemnestra. Prometheus and Antigone? Or do they only seem so to us? For it is significant that these two pretty nearly exhaust the unqualified enthusiasm of the modern for ancient tragedy. I omit to mention Philoctetes and Œdipus Coloneus because the " happy " tragedy in which they figure is as anomalous to our experience as the tragedy of evil or turpitude was to that of the Greek, and hence lends itself as little to comparison. But if Antigone and Prometheus were, in reality, " sympathetic " characters originally, they at least were so by disposition, not by theatrical necessity, as is the case with their younger colleagues. As for Hamlet, I sometimes wonder, for example, whether he was actually so " sympathetic " as he is painted. The remark is fatuous, of course, since Hamlet is just what Shakespeare has made him, no more, no less. But it serves to illustrate the point, if the point is worth making at all, since it assumes an effect entirely at variance with Aristotle's first-hand impression. On the authority of this one deponent, whose competence I fancy no one will question, the Greek protagonist, while laying claim to the pity of the audience for his reverses, was effectually disqualified as a " sympathetic " character by the horror that he excited by his misdeeds. The evidence is conclusive: the " sympathetic " protagonist, with the sentimental reconciliation of which he is an outcome, is a persistent characteristic of modern, in contradistinction from ancient tragedy.

With these preliminaries disposed of, it is possible to examine the specific physiognomy of Racine's characters a little more closely. From this brief survey I need hardly apologize for omitting *Alexandre* and *La Thébaïde* as well as *Esther;* the reasons for doing so are sufficiently obvious. *Athalie,* too, well worth consideration as it is in itself, seems to lie outside of its author's professional career. Racine's tragedy I have already called a *tragédie des femmes.* It is not merely that so many of his title *rôles* are filled by women —Andromaque, Bérénice, Iphigénie, Phèdre; yes, and Athalie, for that matter; or that women so uniformly preëmpt the center of his stage. It is that women come so near to exhausting his interest and invention. *Britannicus,* to be sure, looks like an exception; but even in this case, though Junie may not be thoroughly engrossing on her own account, she is at least responsible for springing the trap. While as for *Bajazet* and *Mithridate,* there can be no doubt that it is Roxane who animates the former as it is Monime who inspires the latter.

In revenge, his typical hero is hardly more than an idealized courtier — not unhandsome, it is to be presumed, and gallant, but rather insipid for a palate accustomed to the gusto of Shakespeare's male parts — the Wertherean Britannicus; the complaisant Bajazet; Achille, *le beau sabreur;* Hippolyte, the *petit-maître.* Even Titus has about him a little something of the operatic potentate:

" Cette poupre, cet or, que rehaussoit sa gloire,
    Et ces lauriers encor témoins de sa victoire."

And while it is a flight of the fancy to think of substituting one for another, still they are all pretty much of a piece. No doubt, there is a kind of disarming candour about Hippolyte — he is so clearly no match for all these designing women, not the least dangerous of whom is the nurse — which sets him a little apart; as is also true of the frank impetuosity of the young Achille. But Bajazet, or even Britannicus, when stripped of his theatrical trappings, is little better than a self-confessed futility.

Perhaps it is too much to expect of an author any way that he should be able to keep the object of a woman's infatuation from looking a little fatuous himself. But to these statements one reservation at least must be made in favour of that wily and bellicose old barbarian, Mithridate, the most virile full-length that Racine has drawn; for Nero's villainy, as I have already noticed, is hardly a masculine villainy as yet — it retains too much of the effeminacy of adolescence. Aside from the dominating and sinister figure of Mithridate, the strongest-featured of all the men are Orestes and Pyrrhus; and it is remarkable that until the next to the last scene of the third act *Andromaque* is comedy — partly, I suppose, on account of the fact that it is something of a *coup d'essai,* but mainly, because of the accentuated characterization of these two principals, whom even the passion that makes the women tragic, only renders a little ridiculous. At all events, Racine never tried the experiment again; and from this evidence — negative, I admit — is it fanciful to conclude that he distrusted his ability to individualize his leading men very strongly without caricature and comedy?

To justify the propriety of such forbearance on his part a brief digression is necessary. It is no secret that the more academic French critics have associated the perfection of their tragedy with the retrenchment from serious drama of two elements — romance and comedy. With Racine's simplification of the action, the plot as such was cleared of the last shred of the romance still so pronounced in the *Cid* and *Rodogune,* and indeed, everywhere in Corneille. And if the result is yet to some extent romantic by reason of the sentimental resolution, the blemish is due to the circumstance that even Racine is a modern, and the modern is incurably romantic by position. After all that has happened in the last two thousand years it is idle to require a perfectly clean conscience even of those who have done their best to expiate the sins of their fathers and to purge their souls of the Asiatic and the mediæval. As for the comic element, that had ceased to be much of an impediment to tragedy already. And yet while the playwright of Louis XIV's time was in no great danger of losing his footing altogether, nevertheless he did slip occasionally, even though he might save himself from actually falling. At least, he has here and there shaken his reader's confidence in his infallibility, like Racine himself in *Andromaque* and Molière in *Le Misanthrope.* To be sure, the outcome is unclouded;

the final impression of *Andromaque* is unambigu-
ously tragic, as that of *Le Misanthrope* is comic.
But there are moments of dubiety, where the judgment is befuddled — just how badly the reader
must decide for himself. And then, aside from these
domestic difficulties, whose seriousness it is hard
for an outsider to estimate exactly — the *genre
tranché* has been an embarrassment to the Frenchman in another fashion. On the one hand, it has
troubled his appreciation of " mixed " tragedy,
like the Shakespearean, which partly on this account Voltaire includes in a common damnation
with the Greek as hopelessly barbarous. And on
the other hand, it has obstructed the understanding
of " pure " tragedy, like Racine's, on the part of
the English, who are inclined to resent the abate-
ment of confusion as a violence to nature and
another arbitrary and crippling convention. If I
embark, then, upon a hasty discussion of the relations between tragedy and comedy, I do so in the
hope of completing the definition of pure tragedy,
since I have already taken account of the
other formally objectionable element, romance, in
explaining the nature of the simple or synthetic
action.

In such an inquiry into the applications of comedy, sketchy though that inquiry may be, it is only
fair that we should place ourselves for the time
being at the French point of view. If the French
critic objects to the admixture of comedy with his
tragedy, it is obviously neither Shakespearean nor
Aristophanic comedy that he has in mind, but comedy after his own kind. Of this kind Molière is

the natural representative; and accordingly to his line the following remarks are roughly hewn.

Considered in this light, the distinction between comic and tragic is not particularly difficult. It is mainly a matter of mood. Just as the ancient artificer might turn his fabrics into a tragic or a comic mask at will, so the dramatist may give a situation a tragic or a comic turn indifferently. To this effect Vinet recalls that the subject of *Mithridate* is identical with that of *L'Avare,* the fifth scene of the third act of the former corresponding with the third scene of the fourth act of the latter. In Walpole's familiar phrase, life is a tragedy to him who feels, a comedy to him who thinks. The subject-matter is the same, what differs is the temper. The one type addresses the heart, the other the head. The emotions aroused by tragedy may vary widely — as, within our scope, between that of ancient and modern times; the passions of the ancient theater being dominated by pity and horror, the agitations of the modern stage being assuaged by sympathy or compassion. But whatever the specific impression may be, it is certain that tragedy undertakes to arouse the sensibilities in one way or another. Comedy, on the contrary, is essentially intellectual. Its characteristic is curiosity; and curiosity is passionless and impartial. A comedy, in the French taste, is a disinterested study of human nature, a sort of critical vivisection, wherein sentiment is misplaced. Once excite the audience to indignation or indulgence in respect of the characters, and comedy is at an end; the play becomes a melodrama. This is the reason that *Le Misanthrope* seems to totter on the verge of tragedy; Alceste is so constantly on the point of conciliating the spectators' good will. At least, such appears to be its effect upon the English reader, whose tolerance of eccentricity has aroused the Frenchman's traditional suspicion of his complete sanity. And indeed, there is not a little in the comic spirit to make it appear malicious and inquisitive in the eyes of the sentimental humanitarian.

On the other hand, we must have an eye to what seems to me the root of the whole difficulty — I mean the confounding of comedy with humour. Properly understood and discriminated, humour appeals to the feelings. It recognizes the frailties and foibles of human nature, not as a subject of interest to the curiosity, but as a subject of interest to the sympathies, as so many evidences of a common humanity. One may view the weaknesses of a friend with amusement, but one's smile is neither indifferent nor unkindly; indeed, it may be deprecatory or even rueful. This is the mood of the great English humorists like Dickens and Thackeray. In reality, humour is a partition of the pathetic; for after all, what difference does it make whether one's affections express themselves in laughter or tears? The point is that we are moved at all, so that in this sense the source of one and the other, of humour and of pathos, might justly be grouped together under a single designation as the touching. On the contrary, comedy, being naturally unfeeling, is, properly, no less insensible to mirth than to grief. Stendhal complains, rather naïvely, that there is so little fun in Molière and other approved comedians of his country — and so much that is merely " *un rire par scandale* " and impertinent. At a performance of *Tartuffe* on December 4, 1822, in which he saw Mademoiselle Mars, the audience, so he records, laughed only twice, and then negligibly. " *On n'a ri,*" he says, " *le 4 décembre.*" But surely, Stendhal is wrong in trying to use this circumstance to Molière's disparagement. That he does so, goes to show that, like most romanticists, he had little relish for the comic as such. As long as the curiosity is interested and the intelligence is busied — as long as the complicated motives of human action are unravelled, with all their contradictions and inconsistencies, for the entertainment of the intellect; so long are the general conditions of comedy satisfied. As a matter of course, the tone of such comedy is realistic and conscientious. It is as serious in its own way as tragedy. The difficulty is that while tragedy finds a relief from its excesses in the purgation of the passions or otherwise, comedy has none, and lacking such an outlet, is liable to become melancholic and atrabiliary. For such a one-sided preoccupation with human inconsequence as comedy demands of its practitioners, must result, at best, in a qualified contempt for the race; at worst, in a kind of moral hypochondria, like that from which Molière himself is said to have suffered during his later years.

For these reasons it is evident that humour, on the one side, is not necessarily incompatible with tragedy. As it is itself emotional and in so far pathetic or affecting, it may, as a matter of fact, be employed to reinforce a tragic effect, particularly in conjunction with pathos in the narrower modern sense, provided it is not discordant with the key in which the passage is pitched. To this end it has been used by all romantic playwrights — I fancy, without exception. It has even been made a part of the romantic propaganda, as witness Victor Hugo and Friedrich Schlegel and Stendhal just cited. Unhappily for its own credit — for there is something peculiarly unpalatable in misdirected or ill-judged pleasantry — it has not always been handled with discretion even by first-rate genius. The grave-yard scene in *Hamlet* has shocked too many judges of taste to be wholly exonerated of offense. But though romantic abuses of this sort may have brought the humorous into temporary disrepute with a certain class of fastidious critics, there is no gainsaying that it has received the stamp of classical approval; it is used by Æschylus and Sophocles, to say nothing of Euripides, as well as by Shakespeare, though much more sparingly and tactfully, and in general though not always, in connection with minor characters. Nor are there wanting touches of it in Racine, in spite of his habitual severity.

In so far the romanticists are in the right: humour has an indisputable place in tragedy. With comedy, however, in its pure idea as represented by Molière — and it is in some such sense that Molière's countrymen must be supposed to conceive it — the case is otherwise. Since its mood is irreconcilable with that of tragedy, there can be no commerce between them. We can not expect an audience to bewail

the plight in which the characters find themselves
and at the same time to preserve an attitude of
nonchalant detachment as concerns their reaction
to those stimuli. It was not without reason that
the Greek tragedian was so scrupulous to neutra-
lize curiosity of any kind on the part of his public
even at the cost of suspense and intrigue. Not
only was he content with well-known subjects, but
he would not infrequently go out of his way to fore-
stall a doubtful *dénouement*. Like the modern
dramatic purists, as we may think of them for convenience, he was up in arms at the mere suspicion
of a comic encroachment upon the confines of his
special province.

Now, one of the most effective of comic motives,
as I have already implied, consists in the elaboration
of the characteristic. Intensive individualization
is an invariable accompaniment of comedy. Compare Molière with our own Sheridan. While the
latter's witticisms are amazingly funny without
much regard to the speaker — in fact, it is related
of Sheridan that he was in the habit of shifting
his speeches about more or less capriciously;
Molière's are so thoroughly in character as to take
their point solely from their appositeness in this one
respect, and to become dull and meaningless in the
mouth of another. The more intensely a character
is individualized, the more completely he is singled
out and separated from others who resemble him
superficially, and the farther he is removed from
common interests and associations. His most distinctive traits are those that are peculiar to him
alone; and they are bound to be " unsympathetic,"

if not actually " antipathetic "; we can like others only in as far as we are like them. Let the dramatist, then, individualize his protagonist to a degree by emphasizing his peculiarities, and he becomes a subject of quizzical scrutiny as far as he continues to hold the attention; for it requires a considerable amount of mental concentration to retain any interest at all in such a character. The very analysis, too, which is responsible for his exhibition, demands a cool and dispassionate exercise of the intellect for its appreciation. While, in addition, since our peculiarities are usually ridiculous to others — " For anything I can see," says Dr. Johnson, "all foreigners are fools " — the process of segregating the character, in converting him into an oddity, has made him a fair mark for the raillery of the beholders.

Hence the more minute the characterization of a play, the farther that play leans toward comedy and away from tragedy, so that the characters of tragedy are always the more general and representative, or " universal.' While comedy is all for the idiosyncrasy, tragedy seeks the mediating term, the principle that relates all the members into an order and brings them under the rule of their kind. The Misanthrope is not mere misanthropy, as revolted by the insincerity of society, but an exception who has fallen into the wiles of a heartless coquette, the embodiment of all the falsity for which he detests his fellows. *L'Avare*, likewise, is the comedy, not of avarice, but of the eccentric miser involved in the extravagance of love. On the contrary, the tragedy of Œdipus Tyrannus is the tragedy of filiation, from whose obligations his extraordinary eminence is powerless to exempt him. While as for Hamlet, indulging himself in his " quiddities " to such an extent that it is too easy to imagine a Hamlet wholly after Molière's mind, his tragedy is the tragedy of a son too — but of a son who can not always escape the comic anomaly of the homicidal moralist.

I have come a long way around; I can only hope that these observations may have gone a little way toward explaining why the characterization of a pure tragedy like Racine's — particularly the characterization of the males, naturally pronounced by reason of their sex and liable on that account to exaggeration — must seem rather subdued to a public untroubled by the dissonances of its most serious literature — since it is probably on these very principles that Racine avoided anything like a duplication of his Pyrrhus and Orestes. In the case of his secondary characters, however, whose relief is lower any way, the habitual flatness of his modelling, I speak relatively, is not, as a matter of course, so noticeable. As sketches they are more suggestive, leaving so much more to the imagination — the warlike and lackadaisical Antiochus, promenading his hopeless infatuation from siege to siege,

" Example infortuné d'une longue constance; "

the devoted Pylade, who whatever he may not have, has at least a genius for friendship, —

" Au travers des perils un grand cœur se fait jour. Que ne peut l'amitié conduite par l'amour? "

and above all, the astute old politician and oppor-
tunist, Acomat, selfish, unscrupulous, circuitous, but
ennobled in defeat by the cool dispassionate courage
of his intellect, —

    " Ne tardons plus, marchons; et s'il faut que je meure,
      Mourons, moy, cher Osmin, comme visir, et toy
      Comme le favori d'un homme tel que moy."

These are vigourous and interesting vignettes if
nothing more.

But even at that, Racine's distinction is not to be
found in this direction. On the whole his men are
accessory; they play their parts acceptably enough
for the purposes of drama, but their parts are not,
as a rule, great ones. His proper theme is woman.
And in this, his own field, he is, it seems to me, un-
equalled. For the English reader the contrast with
Shakespeare is unavoidable. Even in ordinary matters of taste an assertion of preference on the part
of the critic is likely, I know, to seem presumptu-
ous; how much more so when not only taste is concerned but the ideals natural and acquired in which
it is rooted! For it is hard to say to what extent
we have moulded our conceptions of female character upon Shakespeare's heroines. Without
prejudice, however, I may venture to indicate certain
differences and distinctions, which may be thought
partly or even wholly national but which at all
events are real enough to merit enumeration.

To begin with, let me freely concede what is
usually regarded as the greatest achievement of the
greatest Elizabethan — the " naturalness " of his

women. My only misgiving is whether, theatrically
considered, they are not too natural. I am not sure
that woman, to be in character, should not be herself a little artificial, whether her most potent attractions are not in the nature of embellishments:
the women themselves have always acted on that
principle. But at least, to the extent that the stage
is an artifice and the drama is a convention, does
not this very " naturalness " of Shakespeare's women
throw them slightly out of perspective on the
boards? And again, I think it a fair question
whether they may not purchase their naturalness,
many of them, at the expense of the highest dramatic verisimilitude and significance. For it is
quite conceivable that a dramatic character may
possess " actuality " or truth of fact, to the detriment of reality or truth of art. Such a character
may have all the interest of a likeness and conduce
to all the pleasure that recognition is capable of,
and yet want the final charm of illusion, that illusion of a higher reality which Goethe speaks of
as the crown or halo of literature. And it is not the
obviousness of those long-legged, loose-mouthed
hoydens in rompers that I have in mind; I am thinking of the population of the tragedies. They are
all so innocently " womanly," so fondly domestic
and housewifely; their career is so obviously matri-
mony and their tragedy to be thwarted of an affec-
tionate husband and family. Neither Desdemona
nor Ophelia nor Juliet are legitimately heroines of
tragedy at all. They are wives and sweethearts
who ought to be happily mated and wedded. Nor
is there any reason in themselves why they should

not be so. As for little Lady Macbeth with the sullied hands, the most tigerish of her sex at first sight, her vocation is not murder but motherhood, and it is only in default of a cradle that she is reduced to spoiling her husband with his bauble crown and sceptre. After the manner of their kind they have little or no imagination — Juliet has a little, perhaps; but indicatively the fancy of the play is Mercutio, who perishes early in the action. And wanting imagination they are almost destitute of coquetry as well. Naturally, they are not without the strength of their passions; but as a rule, they are singularly free from sexual jealousy; that from the Shakespearean point of view is a master passion — characteristically, feminine jealousy is to his mind a comic, not a tragic motive. Altogether their outlook is pretty well bounded by the hearth. Cordelia is as representatively the daughter as Juliet is the mistress or Desdemona the wife. Isabella seems to have tragic possibilities — though she falls under the spell of her brother, the dominant male, for a time; but in any event her dramatic destiny has cut short her natural career by forcing her into comedy and wedlock — unless, indeed, her marriage is her tragedy, as may well be with her disposition. Cleopatra is, of course, another story altogether; and with Cressida — to glance from my subject an instant — affords a brilliant example of Shakespeare's versatility. But to reverse the common phrase, the women for whom he is most renowned, are men's women — a circumstance that may incidentally have enhanced the popularity of his female characters with the critics. Of all the great drama-

tists Shakespeare is the most subject to the current
masculine illusions about women. As a result, they
take their cue from their masters, just as Racine's
men take their cue from their mistresses. And
though much more strongly charactered than are the
latter's heroes, as they are more " natural " than
his heroines; nevertheless they are comparatively
simple and intelligible when read in these terms.

That it is not for this type of woman that one
admires Racine every reader will agree. Who would
dream of turning to him for a pattern of elementary
domestic virtue — of mother, wife, or daughter?
Unless it be Andromaque; and how much more
Andromaque has in the back of her head than
Constance!   Monime, perhaps, and Iphigénie and
Junie may be made, by some retouching, to take on
a deceptive resemblance to their English rivals; but
it is only that for an instant their helplessness and
dependence simulate a kind of simplicity which
might pass superficially for " nature," just as Cleopatra's promiscuous experience might be momentarily confounded with the subtlety of a delicate and
discriminating *savoir vivre*. In reality their texture
is very different. The interest of Racine's women
— no matter of what sort or degree it may happen
to be — the property whereby they attract and hold
the attention, their very " femininity," in short, is no
unaffected grace; it is an accomplishment, which
is capable in their hands of becoming an effective
weapon either of offense or defense as the occasion
may require. In this sense and to this extent they
are creatures of artifice, if one likes to call them so
— that their character in its final effect is an

achievement of care and cultivation. They are thoroughly aware of themselves and their attainments; and yet their refinement, though an acquirement, is not an affectation, but a second nature. For all her transports one can not conceive of Phèdre's lapsing into the " fair " Ophelia's unpremeditated ribaldry under any circumstances. Roxane, as the inmate of a harem and the despot of slaves and eunuchs, is used to terrible atrocities, no doubt, but it is difficult to imagine her so far forgetting herself as to bedaub the bloody faces of her abjects with her own hands. Such an abomination would suit better the character of Clytemnestra or Electra. That Racine wrote for a conventional society and chose his subjects from such a *milieu* does not to my mind affect the issue. Nothing could be more " artificial " to our view than the status of the Greek women; and yet the women of Greek tragedy are much more " natural " and " Shakespearean " than Racine's. On the other hand, paradoxical though it may sound, the latter's passions are elemental enough — more so, if anything — or at least, more integral than Shakespeare's by virtue of the superior proficiency of the characters. In any event, the fact remains that the personages whom he creates — whatever the vehemence and consistency of their emotions — have not the sheer, unalloyed " womanliness " to which we have been habituated by Shakespeare; they are much too intricate and enigmatic. With passion as his theme and tragedy as his *genre* he confines himself pretty strictly, since woman is his protagonist, to the representation of the sex as a fatality, and of the female as the shrewd and not always scrupulous adversary of the male. No creature can transcend its creator. Great writer though he was, it would be absurd to credit Racine with the demonic genius of a Shakespeare. There is no cause for surprise that the distinction of his heroines, like that of his craft, should be the result of calculation and study. And yet within these margins — narrow as they may appear to the modern primitivist — he has, if not actually created, at least given its classical illustration to a certain female type — the woman of sophistication, whose ends are in herself and not in man.

Of this type Phèdre is the consummation as the play itself is the consummation of modern classic tragedy. I would not be thought by this statement to belittle *Athalie;* it is an admirable piece and can hardly be overrated. I recognize, too, its remarkable analogies with Greek drama — particularly, the divinity that shapes its ends. But withal, its perfection seems to me misleading — not that imperfection is a merit in itself as the romanticists would hoax us into believing; but that the flawlessness of its structure distracts attention from what is, after all, its factitiousness. In a word, it lacks the *desinvolture,* the warmth and animation and expressiveness of *Phèdre.* And not only is it distant and austere, it is in a manner out of space, out of time altogether; it belongs neither to its own period nor to its own stage. In consequence, my admiration is always a little dampened by my consciousness of it as a *tour de force,* like the *Samson Agonistes.* But whether my opinion is right or wrong is of no great consequence at this juncture, save as a favourable allowance may be held to excuse my neglect of the play as lying outside of the *genre* that I have been discussing; the question itself has nothing to do with Phèdre as representative of her kind.

I have often wondered whether any playwright is capable of depicting more than one female character intimately and whether his several heroines of the first plan are not merely this one daughter of his imagination exhibited in different poses and at different stages of growth corresponding roughly with his own development. In Ibsen's principal plays I seem to see, for all her disconcerting caprices, a single woman growing up into a malign prodigy. I do not question the theatrical effect; it is, doubtless, that of multiplicity, — any woman has a sufficient number of facets to supply at least one complete repertoire. But in reading I persist in seeing a kind of identity — or at all events, a family likeness. And so, to a certain extent, with Racine. Roxane, so Vinet thinks, is only Hermione " *approfondie.*" The propriety of Monime, the ingenuousness of Iphigénie, the restraint of Andromaque, the diffidence of Junie, the petulance of Hermione, the circumspection of Bérénice, the frowardness of Roxane, the langour of Phèdre — these traits would seem to be about as diverse as traits well can be. And yet these expressions of a variable temper serve but to dissimulate the persistent features of an unmistakable consanguinity. Unlike Desdemona and Ophelia and Juliet, these women are all tragic, not as they happen to have been overtaken by the dangers of a general mortality, but by disposition and necessity. They are fey. Like Clytemnestra and Electra and Phædra and Antigone, they are born calamitous; and they share with them the sinister dignity of predestination. But they are themselves again and of their own house by their air of sensibility and personal elegance — by the impression which they manage somehow to convey of an inviolable feminine privacy and reserve even in the midst of their most shocking disorders.

SHAKESPEARE AND SOPHOCLES

UNIVERSAL as is the recognition of the respective values of Shakespeare and Sophocles, yet it is hardly recognized how wide is actually the divergence between the kinds of thing that they stand for. The instinct of our generation, which is all for confusion, is to slur it over. That they represent two different attitudes of the human spirit is clear enough. But it is often overlooked that the two attitudes which they represent are not only different but more or less antagonistic. They personify two diverse and inimical ideals of life and literature. Aside from what is eternal and timeless in them both, the one is modern, the other ancient. And as far as these categories are significant, modern is to be understood, by the light of its genealogy, in the sense of popular and natural; ancient in that of humane and moral.

In order to get my bearings to begin with, I must recall, however perfunctorily, the lapse of the great classical tradition, the tradition of humane culture initiated by Greece and transmitted by Rome, which is the great outstanding fact of the Dark Ages. During that period, which was marked by the general suspension or abeyance of literature and art, there was gradually evolved a new and independent civilization and " culture," in the narrower or sociological sense of that word of many evil connotations.

I will not call it Christian; though as far as it has
any universal character, it was determined in a great
measure by the Roman Catholic Church and by a
kind of thought whose subject-matter was mainly
theological. Its exact composition, however, I have
not the erudition to analyse; nor is it particularly
in my way to do so. Suffice it to say that along with
Roman Catholicism and scholasticism the great institutions of feudalism and chivalry illustrate approximately its general disposition. In course of
time this new and peripheral ideal of culture began
to generate secular and vernacular literatures, which
in some cases attained considerable proportions.
The temptation has been to exaggerate their importance, especially the German contribution, by motives of patriotic and particularistic prejudice. But
such monuments as the *Nibelungen Lied,* the *Song
of Roland,* and the Mystery Plays of England are
sufficient to suggest what might have been the result,
if these germinations had been allowed to come to
fruition without the intervention of the Renaissance
and the Revival of Learning.

Under the circumstances, however, the growth of
mediævalism was checked and diverted, where it
was not subdued and overcome, by the recrudescence
of classicism. Instead of having but a single tradition and a single line of development the human
spirit might now choose between two; or by dividing
itself variously it might find any number of outlets
for its activity. And at the same time, there was a
split in another sense — between the learned and
the lewd. It would be the scholars, the men of
education, the curious and the critical who would

be the most likely to revert to the broken tradition
of Greece and Rome; while the people, the ignorant
and the credulous would naturally continue to move
with the stream on which they had been floating for
centuries — and in the same direction. It was inevitable, then, that where literature came under the
patronage of a court and an official criticism, it
should react powerfully, in the interest of distinction, in favour of the classic ideal; where it was addressed to the people, however, it would persist in
the mediæval sense, though its expression might be
modified by the precedents of restoration and reform. The former was the case with French drama;
the latter with English. There were courtly and
scholarly poets and essayists scattered up and down
the English Renaissance imitating Seneca and ridi-
culing the absurdities of popular playwrights. With
suitable encouragement and organization they or
their successors would have been capable of producing in time a classical English tragedy, such as the
French produced a century later. But the temper
and the habit of the nation and the example of
Shakespeare were decisive. The case is often mis-
conceived or misrepresented. Shakespeare was not
a great poet because he was a romanticist, nor was
Ben Johnson his inferior because he was a classicist. That Shakespeare was a superlative playwright is merely the reason or one of the reasons
that romanticism prevailed in England; if he had
been an ineffectual one, it might not have done so.
Whereas if Ben Johnson had been sufficiently imposing, classicism might have attained the preëminence it did across the Channel with Corneille.

In this way it was the people who made English drama through their favourite poet. If the court had any official influence, it was probably exerted, in accordance with Elizabeth's usual policy, to the encouragement of the national and popular inspiration rather than the humanistic. And the people were the issue and the posterity of mediævalism. They cared nothing about antiquity and knew less; their " culture," such as it was, was inherited from the Middle Ages. They had been brought up on the mystery and miracle plays. Better things they might appreciate; but those better things must appear in recognizable ways as outgrowths and improvements of the kind of thing they were already used to. And so their choregus would find himself committed to a certain kind of conservatism in entering upon his succession. Shakespeare was no radical, no reckless innovator; his invention as distinguished from his imagination was notoriously slight, as seems to be the rule with genius. Critics have exclaimed over his borrowings and imitations. Undoubtedly, he was affected himself by classical communications. It is impossible that living when he did live, in an atmosphere of such ideas, he should not have been affected by them. The Battle of the Books seems a silly altercation on the one part, if you happen to think that without the ancients there would have been no moderns to boast of. And it is equally undeniable that without antiquity Shakespeare would not have been so wholly Shakespeare. Nevertheless, whatever secondary influences he may have been exposed to, his direct tradition is the mediæval tradition and his handling

of it is such as to have made him the supreme representative of modernity, to whom every romantic
revival has [turned back] instinctively.

Without attempting to define mediævalism any
more closely, then, I may point out what there is
in Shakespeare which is not in Sophocles. In the
first place, modern life — to give the word *modern*
its fullest extension as including whatever is novel
to antiquity — is tremendously more complicated
than ancient life ever was; and in the second place,
our manner of looking at life has changed tremendously, to take no account of the advantage the
Greek has had over all other races in clarity of mind
and penetration of vision. Consider, for one thing,
how little the ancient knew as compared even with
the contemporaries of Shakespeare, how small his
stock of information. He was acquainted only with
an infinitesimal portion of the universe; of the globe
on which he walked he knew only an insignificant
corner bordering on the Mediterranean Sea. Of the
denizens of this earth, of its flora and fauna he was
equally ignorant; while its shape, size, constitution,
and manner of conducting itself were to him mainly
matters of guess-work. He had by no means discovered all that the naked eye was capable of discovering, if properly used, to say nothing of that
vast accumulation of fact which has been added to
modern discovery by microscope and telescope and
one and another ingenious contrivance for the
multiplication and extension of the senses.

Nevertheless — I may as well anticipate the objection — every ancient literature is not clear and
simple. And while the complexity of modern life

has done much to make chronic a confusion and sophistication of mind to which every age and race is liable; yet the relative lucidity of Greek literature is due also to the quality of Greek thought and to the nature of its ideas. It is not only that there is more fact nowadays, but that some minds — modern minds particularly — are so constituted as to be more easily impressed and dominated by it. For it may be said with a degree of plausibility that beyond a certain narrow limit life is equally plethoric for every mind in proportion to its capacity, as a sponge of a certain size will hold only so much water no matter how much there may be in the ocean. But the comparative intellectual simplicity and lucidity of the Greeks is one of the fundamental data which can not be accounted for historically; it can only be noted and taken for granted. For that reason I have nothing to say here about the Greeks' preoccupation with the moral issue, which simplified life so wonderfully for them. While the circumstances surrounding this essential fact become merely a complication of the subject itself.

As another such incidental circumstance, then, it is to be remarked that along with this accumulation of physical fact has gone a constant accumulation of what may be called psychological fact. Not only do we know more about man and his motives and general mental machinery, but our heads have become a depository of creeds, superstitions, hypotheses, and opinions. No idea that once comes into the world ever dies quite out; no matter how false or erroneous it may be or how often exploded, its ghost still walks, reappearing in one form or another to haunt and unsettle the mind of posterity. And their numbers are always multiplying; for naturally enough it is impossible to increase our supply of information without also increasing our explanations and thereby adding to our theories, systems, and philosophies. Given the facts, the impulse to account for them and dispose of them is irresistible; and hence the swarm of dogmas — moral, religious, physical, metaphysical, social, economic, literary, artistic — which in succession have bewildered and perplexed the world and whose crumbling remains can never be wholly dispersed but serve as a foundation or soil for their successors so that under the churches of Christendom you shall find the ruined temples of Paganism and under the laboratories of science the rubbish of transcendental superstition, the broken alembics of the alchemist and the mouldy horoscopes of the astrologer. And all the while we are endeavouring to adjust our conduct to our discoveries and our principles, until our relations at large — our society, our culture, our civilization — become ever more involved and intricate and unreliable.

In contrast with all this multifariousness how simple seem the life and the thought of the Greek, subtle in his way as the Athenian was. According to Plato (or whoever wrote *Alcibiades I*) Alcibiades' education comprised three subjects — grammar, including reading, writing, and literature, as we should say, wrestling, and the cithera. To be sure, he might have learned the flute also if he had cared to do so. There was little positive knowledge to be acquired; no deep historical deposits to be unearthed for history had but begun. Religion and philosophy were still elementary; — or at least the Greek saw them clearly and in high relief, unencumbered with very much lumber — philosophy, particularly, in an array of sharp antitheses — the one and the many, the same and the other, rest and motion, being and becoming. And in this wise being unembarrassed with a thorny undergrowth of exceptions and variations, he was able to frame a scheme of things which has never been surpassed, on the whole, for its bold and distinct projection. No doubt, he would have done so more or less successfully whatever his materials, such was the character of his consciousness; but he was assisted in doing so by the circumstances in which he found himself. Even the Sophists have come to look to us like innocent and transparent prestidigitators with very little harm in them after all.

Nor was his practical life and conduct more involved than his religion and philosophy. The citizen of a small and isolated city in a comparatively easy society, he was mainly engrossed by his relationship to the polity of which he was a member and the maintenance of his position and credit as a free man in a democracy raised on a foundation of slavery. His intercourse and association were mostly public and by so much the more general and ideal; while his private existence was itself narrow and reserved. His interests were correspondingly broad and obvious; his cares and joys were reduced to the measure of the community. In short, his consciousness was at the same time more abstract and intense than any we are now familiar with.

To emphasize the contrast between this generic integrity in which Sophocles must have shared and the circumstantial diffusion of modernity in which Shakespeare had his part — a contrast admirably visualized in Greek temple and Gothic cathedral — we have only to recall the three great institutions of feudalism, chivalry, and Roman Catholicism which stand behind the mediæval tradition, with their subtle and elaborate conceptions of the relations of man to his fellow men — inferiors, equals, and superiors — to the state, and to God and the Church, along with the etiquette, ceremonial, and ritual in which they sought to symbolize those ideas. And if these institutions had early begun to lose a portion of the influence which they exerted during the Middle Ages, yet they had at least produced an effect not to be easily obliterated and in yielding finally gave way to other systems no less intricate than they themselves.

This is no attempt, of course, at anything like a complete account of the matter. Nevertheless, it must be apparent that herein lies a fundamental difference between modern and ancient — between the new or romantic, that is, and the old or classical literature, and in so far between Shakespeare and Sophocles — namely, in this immense accession of fact and the tremendous prolixity and sophistication of experience and consciousness, both personal and social, which results directly from it. In other words, the data which even a writer of Shakespeare's day had to master and take care of, were increased to such an extent as already to make a significant presentation of life a problem of incredible difficulty.

And indeed, such an effect is visible in Shakespeare's own drama at the most superficial glance. Everywhere, as compared with the work of the classical dramatists, his plays are marked by an abundance, a superfluity of fact and a consequent diffusion of thought and expression. Not only is his " story " twice or three times as long as Sophocles '; it is crammed with incident and observation of all sorts, congruous and incongruous, pertinent and impertinent. Whereas Sophocles has five or six characters to a piece, Shakespeare may run to forty or fifty; and these characters, instead of being confined to a single set of principals and their suite, are drawn from various companies and from all levels of society. The motives, too, by which these characters are actuated, are, in the one case, relatively simple; in the other, numerous and inextricable. About the classical character there is something diagrammatic or figurative, like a silhouette; about a Shakespearean character there is likely to be something abstruse and problematic. And finally, while the intention of a Sophoclean play is more or less evident on the face of it; that of a *Hamlet* or a *King Lear* is dark and mystifying, and is engaged confusedly with the elements themselves and immanent in them.

So it is that as the amount of fact for which the writer has to account, increases, his difficulties in disposing it into a satisfactory system and of disengaging a distinct idea will increase also. As life becomes more and more miscellaneous, and as the thoughts and emotions with which we contemplate it grow ever more comprehensive, and our speculations augment in subtlety and extension; it will be harder and harder to express them even piece-meal, to say nothing of composing an intelligible present-ment of the society into whose existence they enter. In other words, it will be ever more difficult to or-ganize into literature and significance the materials which experience has to offer. And simultaneously with the rising welter of existence, it will become the more difficult also to arrive at a clear comprehension of its import. The weight of the facts will tend to overload and paralyse the imagination. And at the same time that the multiplicity of particulars will obscure a perception of their import, it will distract the attention to the mere observation and notation of discrete peculiarities. The principle which pur-ports to guarantee the external consistency of such a world, be it evolution or *élan vital*, is altogether too vague and rarefied to make sense of our artistic and literary epitomes and microcosms.

Such, it seems to me, is at least one vital distinc-tion between humanism and modernism, between the art of Sophocles and that of Shakespeare. Whatever is produced in the spirit of the former is incited by the desire to make sense of experience. For such an art circumstance is merely illustrative. What counts is the large bold block of meaning; fact is expressive only as evidence of idea. On the con-trary, the art of a Shakespeare proceeds from a spirit more or less under the domination of actu-ality and subdued to what it works in. It repre-sents an order of literature in which the conscious-ness of life is no longer integral and consistent, but is distributed into particular moments or phases. It is the picture, the image, the impression — the illusion of swift and discontinuous succession which is accentuated. Even Shakespeare's vision is fractional; it penetrates and informs the single manifestation and is dissipated with it.

Naturally I have no pretension to know how Sophocles conceived his plays; but the fact that they can be viewed severally in the light of a problem, and a problem with a solution, is sufficiently indicative of the distinction that I am drawing. With other speculative spirits of his time Sophocles would appear to have been profoundly impressed by the observation that man is actuated by two paramount desires — he has, as it were, a passion for happiness and a passion for righteousness or justice; and it is difficult or impossible for the high-minded observer to contemplate with patience an existence which fails to provide for the gratification of both. Even in fancy the misery of the virtuous is revolting; the prosperity of the wicked dismaying. Hence the urgency to reconcile the two ideals in the face of such opposition and contradiction as were tauntingly voiced by Callicles and Thrasymachus. Plato, to be sure, settled the matter to his own satisfaction by asserting the absolute identity of happiness and justice — the state of virtue, so he rules, is the state of felicity, irrespective of material circumstances and independent of the approval of the gods themselves. But he offers no proof of this declaration, save an implicit appeal to consciousness. Of course, if one feels so, that is the end of it; but it must be acknowledged that appearances are often against him. At all events, Sophocles, who as a dramatist had to deal with outward manifestations rather than inward convictions, is neither so bold nor so dogmatic. Perhaps he was not quite so certain. But in any case, it was a rather different aspect of the subject which would thrust itself upon his attention. As a tragedian he would be preoccupied, rather, with human mischances and calamities. On the whole, the question put to him by his sort of theme is, not so much a question about the character of the happy — whether he is virtuous or not — as it is a question about the character of the wretched — whether he is invariably unjust. To be sure, in his extant plays he does face the former question twice — in *Philoctetes* and *Œdipus Coloneus*. But in every instance he answers the question, and he answers it in the general sense of Plato, though less explicitly. Happiness and righteousness, he seems to think, are somehow paired together in the constitution of the cosmos, so that the former exists in some manner by virtue of the latter. Nor is such a conception in its large outlines unfamiliar to pious souls in every age. Only there are these two differences to be noticed. First, in Sophocles' view the misery of injustice is not referable to the judgment or visitation of an indignant or offended deity. The execution of this or that ordinance or the punishment for its violation may be entrusted to the agency or instrumentality of some particular divinity, who comes in this way to represent it, as the Apollo of *Electra* or the Furies of *The Eumenides*. But the inviolability of the entire order or the constitution itself is an impersonal and inevitable law; for Sophocles' nature — and here is the second point of difference — is fundamentally moral and relevant without coincidences and exceptions on the one hand and without impertinences and miscarriages on the other. To Philoctetes and to Œdipus at Colonos it assures the blessings of a reconciliation with righteousness; and the others it leaves, in their several degrees, convicted of misdoing, as plunged in disaster.

But this is all an idea. What Shakespeare has to say about the facts is something very different. Shakespeare is a mediæval overtaken by the immense perturbation of the Renaissance — a perturbation so vast that its agitations have not yet wholly subsided. Its immediate effect, however, was the erection of incongruity or disorder into a vital principle. In reality, there is a certain moment of the Renaissance which is fully as responsible for romanticism as is mediævalism itself, though it seldom or never gets the credit to which it is entitled. For the time being the rule of regularity and consistency was pretermitted; the solidarity of character was broken up. Man ceased to think and act in the spirit of any one maxim, but gave license to all sides of his being indifferently, without concern to discriminate between them. He was no longer *integer vitæ*, a single and indivisible will, but an *être ondoyant et divers*. The duplicity of Shakespeare's characters is a commonplace of criticism; and many and ingenious have been the essays to derive their tragedy from the disaffection within their own souls. Though one may not like the association of ideas, one is perforce reminded by these attempts of Tennyson's " second-rate sensitive mind not in harmony with itself." But in that case why not call them multiple and dispense with all but the protagonist, who comprises a privy conspiracy in himself? Not that I would deny to Shakespeare's characters a share in the distemper of their time — the *aperçu*, when properly guarded, is a suggestive one; only Shakespeare's is not primarily a psychological drama, and to interpret it as such — as a study in " multiple personality," for example — is to denature it.

The inconsequence that struck Shakespeare most, it seems to me, was not so much an inconsistency of character — though he is sensitive to that also, as every one must be who has any experience of modernity at all — but rather an incompatibility of nature. It is not exactly a case of maladjustment, as I see it, or of a faulty adaptation of the creature; though that is necessarily involved, it is a secondary matter. The point has to do with a failure of continuity in creation, a kind of incoherence or inconsecutiveness in the transition from the material or physical to the sentient or human. Sophocles avoided the difficulty by giving the universe a moral bent or turn consonant with that of humanity; the Renaissance relaxed the law for man even within the confines of consciousness. Hence a dissonance, a perpetual contradiction and confutation of reason by circumstance, an irrational and preposterous frustration of human aspiration and endeavour by accident and fortuity, which being essentially casual and unintelligible, has an air of grotesque and idiotic triviality. There is something insufferably stupid and odious about it. It has the effect of an indignity, of an outrage to human nature.

What an ignominious business is that in which Hamlet finally loses his life, for a man of his parts — and how Shakespearean! Nor is the end of Lear less inopportune and futile. Even the sonnets are drenched with this same feeling of perversity and humiliation.

But mark that this sense of incongruity is not an idea, like Sophocles'. It is an impression, or perhaps, a notation. No doubt, Shakespeare reinforced the effect; but the incongruity has its roots in the indiscrimination of life itself. It is not that he makes it appear so, but that it actually is so or looks so. And particularly does it look so when the items are viewed severally and successively, cinematographically, in the modern manner. In other words, incongruity is a property of actuality not of art. Racine is not incongruous; or if he is, he has blundered. Sophocles is not incongruous. To them incongruity would have meant vicious architectonics; for incongruity is impossible without a mass of disorderly detail. Hence wherever incongruity is discernible in a work of art, it argues excess of fact and indifference to design for there is nothing conclusive about incongruity; on the contrary. Similarly, wherever the conclusion of a piece of literature is unconvincing, the piece itself is deficient in idea or intention. And so I can not help thinking that Shakespeare was, as I have implied, concerned rather to reflect life than to interpret it. He was more interested in posing the problem than in solving it. And a more vivid, intense, amazing image — a more suggestive and provocative statement of the enigma has never been known than Shakespeare's.

That such a literature, however, is incapable of affording the highest satisfaction possible to literature, I hold to be indisputable. As is the case with experience also, its very lack of finality is against it. For life itself is never finished but ever lapsing. No transaction ever actually concludes; it evolves. One incident is prolonged into another, and so radiates and ramifies that to bound or delimit it is impossible. And even in those rare cases where an affair seems to have reached a period, the end is splintered and ragged — is anything but such a clean and tidy cleavage as we expect of art; nothing is definitely settled, nothing or very little is decided. The players of all the world go on much as before; the lover is rejected or finds his faithless inamorata coquetting with some one else and leaves her for another more appreciative of his attentions, or for no one at all. Or they fall in love against their parents' wishes, and marry each other or the contrary — it makes little difference in the long run either to themselves or any one else — they merely become the centre or the centres of a new vortex or the dilation of the preceding. Such are the facts, objectively indifferent and indeterminate. And so the writer who pretends to take things as they come, κατ' ἀνάγκην ὑπὸ δίνης, in accordance with necessity, by force of the whirl, must either leave his work at a loose end or else stitch it roughly into some conventional selvage at variance with the regular pattern of events.

There are several plays of Molière's — by no means his worst — plays like *Tartuffe* and *Le Misanthrope,* which the reader finds it impossible to lay aside without a sense of disappointment. In the case of *Tartuffe* the annoyance is particularly sensible; the close of the piece is so obviously mechanical and factitious. It looks as though his characters had finally been drawn into a predicament from which no ingenuity was capable of extricating them by natural means growing out of the premises. There is nothing for it but a special intervention, for whether the work of *Grand Monarque* or Olympian, the issue is equally miraculous. It is neither according to necessity nor probability, physical or moral; it is not δι' ἄλλ ηλα, by consecution at all. But Molière in his degree is a realist. He may not appear so in comparison with Shakespeare, whose eye for the phenomenal is so marvellously prismatic; but he does appear so in comparison with Racine, and also in the comparison of tragedy and comedy, the latter of which is necessarily more photographic than the former. *Tartuffe* may be satire; but none the less does it disclose a minute recognition of the *mores* of the period. In life, however, such knots as that into which Orgon is tied, are indissoluble. The Orgons of reality fare like flies in the meshes of the Tartuffes. If Molière had wished to close his play in the sense in which he had been conducting it, he should have left his dupe to flounder hopelessly in the web into which his credulity had betrayed him. Such a cessation, however, was impracticable; the audience would not have put up with it. Overborne by custom, Molière was reduced to flouting plausibility and forging a conclusion, the most unlikely conclusion to what might have been one of the most likely plays he ever made.

In *Le Misanthrope,* on the other hand, the case is reversed: the conclusion is equally inadequate but for just the contrary reason. With the exception of the engagement of the two " confidants," Philante and Éliante, which is again, as far as it goes, a thoroughly conventional expedient intended to give the piece a deceptive appearance of finality — with this exception *Le Misanthrope* ends very much as such an affair is likely to end in reality — it breaks up. Célimène is exposed and Alceste makes his exit. There is a fine off-handedness about it; and that is all. Nothing in particular is illustrated in spite of the circumstance that the play proposes a very pretty problem. And it is on this account that the close is so teasing — that it does not answer the very question which the action has tacitly propounded; if anything, it raises others. Hence it is not surprising to find that the significance of the comedy and even its status as comedy have been a subject of discussion; for it seems hardly to substantiate an idea at all, but rather to moot certain of the dilemmas and paradoxes of social ethics.

Nor is Shakespeare any less liable to this sort of dislocation — he is rather more so, perhaps, though in his case we are not so likely to be conscious of discomfort because we have become more thoroughly accustomed to his dramatic mannerisms. But to take only a single instance, *Measure for Measure.* It is not one of Shakespeare's great plays, to be sure; but the subject has great possibilities over and above those of which he has taken advantage. Why he should have chosen to make a " comedy " of it, is an idle inquiry, though it seems from the tone and atmosphere as though he must have done so against the grain. But having once chosen, he was fatally determined to a counterfeit and disingenuous conclusion. For such marriages as those of Mariana and Angelo, Isabella and the Duke there is no excuse other than the artificial criterion which assigns to every romantic comedy its quota of arbitrary weddings as to every romantic tragedy its quota of violent deaths. They are neither inevitable nor intelligible, neither nature nor art. At best they serve to dissemble after a fashion the inconclusiveness of nature apart from principle.

And yet there is one exception — in the case of tragedy in the English sense — that kind of a tragedy, I mean, which has a fatal outcome. As a matter of fact, death is a termination if not a consummation; it is at least a bound if not a bourne. It may answer no questions, it may provide no solution for our perplexities; but it puts an end to us and our problems — it stops our mouths forever. And in so doing, it simulates a kind of finality, even a kind of fatality. In this respect, therefore, as far as " naturalness " is concerned, there is no reason to complain of the catastrophe of Shakespeare's tragedies. In following life itself, he has come — without more ado — to the one foregone conclusion. In this sense there is nothing disappointing about the *dénouements* of *Othello* or *Hamlet* or *Macbeth* or *Romeo and Juliet*.

It is only from the moral point of view that they leave something to be desired. And from this angle I confess that to my mind they are not wholly edifying. I use the word advisedly; though I am glad to be aroused by tragedy, I want not to be left unsettled but composed. Of *King Lear* I say nothing; the last act is obviously a blunder. I can imagine nature in her stubborn courses stumbling into some such blind and bloody shambles; that is not the difficulty — the untowardness of insentiency. But I can not recognize in *Lear* the logic or *raison d'être* of the *genre,* the bare technical congruity of the literary " form " which is evident even in the most brutal Zolaesque impressionism. A box is a box whatever it does or does not contain, and is possessed of a kind of mechanical integrity as such. But the deaths of Cordelia and her father are impertinent not only morally but theatrically; they are extrinsic and superfluous. It is impossible to take them up into one scheme with the preceding acts of the play; they do not coalesce. I do not deny that the tragedy has its grandeur, as stupendous at moments as a chaos of the elements. But as a whole, it is inconceivable on its own showing. And so I say that Shakespeare has blundered somehow as he has seldom done elsewhere in tragedy.

To a certain extent, however, *Romeo and Juliet* seems to me another case in which he has failed to carry out his own premises. It is a young man's tragedy: even the poetry, splendid as it is in passages, and the admirable humours of Mercutio and the nurse are immature for Shakespeare. Under these circumstances, it might seem unfair to require any very strict moral necessitarianism of its author, if such were Shakespeare's way in any case. But I should have liked to see the same fatality which passes through Mercutio find its mark at last in hero and heroine. For the sake of dramatic effect if nothing more Mercutio's fate should prefigure that of his friend. But Mercutio dies in a vain skirmish. The hostility of " both your houses " loses its drive little by little until it ceases to penetrate the play and dwindles into a mere pretext for the sorry over-sight or misunderstanding which is actually account-able for the catastrophe.

But the failings of *Romeo and Juliet* are technical. As an illustration of the indeterminateness inherent in " natural " tragedy *Hamlet* stands unrivalled, as witness the proverbial character of the hero. It has all the points of a primary and spontaneous romanticism — the " problematic " temperament, the " psychopathic " doubt and *défaillance,* the " picturesque " background, the " morbid " atmos-phere, the " suggestive " treatment. Think what could be made of an introspective Orestes with a scruple, and what an illusion of profundity and modernity might be created with the *Electra* as so transmogrified. And on the other hand, compare Bourget's *André Cornelis.* The theme is virtually identical with that of *Hamlet;* but what a difference in effect! In the latter the remote fantastic setting of feudal life and customs; the legendary castle of Elsinore with its heavy mediæval shadow, ghost-haunted and visionary; the arras-hung apartments, the barbaric display of royalty, the adventurous in-cidents, and the distant echoes of the outer world, of young Fortinbras and his marching armies. In Bourget's novel, on the contrary, the din and clatter of a nineteenth-century city, the populous streets,

the comfortable houses of the rich and idle, the intrigue of a vitiated society, the commonplace of
" civilization," and above all a kind of French clarity and sharpness and assurance quite remote from
the thick and foggy sea air of Denmark. There is no
question about it: *Hamlet* is a tale of human fatuity,
not in the ancient but in the modern sense. It is not
that Hamlet deliberates to kill his uncle; he is well
within his dramatic rights in doing so. Nor is it that
he does actually kill his uncle before he is through
with him; that also is his dramatic right. It is the
indifference of conscience and choice — of everything save coincidence alone — in the final result;
it is the affront to liberty and the freedom of the will
in that finally his calculations, his delays and hesitations and reluctances should all go for nought and
that he should find himself at last tricked on such
frivolous occasion into an assassination so unpremeditated, so flippant even, as hardly to bear the
character of voluntary action at all. How uncon-
scionable, and yet with what consummate plausibility it is carried off! It makes not only the most notable example of Shakespearean irony but quite the
most " interesting " tragedy extant. Small wonder
that no two commentators have ever agreed as to
its intention.

Let us suppose a chorus of sententious old wise-
acres, after the antique fashion, gaping and gossip-
ing over the issues of the action; in what apothegm
or adage do you suppose they would sum up their
impressions? Horatio, who serves as a kind of
epilogue, speaks of it as a skein

" Of accidental judgments, casual slaughters."

But can we think of a valedictory more inaccept-
able to the sober wisdom of antiquity? There is a
phrase of Hamlet's own toward the end of his
journey — an expression not inconsistent with the
spirit of the play — " the readiness is all," which
we should have no great difficulty in imagining a
Greek chorus' elaborating in the sense of Edgar in
King Lear;

> " Men must endure
> Their going hence, even as their coming hither;
> Ripeness is all."

It offers no apology for the excesses of a conscienceless eventuality; but it supplies a rule of conduct —
not wholly foreign to the Greek temper — in a
world of careless and improvident possibilities, so
that it is not astonishing that Shakespeare should
have repeated the sentiment in the two plays of his
which are of all the most unpunctual and inscrutable.

Macbeth, on the contrary, while thoroughly
Shakespearean and " natural," seems to present the
least difficulty to the anxious aphorist. For my part
— to take my slight exception at once — I am not
wholly satisfied with the interpretation which sees
in Macbeth himself but an evil-doer justly punished
for his crimes, though such an explanation, as a
" probable opinion " and relatively true for the final
scenes, may serve its purpose as a rough and ready
means of disposing of the play. But if such is the
case, why has not the playwright launched the protagonist as a criminal after the fashion of *Richard
III?* The more I think of it, the more strongly I
feel that Shakespeare intended to represent a good

man gone wrong — so that to a certain extent *Macbeth* is by way of being a pendant to *Hamlet*.

Of course, the motives, sentiments, and circumstances of the two tragedies are very different. But as far as the mere argument is concerned, Macbeth is Hamlet with the inhibition left out. He is susceptible, like Hamlet, to "supernatural" suggestion; he is equally irresolute — "infirm of purpose," his wife calls him. No doubt, his profession, as well as his later insolence, tends to obscure the perception of his weakness; but a man may be a courageous soldier and an indecisive character, while indecision is not unusually violent in extremity — as, indeed, it is with Hamlet. In addition, if Macbeth has not Hamlet's introspection, he has something of the latter's abstraction, and — I think it is Professor Bradley who has noted the fact — not a little of the Dane's native amiability and courtesy, when in his right mind. Need I call attention to similarities of setting — the castellated background and the air of ominous dubitation which are common to the earlier scenes of both plays? So close is the likeness at instants that one is tempted to read in Macbeth's career the secret of Hamlet's fate, had the latter done similar violence to his conscience — as some commentators seem to wish — at the promptings of an equally questionable apparition.

But it is at this point that the dramas diverge. Macbeth differs capitally from Hamlet in his reaction to opportunity — a parcel of demented old women on a heath, an ambitious wife, an old man, and a throne. That is the pity of it. Nevertheless he incurs the odium of his villainy; and since he has come to be what he is, there is no denying the justice of his damnation. It is at least the consequence of his own choice. In this respect the tragedy has a Sophoclean relevancy, which I would not belittle, though I must add immediately that there seems to be no higher motivation for his delinquency than chance and tide. And is it not true, by the way, that to the consistent " modern " *artist* the punishment of evil-doing is a " conventional " rather than a " natural " climax? But then the modern artist is not particularly consistent.

Of *Othello* I have little to say; it is self-explanatory. And that, perhaps, is the reason that in spite of its greatness it is one of the least " interesting " and " suggestive " of Shakespeare's great plays. A famous general, a noble though simple nature, with occasional flashes of poetic fancy and language, who stifles his bride in the back room of a barracks in a fit of jealousy and forthwith stabs himself, because he has fallen in the practice of a malignant villain — the police court is too full of such misadventures to permit a doubt of their authenticity. Nevertheless, my spirit is disquieted as well by the deaths of Desdemona and Othello as by those of Cordelia and Lear, Ophelia and Hamlet.

My *rôle* has been an ungrateful one; it is so much easier and pleasanter to praise an author's merits and excuse his faults than to apportion the defects of his qualities. But to this latter task my subject has confined me far longer than I could wish. There is one reproach, however, that I would not willingly incur. I would not be thought to imply that the closet is more than a kind of appellate court for tragedy. The court of first instance is the theatre. And it may be that under the latter jurisdiction my dicta seem weak and fanciful. In stagecraft Shakespeare has never been excelled. The difficulties of *Hamlet* are figments of the student and dissolve in the acting; the spectator knows nothing of them. The " double time " of *Othello* is a problem of the study, not of the stage. Nevertheless, while the text is not the play, it should be capable of withstanding a certain sort of scrutiny. Though it want complete verisimilitude — a verisimilitude which perhaps no reading, however " visual," can wholly supply, it ought to evince the writer's principles — for he wrote it after all. And in the same sense in which he may test his manuscript impressions in the theater, we have the opportunity to test our theatrical impressions by the text. I know that the line is hard to draw between legitimate cross-examination and captious inquisition; but I have tried to keep well within bounds by sticking to the more obvious issues of literature.

Obviously, there are two sources of literary interest — the likeness or the image and the idea, corresponding with the two kinds of subject — fact or " nature " and truth or import. A regard for the latter presupposes a recognition of the former; but a concern for the former does not necessarily imply a sense for the latter. At the same time, it is probable that a devotion to import may incline to an accommodation or " arrangement " of actuality, just as an absorption with actuality leads to a neglect of significance. The vehicle or agency of likeness is imitation or representation; of truth, interpretation. What Aristotle had in mind in defining poetry as an imitation I do not pretend to say. I would merely suggest that the term was traditional and that to a youthful art or criticism the securing of a recognizable likeness to the subject is a matter of first and disproportionate importance, on which account the term *imitation* has been supplanted by representation agreeably with the increased facility of the artist. Still even at that, I fancy from Aristotle's own words, as when he calls tragedy more philosophical than history, that his imitation was less an imitation of reality than of ideality, of fact than of truth. But however that may be, I have no intention of using the word otherwise than in its ordinary compass.

Where the source or subject of literary interest corresponds with this process of reproduction or exhibition, the gratification will consist in recognition; otherwise in comprehension and illumination. On the part of the author, the one demands an act of perception, which may be characterized as emotional and ethical; the other, an act of intuition, which I will not call philosophical lest it be confounded with metaphysics, but rather moral — yes, I will go so far as to call it religious also. It was not an accident that the greatest tragedy ever produced was of a distinctly religious strain. There is something more required for the production of great tragedy than an eye for " social " values: there must be divinity in it somewhere.

On the one hand, the aim of literature can hardly reach beyond the enhancement of actuality, whether emotional or sensational — " scientific " Zola would call the latter; its highest achievement will consist in eliciting all the " human " or in registering all the " interesting " manifestations which the subject is capable of yielding. That the human degenerates into the animal and the interesting into the shocking is of no great consequence to the later practitioners of the arts of realism and naturalism. On the other hand, literature will aim at creating what Goethe calls the illusion of a higher reality by informing its subject-matter with moral relevance and consistency, — the business of the dramatist being to produce, in the diversity and confusion of sense, a distinct type or expression of human significance. There is no higher verisimilitude than that of truth; " documentation " is ineffectual in comparison. Where the informing spirit of moral and religious significance is absent — either because the author's vision is dull or is distracted by the importunities of fact — the work, taken as a whole, seems singularly dense, abstruse, and incommunicative. It comes to resemble some substantial physical formation or impersonal aspect of matter — a great body of water reflecting the landscape of its shores with an effect profound, scenic, and non-committal.

And so it is that for all his " depth " Shakespeare, as compared with Sophocles, is at once the more reserved and the more suggestive. The remark is true of the whole movement which he heads. While the ancient is the more disinterested and expressive, the modern is the more curious and exciting. I have tried to show how equivocal are Shakespeare's *dénouements*, either because they are reluctant to pronounce a verdict or else because they turn out to be conventional and specious when regarded as solutions. At the same time, a performance which fails to conclude, may still raise the question and raise it in a thoroughly arresting manner. To be suggestive it is necessary only that the writer should be himself " suggestible " — that he should be sensitive to outward influences and should model his drama directly upon his impressions; for inasmuch as experience is provocative in proportion to its immediacy, that literature will be the most suggestive which comes nearest to writing itself. Such automatism we are accustomed to glorify as " inpiration." In short, suggestion is a character of indetermination, which is in turn apotheosized with the epithet " infinite." A cloud may hint a thousand things — a whale, a camel, a face, a wall of battlements, a range of mountains; but let it subside into a single positive shape, if it will, and it ceases to be portentous. A corner is only the more mysterious for being obscure; the " wonder " varies directly with the uncertainty. As far as Shakespeare is a piece of nature, his " magic " leaves us in the end very much where life itself leaves us and with very much the same sense of mirage.

Among all the many emotions inspired by this mirage of actuality, as distinguished from Goethe's illusion of a higher and significant reality, there is one so indicative of modern literature, as of modern life, that it deserves a few minutes' consideration to itself. Perhaps the most persistent and invariable sentiment which a direct and inconsiderate contact or " communion " with nature leaves with

the " communicant " — shall I say? — is that inef-
fable longing, that insatiable and aimless desire, that
" homesickness of the soul " which we have learned
to call nostalgia. Like the *tedium vitæ* of Tacitus,
the ἀθυμία of Chrysostom, the acedia of the mon-
astic Dark Ages, it represents the inevitable reaction
of the human spirit to the complete inanity and vacuity of a phenomenal and inconsequential existence.
But unlike them, it is no mere symptom of an occasional or sporadic disease or even epidemic, but
rather of a chronic lesion in modern life and art.
Nor is the modern nostalgia, like its older counterparts, a mood of simple disillusion — an awakening
from the beguiling delusions of sleep to a realization
of the cold, drab desolation and bereavement
of day. It is, on the contrary, the mood of
deception — often of perverse and voluntary deception, of forced faith in impotent simulacra and
spurious oracles. It is an invariable penalty, for
instance, of the pursuit of " beauty " for its own
sake, and lies at the bottom of the melancholia and
distemper — or " temperament " as we like to hear
it named — which vexes every " artist " who will
hear of nothing but his art.

As a matter of fact, this feeling of nostalgia,
though familar enough to common experience in
connection with landscape, is most noticeably dramatic, perhaps, in the presence of a crowd: there
is nothing so baffling, nothing quite so hopelessly
convincing of the inability of man to find satisfaction in the mere spectacle and raw material of
life. Here on the pavement has happened together
in some way a number of people. They are to all

appearance individuals, separate and distinct entities. Each moves by what we call his own volition; independently of the others he is going about his own business. What that business is you do not know; nor do you know his past or future any better than his present. And more bewilderingly still, he has concealed in his head, in that hollow box of bone which houses his mind, all kinds of motives, impulses, interests, many of which, we are told, he is unconscious of himself. To every one, including himself, this " poor inch of nature " is little better than a riddle. And to add to the confusion, all these secretive little cellular beings, these intensely animated and vivacious automata seem to have nothing in common. As far as can be detected there is no principle of association, no formula or equation, no single expression which will take up just these atomies here present and bring them together into a system and account for their presence or doings, their concurrence in just this spot in just these numbers at just this time. They have no common denominator. They are like a swarm of motes in a sunbeam: the flicker in and out; they flit and fade; and they never reassemble identically or simulate again the same set or combination as before. They unite in no one idea; they make nothing but a phantasmagoria. Such is the throng; it is absolute illusion — or I should prefer to say in distinction from that other higher illusion of law and significance, it is mirage.

How much of the glamour of Shakespeare and of modern poetry as a whole is owing to this mirage, it would be hard to say — certainly, a great deal.

It is not Greek: at least when it appears in Greek, and that rarely, we speak of it exceptionally as romantic. In itself it is an evidence of imperfection, whatever pleasure we may receive in abandoning our minds to it; and it indicates a failure to discover, amid the shows of things, a home or residence for the vagrant spirit of man. It inspires, first, nostalgia, and then, satiety and distaste and skepticism until succeeded by the affirmation of a higher and more purposeful vision.

Here, as far as revolutionary romanticism is concerned, the matter might be left. But with Shakespeare in the case it is necessary to enter a qualification. If we consider, as I have done, that what Shakespeare was most apt to represent is the mutable many, the absolute illusion of the throng, without attempting to inform it further than is essential to herding it into the five acts of a play — though this, to be sure, requires no small amount of contrivance in itself — if we suppose that at best he attempts no other interpretation than this fairly literal translation into the dramatic *genre*, respecting otherwise the broad unconscious indifference of nature; and if we suppose that in this manner he has produced the most startlingly suggestive panorama of life that was ever unrolled — in a word, if he has rendered the mirage of actuality with almost incredible vividness: — still we must add that there are times, and those by no means infrequent, when he rises to a higher altitude, when he gets clear of all this lower atmosphere of fog and and cloud and obscuration, and sees the world for what it is — a phantasm, a hollow and deceptive

show in spite of its apparent bulk and solidity. He
has still no counsel of detachment, no pattern of
perfection or consummation; but at least he un-
masks and discovers it for what it is, for what every
supreme philosophy and religion has taught that
it is — a vain and disquieting shadow thrown upon
mist and resolving, like a little vapour, into nothing.
Such is the sense of his noblest and most memorable
passages:

> " These our actors
> As I foretold you, were all spirits and
> Are melted into air, into thin air;
> And like the baseless fabric of this vision,
> The cloud-capped towers, the gorgeous palaces,
> The solemn temples, the great globe itself,
> Yea, all which it inherit shall dissolve
> And like this insubstantial pageant faded,
> Leave not a rack behind. We are such stuff
> As dreams are made on, and our little life
> Is rounded with a sleep."

And I can not refrain from giving myself the satisfaction of the following quotation also:

> " To-morrow and to-morrow and to-morrow
> Creeps in this petty pace from day to day
> To the last syllable of recorded time,
> And all our yesterdays have lighted fools
> The way to dusty death. Out, out, brief candle!
> Life's but a walking shadow, a poor player
> That struts and frets his hour upon the stage
> And then is heard no more; it is a tale
> Told by an idiot, full of sound and fury,
> Signifying nothing."

This is the Shakespearean skepticism. And it is as much a part of Shakespeare as his irony and his nostalgia. Like them it is born of the mirage; but it has the advantage of puncturing the bubble, of riddling the deception. And not only occasionally and in passages of this extent, but in brief snatches also, every here and there, like momentary flashes of lightning, stabbing into the obscure corners of existence and lighting up their vacancy with revelatory glare, plays this merciless skepticism of the greatest playwright that ever undertook to stage this show of earth. There is no firmament, no distinct source of steady and beneficent illumination to infuse the troubled scene with orderly chiaroscuro and perspective — nothing but the rocking sea and the intermittent lightning. There is no vision of an immutable pole, no reassuring intimations of system and gradation. His inspiration is still dispersed among the several moments of his conception and is inseparable from the elements in which he works. His ideas are immanent. Every case is individual and exceptional; and his " art " is essentially " descriptive." Nevertheless while skepticism may not be the end, it is the beginning, of wisdom; it confounds both matter of fact and common sense, and lays bare the imposture whereby the mirage practises upon the vulgar credulity of mankind, pretending to reality itself when the sole reality is by virtue of the rational intuition which transcends and transforms it.

CALDERON

IT would be too much to say that Calderon was ever popular outside of his own country. But once upon a time he did enjoy a kind of exclusive literary vogue or fashion. Seventy-five to a hundred or more years ago in Germany and to some less extent in England and even in France he was an object of interest and mild enthusiasm to the lettered and sophisticated. In England he was happy enough to attract an archbishop, who wrote a little book about him, and to inspire a man of taste to translate or adapt half a dozen of his plays. In America Lowell celebrated his name in verse. Already in Germany, the source of this tepid conflagration, a group of criticasters had been busying themselves with their work of exhumation. Even in France, the country least susceptible to his peculiar appeal, an occasional *littérateur* would condescend to favour him with his notice. I say nothing of Spanish influence upon the earlier drama: that is another subject altogether. But I ought not to omit a reference to the Spanish obligations of a writer so late and so considerable as Grillparzer.

About all this repute there has been something decidedly artificial. Not only were his staunchest admirers so unmeasured as to provoke suspicion and

objection; but the interest itself has failed to stand
the test of time and cold blood. As a matter of fact
it has come to look a good deal like propaganda until
it is only as a scholium of German Romanticism
that the cult of Calderon appears of much importance.
At all events it was to this movement that he owed
his revival in the first place. With Shakespeare and
Dante he served to form a strong opposition to
classicism and to give the Romantic School a consistency which it wanted of itself, and a literary tradition which it pretended to despise but found that
it could not do without. It is in this manner that he
figures to A. W. Schlegel, who was probably the first
to resuscitate his fame, as "der letzte Gipfel der ro-
mantischen Poesie" and as the prime representative
of the "Religionsgefühl biedrer Heldenmuth, Ehre,
und Liebe," which constitutes its groundwork. It is
to be supposed that Schlegel was thoroughly familiar
with his author; but his remarks on the subject in
his "Vorlesungen über dramatische Kunst und Litteratur," which were as much as anything the immediate occasion of the Calderon fad, are more
conspicuous for zeal than accuracy.

About Calderon's work, he says, in spite of its
quantity "there is nothing random or topsy-turvy:
it is all worked out, in masterly fashion, after
established and consistent principles, with the most
profound artistic intentions. This fact can not be
gainsaid, even when the pure and lofty romantico-
theatrical style of Calderon is mistaken for manner-
ism and his daring flights of poetry to the very bounds
of the conceivable are regarded as aberrations. In
particular he has turned back into matter what his

predecessors took for form. (Denn Calderon hat überall das, was seinen Vorgängern schon für Form galt, wieder zum Stoff gemacht.) Nothing less than the noblest and finest flowers satisfied him. Hence it is that he repeats himself in many expressions images, similitudes—yes, in many a turn of situation [in manchen Spielen der Situationen] for he was too rich else to need borrow from himself, to say nothing of others. The stage-effect [die Erscheinung auf die Bühne] is his first consideration; but this concern, which is with others a limitation, is in his case wholly positive. I know no dramatist who, understanding how to poetize the effect in such wise, has been at once so sensuous [sinnlich kräftig] and so æthereal."

Such is Schlegel's opinion. Like most romantic appreciation it is characteristically vague, general, and adulatory; above all it has caught the trick of capitalizing defects and failings. But such as it is, it was in its time taken up into criticism and came for a while to constitute the official estimate of the dramatist. Needless to say, however, it is impossible to sustain him at such an altitude, though it must be acknowledged in the next breath that the romantic position was of itself well taken. In one respect at least, as I shall try to show, Calderon is no despicable example of the spirit that he was chosen to illustrate; he is above all and most exclusively the dramatist of mood.

It is generally admitted that Calderon is no delineator of character—and it is the delineation of character that we incline to make the point of genius nowadays—that on the whole his interest is less

with character than with action. Indeed, the preference for action is often referred to as a feature or
symptom of the whole romantic drama, as of romance, including Shakespeare's as well as Calderon's,
in distinction from the classic. And yet Aristotle declares explicitly that the mainspring of tragedy is the
action. It is evident, then, if the word *action* is to be
taken as idiomatic both of romantic and of classic
drama, that it must have different meanings in both
cases, since a merely superficial comparison shows
a wide discrepancy in this particular between the
two sorts of plays. The fact is that under the name
of action we think more of story, the romance, whereas
the Athenian thought of the moral juncture. To our
modern minds the essential matter of the action is
incident, the moments of which it is composed; to
the Greek, the urgency of the occasion. Conformably
with our different mental attitudes or habits, we see
the action as an affair of interesting elements; he saw
it as indivisible emergency. Hence the distinct feelings which the two kinds of action aroused; Shakespeare's, curiosity and suspense; Sophocles', conviction and reassurance. In short, what the Greek saw,
was its moral import; the romantic poet, its sensational effect.

Naturally, this difference in the point of view produced a decided difference in the technique or the
"art." The romantic dramatist has been tempted to
dwell upon his action for its own sake and in detail,
to elaborate and draw it out, to lavish his invention
and fancy upon it, to complicate and embellish it—
in a word, to develop it into a plot or intrigue. In fact,

the tendency of his excess, as he has tried to stress his story and yet keep it fit for the stage, has been to make it theatrical rather than dramatic, just as the defect of the Greek was to shrink it into a mere situation without conclusion or issue, as Euripides inclines. To be sure, Shakespeare seldom runs into this extreme; when he drops too far into romance and his plays begin to lose their dramatic virtue, he leaves the stage. But it is Calderon's vice exactly; he is invariably and successfully theatrical.

In so far Schlegel is right: a sense for romance and for the theatrical Calderon has unquestionably. But dearly has he paid for it—at the expense of the dramatic. He is quite lacking in dramatic concentration and development. Even a long play, like Shakespeare's "Macbeth," may have dramatic concentration. But Calderon's plays are unexceptionally diffuse: they spread like water; their movement is centrifugal. Nor has he any particular instinct for development: one thing simply follows another, runs into it fluidly and without consistency; there is no necessity about it of any sort. Like all this Spanish comedia his plays have subjects but no themes; they are tales told in tableaux for those who can not or will not read. That is the worst of a popular drama, or rather stage, that it addresses and must meet just this kind of public. The Elizabethans suffered from the circumstance, though not perhaps so much as the Spaniards. And it is as a result of this sort of determination, at least in part, that Calderon wants reality. His plays are in a manner spectacles and are, almost without exception, morally unconvincing.

Now, a play may have verisimilitude and yet be morally impossible; or on the contrary it may lack verisimilitude and possess moral probability or even inevitability. The latter is peculiarly the case with Shakespeare's "Twelfth Night"; the former with Calderon's "El Mayor Monstruo." It is a matter not merely or solely of action or yet of character, but rather of the relation of the two. Or better, the nature of the action itself is relieved only in its relation with character.

That in Greek tragedy the characters played as such a secondary *rôle* or what we should consider such, is undoubtedly true, and Aristotle is unquestionably right in saying so. Themselves they were more or less representative, generic rather than individual. And what they stand for, too, are not so much common types and species of human beings as the changes and vicissitudes of human experience. Hence they serve as a signature or index of the significance of the action. In the Shakespearean drama, however, it is the action or at least its issue which comes to appraise the character; the character results in the action and is on this account incapable of evaluating it. He is standing trial himself. But in Spanish, again, not only is there no gauge at all of the moral import of the action save and only a story—in Calderon the action neither measures the character nor is measured by him. It only gives rise to a succession of passing impressions, whose fluctuations lend the play its idiomatic interest. In other words, it has no inherent ethical significance—or rather, just as Calderon the playwright turns theatrical, so Calderon the man turns theological. What little moral sense his theatre owns is extrinsic and is caught up by the way in the dialogue, not involved in the constitution of the play. Juan Valera is quite right in contending that the Spanish drama is at all events unmoral if not actually immoral; though how in the face of such a conclusion he can maintain its literary pre-eminence is a wonder to any one who is unfamiliar with the vagaries of romantic criticism.

On the other hand, while the characters in Greek do indeed have this secondary or accessory *rôle* which makes them moral exponents of the action, they still have a distinction and distinctness of their own even while they themselves are strictly coterminous with the drama. Œdipus, Orestes, Antigone are clear enough and discernible through the stream of the action, although unlike Othello, Hamlet, Macbeth, they fail to protrude above its surface and are not, any of them, "characters" in that limited sense in which we sometimes speak of a man to-day as such by force of his standing out conspicuously and in high relief from his surroundings and circumstances —or as the Elizabethan might have said, a "humour." But in the Calderonian drama the characters neither project like Shakespeare's in the manner of the figures in a frieze nor do they resemble, as is the case with Sophocles', a pattern interwoven with the texture of the fabric but always distinguishable from the background; they are, rather, like the shadings of a watered or changeable silk in which the figure is continually losing itself and reappearing more or less uncertainly or elusively like a shadow on the surface

of the stuff. In such a manner do Calderon's characters tend to run into his action and lose any singular
identity of their own that it not infrequently seems
as though they had been thrown up momentarily by
the force of circumstances alone, to fall back upon
them and be reabsorbed like bubbles in the stream.
Such discriminations are not easy; but it ought to be
reasonably clear that this treatment of character is
quite different from the Greeks'. And it is conditioned, I believe, by a peculiarity that the critics of
Calderon have failed to notice.

To speak as though Calderon had himself but little
interest in his people or attention for them and were
entirely absorbed by his "fable," is an illegitimate
conclusion. All his masks—it would hardly do to call
them portraits after what I have been saying, and in
fact they are rather masks than portraits—are
carefully finished in his own manner. To be sure,
great numbers of them bear a strong resemblance to
one another—indeed, like his situations they are
scarcely distinguishable in themselves, if they are
not actually identical. But this effect is mainly due
to the way in which the interest is focussed. To speak
properly, it is not character as such for which Calderon is concerned except in the subordinate and
ancillary fashion, which I have tried to explain, as
chips on the current or straws on the wind. It is
hardly too much to say that he assumes the character or takes it ready-made; whence his collection of
easy types—the man of honour, the gallant, the
jealous husband. No, it is not character with which
Calderon is preoccupied; it is mood, the transitory

and unstable feelings and emotions, the mental fluctuations corresponding with the incidental fluctuations of intrigue and plot.

To this sort of human interest the Greek was
hardly awake. It was the steady bearing of character
or disposition with which he had to do. His interest
was structural. The momentary impression, the shifting play of consciousness, the fits of resolution and
infirmity found no echo in his drama. Only occasionally will you find anything like a note of mutability
in his tragedy, and that late. As has been so often
pointed out his personages go through their work
with a single mind and with nothing that can justly be
called a vacillation or change of heart. The words,
"Τί δῆτα δρῶμεν; μητέρ' ἦ φονεύσομεν," which Euripides puts into the mouth of Orestes at the very
instance when his scheme is succeeding and his
mother walks into the trap prepared for her, this
expression, "What then to do? Are we to kill our
mother?" is the only example that I can recall of
such an agitation. And while Shakespeare has by no
means ignored mood—while the fascination of his
theatre is due in part to this motive and the prismatic
play of consciousness which it introduces; yet the
moods of his *personæ* have been deduced from their
character and are regulated and supported by it.
"Hamlet" itself, not to mince matters, is almost
exclusively a study of mood; its significance lies in
its sudden alterations and revolutions of temper.
But at the same time all moods are Hamlet's;
they arise out of his nature and subside upon it so
that finally they compose a characterization of that

In short Hamlet is, in the jargon of our day, a temperament.

By comparison, then, we have in Calderon a dramatist of mood for its own sake. Not that his moods have no background at all, but that the background is relatively insignificant. For the fact is that Calderon's figures are so purely conventional, so "stock," that the sense of character virtually vanishes in a wholesale reading and leaves the perception of mood alone recognizable. Read any one of his comedias, "A Secreto Agravio Secreta Venganza" or "El Médico de su Honra" or even "El Escondido y la Tapada"; and the sense of character is penetrating enough to a foreigner. They are all Spaniards of the sixteenth century, infected with the *pundonor*, the punctilio of their kind; and in as far as they are neither Anglo-Saxon nor Nordic nor Anglo-Celtic nor whatever we like to think ourselves, they appear, taken one at a time, as sufficiently individual on the strength of their unfamiliarity. But read all these plays—or better yet, any half-dozen—and notice the resemblance, if not the identity of the essential traits or lineaments, see how the one person repeats himself again and again, until you turn your attention from the personality to its affection. In other words, the character remains a constant in every equation; once admitted, it is negligible and neglected.

Dramatically considered, character is another element than action; hence its development may become detrimental to the drama—if the play is indeed the thing. Many a strong character has ruined a good story. Unless the characters concur with the action—as was the case with the Greeks', where they swim with it—they are likely to have a disturbing influence. Their doubts and hesitations, their scruples and compunctions, may well impede the course of the drama, their wills resist it. This is one of the causes that Shakespeare's plays or so many of them appear when read to be ill constructed; his characters get in the way. They interfere with his action; not with the course of human events which he mirrors, for the fiction or myth, as distinguished from the play, results from the "oneyeriness" of his characters—but with the dramatic economy they do interfere. Whereas mood, on the contrary, arises directly from the circumstances of the plot; it is the effect of the incidents upon the person concerned. And further, since mood is itself transitory, shifting, unstable, changing with every incident; it naturally will blend with the action, becoming itself a part of the general current. Hence the peculiar shimmering watered appearance of Calderon's fabric, where his *dramatis personœ* seem to run into his action and lose themselves.

On these considerations too it is possible to explain the curious habit of repetition which marks his drama so singularly to a foreigner. Nothing would be easier than to make an extensive list of parallelisms in which the one sentiment recurs again and again in virtually the same words. But then, as I have said, Calderon was not concerned to show an individuality asserting itself amid the flux of circumstance, but rather the feeling of a pretty well-defined and limited kind of man, the man of honour

after the Spanish fashion, in a few representative
situations. And since these situations are in the
nature of the case recurrent, their affects and expressions in that one nearly invariable type will be recurrent too. Not that every capital situation in Calderon
is identical with every other, though there is a likeness among them all. But it is hardly too much to say
that the foundation of the Calderonian Comedia is
formed by a small set of stock situations.

> "¿Es comedia de Don Pedro
> Calderon, donde ha de haber
> Por fuerza amante escondido
> O rebozada mujer?"

There is always the lover, frequently surprised by
the husband who, unlike the French *mari,* is usually
the heroic and sympathetic personage, under more or
less compromising circumstances for which it be-
hooves him to exact vengeance for the satisfaction of
his honour. But the skill with which these commonplaces are varied so that a little shading is introduced
into the collection, is remarkable, it must be granted
And as the minute ingredients of the same old salad
change a little, the emotional responses of the characters, in the technical sense of the word, change also,
even while the language remains much the same, in
a manner easy enough to appreciate though not very
easy to define. There is in this wise an undeniable
subtlety in Calderon's drama, which the cursory or
partial spectator might fail to notice. But on this
score we who are of the Shakespearean tradition can

hardly afford to throw stones. And I suppose that
the observation is true of any great literature after
its kind, that it carries two messages—one obvious
and superficial, the other difficult and recondite.

And so while the Spanish comedia has no great
sense for the thematic either in character or plot, its
sensibility to mood and its expression does result in
the creation or realization of a certain kind and
into the collection, is remarkable, it must be granted.
number of situations—mood-situations, perhaps I
may call them to mark their affiliation with the affections of the *dramatis personœ* and their distinction from anything constitutional or organic. As such
they may be described as a kind of convulsion, a
sort of spasm affecting action, as mood is to be viewed
as a kind of spasm affecing personality. In other
words the Spanish action is as temperamental as the
Spanish character and equally excitable. Or is it the
other way around? Was it this taste for pointedness
of incident which developed the *penchant* for mood as
its best means of exhibition?

At all events it is a fretful drama. And the impression is not a little enhanced by the verse in which it
is written. To the English reader it seems quite impossible that what is virtually a ballad measure should
ever be susceptible of tragedy. Certainly it lacks
solemnity. And besides, it wants the long dramatic
crescendo to which we are accustomed in English and
Greek, and in French as well—in short, in the languages on which we have formed our taste. But it
served the purposes of the Spanish theatre nevertheless. In spite of the fact that eloquence and majesty

are impossible to it, there is a kind of rough and
ready poetry about it, such as we have brought ourselves to admire in Percy. It is not epigrammatic
but it is capable of making a point—it lends itself
to the quip or quibble, the sort of theatrical casuistry
to which the Spanish were addicted:—

> "Y así vengo, cuando yace
> En el supulcro del sueño
> Toda mi casa cadáver";

or better, perhaps—at least more in the Shakespearean vein, though without its impressiveness:—

> "¡Qué mal hice quando necio
> De amor, y de su violencia,
> Culpé á Antonio que adorase
> A aquella gitana, á aquella
> Que en los teatros del mundo
> Hizo la mayor tragedia!"

I have been speaking of Calderon very much as
though it were all a matter of tragedy or serious
drama exclusively. Such, however, is not the case.
And yet the great illustration of Spanish comedy, of
course, is Cervantes, not Calderon. Even as a playwright Calderon is inferior to Lope de Vega. On the
whole, "El Alcalde de Zalamea" would be considered, I suppose, Calderon's best piece. In point of
fact it belongs to Lope de Vega. There is nothing, at
least there never has been anything against one
dramatist's appropriating another's subject. But in

this case the *procédé*, the facture of "El Alcalde" is not Calderon's; he has not made the play his own—it is quite anomalous and of another technique. And in comedy Lope's superiority becomes particularly evident. His "El Perro del Hortelano" is the most entertaining play of the period that I have read in the language. It is not so very unlike Marivaux somehow; for instance "Les Fausses Confidences." Nor is "Los Melindres de Belisa" without a good dramatic core. The difficulty lies in what we should esteem the curious dramatic irrelevances with which the plays are developed. Their faults are those which I have just been discussing—extravagance, lack of verisimilitude, moral improbability, and in this case a misconception of the properly comic and a preference for the accidental and coincidental, for misapprehension and *contretemps*—to say nothing of the diffuseness which comports so ill with the charter of drama.

For these reasons among many Cervantes is the Spaniard who ministers most agreeably to our sense of comedy, that sort of comedy which is so saturated with humour as to be hardly distinguishable from it. For this *genre,* if it may be so called, narrative is in itself a much better medium than drama; it is ampler and much less constrained, and is capable of broader effects. To be sure, there is a great deal to be overcome in "Don Quijote." As a burlesque of the chivalric we can only make the best of it. And no doubt, too, Cervantes' fun is often pretty rough and obstreperous for a twentieth century stomach wonted to the titillations of innuendo and insinuation. Nothing ages so rapidly as the fashion of mirth, and the jest that tickled the father may nauseate the son. The eternal heckling to which the Don is mercilessly exposed for two thousand pages or so but works its own reaction. Naturally these seemingly interminable wastes of buffoonery and horseplay and slapstick have their oases. I would mention only the gathering at the *venta*, with the tales of the Cautivo and the Curioso Impertinente. About this episode in particular there is at least something like poetic verity; it builds up in the imagination into a sort of illusion which persists in recollection—I had almost said like a situation of Dickens', different as the two humorists are. But it is only a respite after all. The public must have been stupider in those days, if that is possible. At least their density was greater than is ours—their molecular constitution more stable, so that it took more to dissolve them into tears or laughter; or it may be that they could bear more laughing and crying without the mood's disintegrating. At all events the effort which Cervantes has expended upon his effect has turned out to be an embarrassment. And to add to our difficulties, the story itself is of the old picaresque or perambulatory type. A marvellous achievement for the age—it antedates "Tom Jones" by a century and a half—it marks nevertheless a relatively rudimentary stage in the history of the art so called of prose fiction.

But after all, while I do not belittle these failings, which the Romanticists in their habitual fashion were quick to capitalize, still Cervantes' humour in any case runs very much deeper. There is about it a

large and luminous tolerance, a profound humanity
—not the humanity which is blind to human foible
and vanity and vice, the silly official optimism of the
professional humanitarian, which blinks the fact of
evil and misery and error—or even, I doubt, that
"touch of nature which makes the whole world kin"
in a universal frailty. But to be disabused of the
deception, without losing interest in the reality, of
life; to suspect that very reality, perhaps, and yet to
retain sufficient indulgence to expatiate at large
upon the momentous trivialities of human experience
—this is in itself a triumph of good humour. Above
all, it is Cervantes' ability to recognize the portion of
illusion in the nobility and elevation of man and of
his civilization which makes of the juxtaposition of
Don Quijote and Sancho Panza an enduring symbol of its kind. He is not a myth-maker like Plato;
but in his amused appreciation of the contrast between his two characters, the visionary and the prag-
matic, in particular their lien upon one another and
its fabulous source, I seem to see a gloss on Plato's
economy of the gold, the silver, and the bronze men.
And so it is that in his wide and at time otiose elaboration of his theme he has won a position as one of
the three or four great representatives of the humorous comedy of life, with Aristophanes and Shakespeare, far and away above his dramatic compatriots.

And yet, in conclusion, this drama itself, so negli-
gent on the whole of theme and character, has endowed modern literature with one of its perennial
motives and one of its immortal characters. For the
latter service the credit belongs to Tirso de Molina

with his "Burlador de Sevilla y Convidado de Piedra," the original of Don Juan. For the former Calderon's "La Vida es Sueño" is immediately responsible. The sentiment is, of course, a commonplace; but to Calderon's development, I think, it may be said to owe in large part its currency—in fact, that very familiarity which makes it a commonplace:

> "¿ Que es la vida? Un frenesi.
> ¿ Que es la vida? Una illusion,
> Una sombra, una ficción,
> Y el mayor bien es pequeño:
> Que toda la vida es sueño,
> Y los sueños sueños son."

Such are the unexpectednesses of genius.

STRUCTURE AND STYLE

O NE OF the most remarkable achievements of the romantic spirit has consisted in the development of a literary style of such refinement, elaboration, and subtlety as to have drawn attention more and more to itself and away from the bolder and solider properties of design and composition characteristic of classicism. While it can not be said that every classic revival has centered directly upon Sophocles in the same manner that every romantic reaction has been made to hinge upon Shakespeare, yet it is generally felt, and felt correctly, that the former is as truly the pole of the one as the latter is of the other; and as a matter of fact, it is just this relative importance and predominance of style as compared with structure which measures the distance between the two. In spite of the felicity of Sophocles' expression — a felicity which after all consists in the happy adaptation of language to idea — it is evidently by his conception that he imposes — the perfect proportion of parts, the large outline of his general plan, the great indivisible block of his meaning. While it is impossible to read Shakespeare without being struck by his extravagance, inequality, and confusion — as impossible as it is not to be thrilled and dazzled by the brilliancy and splendour of those frequent sallies on which it would seem that he must have relied, in the exuberance of his genius, to redeem the impression of his faulty and careless economy.

Even among living literatures those prevailingly romantic are comparatively indifferent or insensible to structure, or composition in the broader sense, as might be shown by a comparison of English and German with French; while the distinctive effect of lyric poetry, which is virtually a creation of romanticism, has been purchased by a sacrifice of form to manner. Indeed, it can hardly have escaped the attention of the most casual observer that poetry as a whole has been completely transformed in the sense of the romantic evaluations of the last century. The old architectural analogies and figures of speech, the plastic tropes and metaphors — heirlooms, many of them, of antiquity — by which literature was once assimilated with the arts of construction and design, have been gradually supplanted by terms of music and painting, arts of execution and expression, almost exclusively. It is no longer the ground-plan, the *fond*, the general lines, the sage proportions, the *ordonnance* of a work for which the critic reserves his enthusiasm; it is the " purple patches," the " tone-colour," the " word-painting," the " visualization," the " melodies " or " harmonies," the " instrumentation." The term *playwright* has no further sense; the dramatist is a maker of *tableaux;* while the poet composes symphonies or sonatas or even " diapasons of colour."

Under the circumstances, since the distinction is not only admitted but approved already, it may not be profitless to trace the consequences of such a preference for style or structure, in the hope to surprise the peculiarities of disposition in which it has its root, together with the characteristics of the literature corresponding and its effects upon the consciousness of the reader.

Now, literary organization is, on the face of it, so largely a matter of selection that there is, if anything, a temptation on the part of its students to underrate other factors of equal or even greater importance. So, to William James mental organization, of which literary organization is only the consummation, seems to consist almost exclusively in the exercise of choice. And if only I may add the qualification *conscious,* I shall be disposed to go a long way with him. For conscious selection implies a purpose or aim, which in turn implies an idea or perception of significance; and literary " creation " is marked, to my mind, by the presence of just such an informing idea or principle. The fact is plain. It is impossible to choose materials of any sort without knowing what is to be done with them; and it is impossible to know what is to be done with them without understanding them, not merely as materials but also as self-subsisting realities or ends in themselves. Choice involves intent, the prevision of an end and the apprehension of the means whereby it may be attained and the will to reach it; and not only that, but above all and principally, it presupposes the sense in which the whole affair is to be taken, inclusive of the subject considered in the light of an independent value or source of interest. Hence organization, involving conscious selection, involves a discrimination in favour of

certain means and against certain others, a preference for certain matter over other matter in view of
a definite appraisal or judgment of the content as
a theme of general human moment or concern.

This, then, is what makes the essential difference
between literature and life; and it is on this account
that the appreciation of art and the appreciation
of nature rest upon entirely different bases. While
our current consciousness is usually flat and colour-
less and tame, a genuine work of art is enhaloed
with a kind of nimbus or aureole; it irradiates a
charm or glamour of its own. It inspires a conviction of finality and completeness. In short, literature produces a characteristic illusion, Goethe's
illusion of a higher reality; while our current consciousness produces no illusion whatever.

" As Esmond crossed over to his own room . . . and
turned to enter in at the low door, he saw Lady Castle-
wood looking through the curtains of the great window
of the drawing-room overhead, at my Lord as he stood
regarding the fountain. There was in the court a peculiar silence somehow; and the scene remained long in
Esmond's memory: — the sky bright overhead; the
buttresses of the building and the sundial casting a
shadow over the gilt *memento mori* inscribed underneath; the two dogs, a black greyhound and a spaniel
nearly white, the one with his face up to the sun, and
the other snuffing amongst the grass and stones, and my
Lord leaning over the fountain, which was bubbling
audibly."

This is not nature; it is not even consciousness —
it is not actuality at all. It is illusion, the illusion

of a higher reality, the effect of significance. And in every case where the organization of material is anywhere near complete, this sense of significant illusion with its penetrating and satisfactory charm is invariably disengaged. It does not occur in our quotidian consciousness because that consciousnesss is not thoroughly organized and hence is not thoroughly significant. Only when man's life is mastered by some great and overpowering purpose which dominates for the time his whole being, does he find anything like this sense of illusion in every-day events. A memory, however, is in its way a work of art and produces an impression of art just to the extent that it ceases to be reproductive and becomes representative. It is rudimentary literature, to be sure, but still it is literature — literature with structure but no style. Indeed, the mood of reminiscence is the mood of literature. And as such recollection is sharply marked off from sensation; it is partially organized. But since this topic is fundamental, since it lies across the very threshold of literature, it is worth while to make a special effort to illustrate it — and the more simply the better even at some risk of over-obviousness.

Everybody recognizes that any work of art — and for the present I will continue to include literature under that head — is made up of a number of different elements or constituents all combined to produce a single large effect. Now, it is impossible to put together even two or three components, let alone a number, without some purpose to serve as a guide in doing so. Even a carpenter can not get his boards together into a box unless he foresees the box into which they are going. And his aim or purpose, as is equally patent in so plain a case, includes also a just appreciation of the value or possibilities of the elements to be composed. In so far it is critical; it involves a criticism of his material. The carpenter would be farcical if he tried to make a box out of pebbles or bricks — and no less so if he used mahogany or Circassian walnut for fence rails or clothes posts. He might still be a good joiner, but he would betray his inability to see anything in his stuff or to make anything out of it; he would prove himself to be a man of no ideas. The competent cabinet-maker, then, has two notions — one of his *genre,* the box; the other of his stuff. The first is a model or pattern, the latter an idea proper.

In other words, it is necessary to distinguish two questions which are commonly confounded and interchanged, sometimes innocently but sometimes mischievously. The one is a question of trade or technique; the other a question of art or criticism. While every art has its trade or craft, it is a mistake, though a frequent one, to assume that the trade or craft which underlies the art, is in so far forth an art of itself. For the competent cabinet-maker the two questions may be phrased in this way: What kind of chest will this particular lumber make? and, What will this chest make of this particular lumber? If a playwright be substituted for the cabinet-maker, however, these questions will read even more pertinently: What kind of tragedy will this subject-matter make? and, What will this tragedy make of this subject-matter? The former is a question of *genre;* it is raised and answered by the type. It is purely technical and banausic, and goes with the trade or craft of writing alone; and it is of comparatively little moment or importance to anyone save the *littérateur* himself, and to him only in the capacity of artisan. In spite of the general publicity given it by certain loquacious romanticists of the third or fourth generation, like Flaubert (indeed, it is this kind of talk which makes them seem so disconcertingly amateurish for all their appalling sophistication) this problem belongs to the study and the *atelier;* it is " shop." The second is the literary and artistic question *par excellence* — What will this tragedy make of this subject-matter? — as it is the critical question also. It is concerned for import and significance. It asks, not what are the æsthetic possibilities of this subject in terms of style and execution, but what is its intelligible interest as representative of idea and life. And the answer is addressed directly to life and its issues.

To be sure, the stuff in which the writer works is not identical with that of the cabinet-maker or the artist; but the same argument holds for both. The matter out of which the novelist or the dramatist is trying to make his story or his play is the matter of experience. The words are merely symbolic; they are not the stuff of his creation; they are but signs of the realities with which he has to do, mere notations, and may even be dispensed with conceptually, as in memory. Properly and exactly, his element is life; and before he can determine it in this sense or that, he must have some definite idea of its significance — not a vague impression of immensity and confusion, a swimming of the head or a ringing of the ears, a sensation of intoxication and exaltation, of bemusement and wonder — but (dare I say so in this generation?) a kind of philosophy, at least a few fundamental principles, if not of life as a whole, at all events of that portion of it with which he habitually deals. And since his whole organization is dependent upon this idea or principle, it must come to constitute the informing spirit of his work.

The pretension of modern romanticism in its more " realistic " and " naturalistic " activities to find the informing idea or principle of literature in " nature " itself so that literature has nothing more to do conceptually than just to shepherd the facts into the fold of some *genre* or other — this assumption is so preposterous to unspoiled common sense as hardly to bear statement, much less analysis. Indeed, it is hard to account for the currency of such a belief, so inconsequent and pointless does actuality appear in its ordinary manifestations — a whir of disorderly sensations, a smear of forms and colours, a jangle of unmusical sounds. Try to digest your impressions for the course of a day — the odds and ends of humanity you have met, the sputters of broken talk you have overheard and taken part in, the momentary vexations and annoyances you have suffered, the passing emotions, the flutter of spirits, the shivers and goose-flesh, the lapses of attention — and yet the minutes of such experience should be the perfect realism, if minutes were but a *genre* as Friedrich Schlegel tried to make them.

Of course, we have come to believe, some of us, though on very questionable evidence and as much for the sake of saving our face as for any better reason, that nature, taken as a whole, has a sort of higher unity in a transcendental idea of some kind. We like to think that there is a universal term or expression which embraces and reconciles and explains away all contradictions and incompatibilities. To an infinite intelligence, we suggest, all this confusion and bewilderment to which we are subjected, would straighten out and present a symmetrical appearance of graduation and regularity. But unfortunately we do not know any such scheme; we merely feign it, we can not detect it for ourselves. We have never yet been able to reduce history to science because we have never been able to discover any rule to which human life as a whole conforms, though just now some of us are much given to mumbling economic rigmarole, while others of us are rather inclined to suspect with M. Bergson that vitality is mainly irrational and unintelligible after all, little as we like his view of the relative importance of that portion of it or his conclusions with regard to the consequences of such a faith. With the physical universe our mechanics have done a little better, if we are willing to disregard certain discrepancies and overlook certain gaps and lapses. And yet we have not banished one spectre — a doubt of the competence, if not of the relevancy, of this inhumane science and of its ability to read the riddle of man.

And yet suppose for the sake of argument that we are on the right track nowadays — suppose that there is an ultimate mechanical or mathematical or scientific principle — if any one can imagine such a thing — under which all nature and life are subsumed; even then such an idea would be too vast, too distended to serve as the constituent principle for just a single isolated work of art or literature. It would transcend the infinitesimal circumscriptions of experience with which we deal and which are too restricted even to enter the law of averages — it would not make sense of a crowd. As far as the author is concerned, he would be just where he was before. Pack nature into your containers as much as you please, it is nature still; you have altered its figure but you have not made sense of it. And until you do so, it is neither literature nor art.

I am ashamed to have dwelt so long on such a subject; it all seems so simple and self-evident. My excuse must be the perversity with which the whole matter has been misrepresented in the interests of a conception of art so narrow and partial and false as to have brought the very name of art itself into disrepute among the serious to a degree unparalleled since the days of Plato. Nevertheless, in spite of these confusions, it ought to be clear to an eye of any discernment at all that the structure demanded by literature requires insight or vision or intuition — the ability to find a meaning or significance for the data of experience; for without such a key there can be no conscious discrimination or selection of material, no point in handling it above the bare dexterity of technique, which makes for artistry, not art. And further, since the subject of literature is principally human nature, it is obvious that this intuition upon which the author depends for the inspiration of his work, must be a rational and moral intuition — not a sensational or emotional one; for all other considerations apart, a sensational or emotional inspiration would never support a closely concatenated fabric of sustained significance. Such an inspiration must be one capable of enlisting the services of the intellect as against the spasmodic impulses of an irrational instinct.

It follows, then, that if we would discover the author's meaning, we must look to his design, for there, if anywhere, it resides. Whatever significance a piece possesses is to be sought in the constitution of that piece as a whole and not in the several members taken singly. It is the plan or plot, as Aristotle implies, which is the index to the writer's vision. And it is this body of meaning for which the name *form* should be reserved, if the word is to have any literary application at all. For language or expression such a term is evidently a misnomer; it is appropriate only when used of the configuration of elements as fixed by the presiding conception. The form is determined by the frame, which is the schema of the idea.

Style, however, is quite another affair; and though it has its own function too, still it is the organ of idea. Properly and in a correct balance of faculties, it presupposes intuition. Only where conception leaves off does style enter to carry out its decrees. Its office is to translate the idea into language. It is an interpreter and is not itself responsible for the oracles it utters under the influence of the vision. It is quite possible that an author should compose his work without ever thinking about style. Racine appears to have framed his tragedies first in prose; there is among his papers an act or so of an *Iphigenia in Tauris* outlined in this manner. Sophocles is reported to have called a tragedy of his completed when he had only thought it through wordlessly. Goethe wrote the whole of his *Iphigenia* in prose before turning it finally into verse. In short, style is nothing more than the practical *procédé* by which some one portion of the design is realized or executed. The phraseology may be very curious, very pretty, very brilliant; but the impressions which it produces, unless correlated into an intelligible pattern, are only partial and disparate at best. And what is worse, they will, if exaggerated, distract attention from the main concern and attract it to themselves to the detriment of the idea.

Still the relationship between conception and style is wonderfully intimate inasmuch as style belongs to the trade upon which literature is reared — the trade of letters. And since language is the sole medium for the communication of ideas, it is style upon which the author must rely exclusively to bring out point by point the significance upon which his illusion depends, and above all to produce the requisite sensible effect from moment to moment. This latter obligation, to take care of the sensible effect of the moment, is the primary duty of style, as it is the primary duty of structure to take care of the meaning of the subject. This is the original and first-hand contribution of style to illusion, and it is inimitable. For this reason the finest poetry is untranslatable. The general conception, the theme, the intention of poetry may indeed be reproduced in one way or another; and from these sources it is not impossible for one who is himself potentially a poet to recreate the characteristic illusion of the original from the beginning. But in as far as the illusion depends upon the appreciation of the proper sensible notes *seriatim,* translation is wholly inadequate. As a matter of fact it is always unsuccessful in detached passages; and it is the more unsuccessful where the imaginative fusion is the greater. The German translation of Shakespeare is a remarkable performance; one has only to turn to Ducis' to see how remarkable — about the German language there is a kind of inchoateness which makes it an unusually good vehicle for translation. And yet with all its merits, it leaves something unmatched when compared sentiment by sentiment with Shakespeare: —

" Mir war, als rief es: Schlaft nicht mehr!   Macbeth
   Mordet den Schlaf!   Ihn, den unschuldigen Schlaf;
   Schlaf, der des Grams verwor'n Gespinnst entwirrt."

The last line is a marvellous bit of rendering: in spite of the fact that it means just the opposite of what the English seems to mean, it comes the nearest of any single line of translation that I know to catching the sentimental thrill of the original. And yet weigh it with the English phrase by phrase —

" Methought I heard a voice cry, Sleep no more!
   Macbeth does murther sleep, — the innocent sleep,
   Sleep that knits up the ravell'd sleave of care " —

and there is a difference of timbre which I can not describe but which is perceptible enough. No; style, together with the sensible modulation of which it has charge, is inimitable — and just so much of the significant illusion too.

To state succinctly the case of style in relation to structure, it is safe to say that indispensable as style is in executing the details of conception, it should none the less take its cue, even as a sensible exponent, from the theme or plan; for what the phraseology of an author discovers is only a succession of distinct traits which are in themselves intransitive and receive their determination solely from their association or fusion in a common design, as characteristics inhere in a character. Style, in short, is an affair of the phrase; it is a strain which fills the ear for an instant and dies away to be succeeded by another equally impermanent. What it does is to render in the fitting sentimental key a single effect called for by the motive or idea. The interest results from the synthesis of all these particulars. But their fusion requires that the moments should dissolve or melt into the solution. Hence a special or extraordinary accentuation of the separate strokes — anything exaggerated or ornate as well as anything merely odd or erratic in the style impairs the illusion, as it disintegrates the form.

Important as they are, the consequences which I have been discussing are not the sole consequences of structure by any means. In addition, design has an intellectual as well as an imaginative aspect. And it is the cultivation of structure in this sense, without vision or insight to inspire and spiritualize it, which is responsible for the rather grim and forbidding air of intellectualism characteristic of pseudo-classicism. In this aspect form itself becomes a matter of technique — a branch of the trade of authorship. It is confined to the notion of a more or less methodical organization or incorporation of members into a common body. Differentiation of parts or organs and integration of functions becomes the criterion of the successful product. And just as the health of the human system inheres, not in this and that organ, but in their integration, so the virtue of the literary composition lies, not in the parts or even in the summation of the parts, but in their coördination and coherence. It is, therefore, essential that the writer who devises the work and the reader who peruses it, should be able to appreciate this congruity. But the perception and enjoyment of relationships is an intellectual exercise. It requires of the writer the peculiar ability to discriminate among a crowd of discrete details importuning his attention simultaneously and the peculiar skill to dispose or digest his selection into a scheme or plan; while on the part of the reader it requires the same faculty only in lesser degree — besides the feat of holding them all together in a single combination. Hence literary construction presumes a certain amount of mental effort, varying with the severity of the organization. It is quite feasible to teach composition, as divorced from vision. Any one with intelligence can learn to put his work together creditably, if he wants to badly enough — every educated Frenchman can do so —

though it is doubtful whether every intelligence possesses the insight which alone makes composition significant, or can acquire the style which alone will make it expressive. The one calls for great power of divination, the other for great sensibility; and these are rare and special gifts, their alliance amounting to something like genius.

At all events, the conclusion is clear. Since structure, considered technically, lies within the scope of intellect, a writer whose character is preponderantly intellectual will naturally stress the technique of composition above style and expression. He will be likely to prefer a clean, tidy, definite, and regular outline to verbal charm or grace. And if his disposition, in addition to being of an intellectual cast and delighting in the working out of combinations and the adaptation of means to ends, the coördination of parts and the comprehension of wholes, is also endowed with moral intuition to divine the human import of his subjects; then will he incline to value design superlatively, not only for its own sake, but as the scaffolding of a rational illusion, whose sensuous elaboration he will confide to the sympathetic instrumentality of style. In other words, since in the balance of literature design is the legislative and style the executive agency, it results that the presiding authority of a sane and well-found literature will be intuitive and intellectual; it will blend insight and reason. Such a literature will not be uncompromisingly intellectual by any means, for it will be tempered by inspiration; but it will be orderly, intelligible, and significant, permeated through all its pores with the illusion of

truth or reality — a solid, substantial, self-sufficient
creation of the imagination, cosmic and substantive
amid the chaotic rioting of sense. Such is the character of that noblest monument of human genius,
the tragedy of Sophocles — and the secret of its
permanency — as it is the character in relative degree of every literature to which the designation
classic is properly applied. And such is the rationale of the classic preference for the plastic and the
architectonic.

In contrast with this massive unitary effect, in
which subject counts for so much, the effects of
style, as I have already indicated, are severally in-
complete and partial, comparable technically with
the dressing of stone or the chiselling of statuary.
As is admitted in the figures of speech affected by
their devotees, their affiliations are less architectural
than artistic in the limited English sense which has
always been disposed to confine art to painting —
colourful, for the most part, and rhythmic; decora-
tive or at all events, accentual. They impart warmth
and tone and splendour to the work of the stylist;
they prick out strongly the high lights; they bear
witness to the writer's eye for appearances; they
magnetize the reader's attention and flatter his
senses like bits of glass in a kaleidoscope or the
pulses of a melody — but they have no sequence, no
coherence; they are without a reason save as they
belong in a composition. In themselves they are an
index, not of mind, but of mood. What they measure are the author's sensibilities and susceptibilities.
Free of logic and volition they have only to follow
his temperament — the instinctive response of his

nature to sensuous and emotional stimulation. In piquant or poignant phrase they recall the prickle of sensation, the tingle of feeling without responsibility for the merits of either:

> " Old, unhappy, far-off things,
>   And battles long ago."

That is the very immediacy of impression; the significance of it consists in no general idea but is concrete and inherent in the sentiment, as it were an intrinsic and specific property of the thing itself, a component part of the perception. Hence its charm is intimate and inexplicable, like that of an admired face which can not be recollected satisfactorily but must be sought to again and again. That is style; and there is no great passage of poetry which does not owe its magnificent isolation, like this, to style and style alone. But its character is evident; it is the pathos of the passage, a pathos owning no obligation to the reason or the will, which stirs the reader; and all the while there is a little rustle, as it were, among the memories of sense and their residues, as though he had but just turned away from some landscape or other spectacle of nature which was still troubling his consciousness. It is an æsthetic effect — haunting, nostalgic, and itself unhappy.

Is it necessary to multiply examples? Whereas the writer of insight and intelligence inclines to make a convincing and comprehensive whole of his subject because he understands it and sees his way through it, while the logical and formal intellect busies itself with the coördination and consolidation of the parts into a consistent and coherent body or organization; the writer of sensibility, on the contrary, excited by the sensual effluences of nature and dizzied by the shifting panorama, the flickering cinema of experience unrolling before the eyes like " a tremulous wisp constantly reforming itself on the stream " — such a temperament is bound to turn from the severe abstractions of the creative imagination to the cultivation of style because it is possible by fastidious refinements of phrase to produce a kind of linguistic iridescence corresponding to the shimmering surface-play of impressions which makes the main interest and gratification of his conscious life.

And this, I suppose, is the explanation of the modern and romantic cult of style; for romanticism is, first and foremost, a literature of the senses and the emotions, of the blood and the nerves, impatient of the control of the inward monitor — *le maître intérieur,* in Fénelon's phrase—and eager to discredit its authority. About such a literature, with its pretention to banish the *tedium vitæ* forever, there circulates a draught of exhilaration and expansiveness which recommends it to the young, the ardent, and the intemperate in every generation. Beside the intent and purposeful discipline of classicism it poses as indulgently broad and tolerant. In competition with the graces of the stylist who charms by the richness and profusion of his effects without much anxiety for their consistence, the precision of the classicist with his conscientious adherence to principle is at the disadvantage of appearing meagre, even sterile at times, just as the formality of a Greek temple may seem austere and parsimonious in contrast with the extravagance of a Gothic cathedral. Between the judicious frugality incident to form and the lavishness and caprice of nature there exists an evident incompatibility. Life is so abundant, so prodigal and licentious that the attempt to reduce it to lean and comely proportions is impossible without a vast amount of excision, simplification, and correction. For the sake of order and measure the classicist must surrender something; and he prefers to surrender what is of least moment to idea — the discrete, the adventitious, the exceptional — whatever refuses to focus and converge and articulate — in short, multiplicity and divarication.

Of this sort of literary economy Greek tragedy remains the aptest illustration. In conception and structure it corresponds as nearly as literature may to the type of the Greek temple. Its purport is unmistakable. Its design is so simple as to be clear at a glance; even the chorus fails to disconcert it. It contains only the emotion proper to the subject. And as a result it leaves the strongest impression of any drama ever produced. The effect is perfectly definite and final. When a play is ended, the matter is settled. The memory is filled with a single image, the consciousness with a single theme, the mind with a single decision.

But such a result is at odds with anything like comprehensiveness of subject-matter or treatment — it is intent, compact, instant; while breadth, whether of content or handling, runs to amorphousness and distention. Take a novel of Thackeray's or Dickens' — *The Newcomes,* for example, which undertakes to represent London society in the middle of the last century, that is, a modern and voluminous subject; and the clear, firm contours which characterize Sophocles' drama are impossible. The outline of such a novel must be elastic, supple, fluid — as winding and sinuous as an indented coast; it must be capable of indefinite expansion like a pouch or pocket. Consider the length of time covered by such an action, the multitude of characters entangled with it, the wealth of incident included. And then remember that a Greek tragedy dealt with only five or six persons, that it accounted for only a single moment of their lives, that it had to do with only one sequence of episodes. How much easier to knead a few ingredients like these into a shapely loaf than to fashion a cake out of Thackeray's material! Or more accurately, how much more difficult to reduce a teeming and plethoric subject to these narrow and punctual dimensions! Indeed, it is hardly correct to speak of such a novel as having a form at all; it has only a kind of rhythm, a pulsation from one incident to the next. And while the later novel has been influenced by science and the drama to a straiter and more methodic structure, it has diminished its content *pari passu,* and without ceasing to be romantic has become only more realistic in its strict preoccupation with " nature " and its idiomatic detail.

Clearly, then, Greek tragedy does not practise this admirable thrift without what is, from the modern point of view, something of a sacrifice. It slights a great many aspects of fact which popular

taste has come to hold in a kind of superstitious
awe as guarantees of reality. In particular, it fails
to make very much of the characteristic provoca-
tiveness of actuality. Many of those feelings of
unresolved and motiveless perplexity, amazement,
and consternation which we require of tragedy because they seem to us the essence of experience
are wanting to the Greek. We must suppose that
life as such went on for Sophocles very much as it
does for us — in the same clutter and at the same
loose ends. We may picture the crowd jostling
him on the street, the grimy beggar or the greasy
demagogue thrusting an equally unlovely face of
solicitation into his, with here and there a still figure
of philosophy musing disinterested and unregarded
amid the hubbub of " practical " interests; we can
imagine the clash of opinion, the cross-purposes,
passions, and suspicions of party politics which
made up the public life of " democratic " Athens
— we may think of the more tousled aspects
of life as present to him as to us. But to
this daily distraction his drama has remained
impervious. To be sure, a good deal of the impertinence of common reality has worked its way
into Euripides, but greatly to the detriment of his
significance and integrity. The issue can not be
dodged. In order to dispose experience structurally
at all, in conformity with the constitution of dis-
course, it is necessary to reject altogether a great
part of the detail to which actuality is indebted
for its piquancy, and to admit only such particulars
as are capable of taking place in the permanent
organization of consciousness. What is unstable,

indefinite, fugitive must be passed over or set aside
as incapable of definition or fixation. All those dim,
uncertain exaltations and depressions, those nameless apprehensions and premonitions, those indeterminate stirrings and impulses which strain our
attention and warp our judgment — all these fumes
and vapours of the brain, many of them somatic,
the classicist is satisfied to ignore; they are neither
constitutive nor expressive. In brief, his literature
is something more than a succession of twitches and
flashes. Nor is it a mere derivative, drawing its
interest and justification from some other source
and having a purely analogical value in terms of
such another variable. On the contrary, it is an
ideal, self-sustaining and self-sufficing fabric built
up gradually and regularly in the imagination from
materials strained and sifted out of experience for
that purpose.

Conversely, the writer who looks upon literature
as a function of life, immediately responsible to existence and the impressions peculiar thereto, as it
were a kind of sensorium for the collection and registration of vital stimuli — such an author will set his
ambition in the conviction which he may succeed
in producing of the characteristic waywardness and
" wonder " of nature. In this view the idiosyncra-
tic, as possessed of superior actuality, tends to become the exclusive subject of representation. Individualization, not typification, is the desideratum.
The strange, the irregular, the unusual engross a
correspondingly larger share of attention. The exception rather than the principle comes to be the
rule. Form as a rationale — as aught but a me-

chanical nexus like a string around a parcel, is considered an impertinence. Metre, rhythm, not to say the *genre* as such, are disqualified one after the other. The laws of association are abrogated; reverie usurps the place of rational intuition or vision. And with the dissolution of the idea, style encroaches farther and farther upon the logical province of composition — until finally, defeated in its attempt to reproduce all the exquisite thrills of sentiency, it abandons the struggle altogether, and ceasing to be expressive at all, becomes avowedly symbolic and suggestive.

Of late the disorganization has proceeded to such an extent as to have crowded pretty nearly the last vestiges of mind from English poetry — which has ceased to be humane or moral — and has left next to nothing for criticism to take hold of. But to those of us for whose youth Tennyson was the poet of romantic sentiment, he will still seem the natural illustration of the tendency. In him, at least, the process, while sufficiently advanced to be conspicuous, is not too far gone to be intelligible — at worst there is always a modicum of sense remaining; and from him I will illustrate it: —

" Then saw they how there hove a dusky barge,
  Dark as a funeral scarf from stem to stern,
  Beneath them; and descending they were ware
  That all the decks were dense with stately forms,
  Black-stoled, black-hooded, like a dream — by these
  Three Queens with crowns of gold; and from them rose
  A cry that shivered to the tingling stars,
  And, as it were one voice, an agony

Of lamentation, like a wind that shrills
All night in a waste land, where no one comes,
Or hath come, since the making of the world."

Now, the point to which I would call attention, is
that these last three verses —

" a wind that shrills
All night in a waste land, where no one comes,
Or hath come, since the making of the world " —

these three lines, I say, have no rational connection
or reasonable association with the theme. They do
not constitute a part of the significant illusion, the
illusion of a higher reality, as such; on the contrary, they create a kind of mirage — an extremely
vivid one but one below the horizon of the subject
nevertheless. They catch just a kind of sudden
sentiment that the sound of mourning might possibly have provoked in the spirit of some musing
on-looker, hardly in that of an intent participant.
In this sense they are thoroughly romantic: they
pick out, like a ray of sunlight,

" Kindling the cones of hills, and journeying on,"

a single eccentric detail to which the eye of the
inattentive traveler is immediately diverted. As a
whole, the effect of the passage is not that of vision
proper but of the romantic substitute, reverie,
where the mind pursues no necessary sequence of
ideas but is seduced from one image to another by a
number of more or less adventitious and arbitrary
cues. It is this vagrancy of fancy which we find so

pleasant in falling asleep: the sounds of the outer
world reach us remotely and vacantly — we hear
the distant clatter of hoofs along the road, the drip-
ping of water from the eaves, the barking of a dog
in the night, the untimely crowing of a cock; but
we connect no definite ideas with these impressions;
our consciousness floats indolently along, with an
hypnotic sense of levitation, on some easy current of
suggestion which they happen to have set flowing,
without the labour or responsibility of thought or
the necessity of arriving at any particular conclusion.   In such adumbrations of a vague and phantasmal reality, which demands little in the way of
concentration as it offers little in the way of content, lies the secret of romantic literature.

" Like God, whose servants they are [Our Ladies of
Sorrow] they utter their pleasure, not by sounds that
perish or by words that go astray, but by signs in heaven,
by changes on earth, by pulses in secret rivers, heraldries
painted on darkness, and hieroglyphics written on the
tablets of the brain.   They wheeled in mazes; I spelled
the steps.   They telegraphed from afar; I read the
signals.   They conspired together; and on the mirrors
of darkness my eye traced the plots.   Theirs were the
symbols; mine are the words."

This is the romantic mirage, as distinguished from
the significant illusion of classicism.   Under the
stimulation of a style which has cultivated suggestion to the neglect of expression, reminiscence is
aroused, the consciousness is suddenly injected with
a flood of sensuous memories and presentments —
the imagination moves; but inasmuch as the mind

has no clear conception before it, the imagination moves aimlessly and without creative activity or effect. It is inspiration of a sort — the sort which Nietzsche has designated as Dionysian on account of the prominence of these very characters and has assimilated to the irresponsible enthusiasm of inebriety. To its influence is largely due the witchery of modern poetry; it is responsible for what Matthew Arnold calls " the magical way of handling nature," —

> " Or magic casements opening on the foam
> Of perilous seas in fairy lands forlorn " ;

and it seems to be the animating spirit of what he understands distinctively as " style." As such it is the achievement of English literature and the crown and triumph of the romantic revival. I pass over its later-day decadence, its final divorce from reason and conscience, and its subsequent inanity and fatuousness — such matters belong to the degeneration of romance. But in measure and at best, it must be rated as an enrichment of literature in general and of poetry in particular — not a clear gain, perhaps, but an acquisition without which we should be the poorer; for within limits a literature, like a race, should be credited with the variety as well as with the perfection of its types.

But I have said as much as my subject warrants. If I have not already succeeded, I can never hope to succeed, in showing that classicism consists in a just balance or equilibrium of the faculties under the presidency of the divinatory reason or intuition and that whatever tends to disturb or disrupt this balance is romantic. Hence the classicist sets great store by form and structure; they are the representatives and trustees of order and proportion in literature. He has a decided intellectual bent, as witness his devotion to clear ideas and his care for the consolidation of part with part in the organization of his materials; but the severity of his logical character is tempered by vision or insight, which inspires him with a sympathetic sense for the human significance of his subjects. As a result of this disposition, he inclines to a marked subdual or lowering of the parts of the composition or to such a treatment of them as shall indicate that they are merely members of an association from whose solidarity they draw their own importance; and he leans to a similar handling of style as an instrument of thought, for the attainment of an ulterior rational end. In like manner he is conditioned to the simplification and contraction of actuality, whenever fact becomes embarrassing either by reason of its proliferation or obscurity. The classic tendency is towards clarification and concentration. And finally, in this instinct for transparency and definition, and in the consequent avoidance of whatever is vague and diffuse, the classic pretends to convey no more than lies within the ability of the author to understand or the power of language to represent; it is expressive, not suggestive. Its aim is to create a significant illusion of reality.

Romanticism, on the other hand, manifests itself in literature by an emphasis on style above structure, because the romanticist himself delights in novelty and variety of detail even more than pertinence and consistency, and it is possible by one sort of phrasal ingenuity or another — the " exquisite epithet," the " purple patch " — to mimic the changing moods of nature more or less successfully. The romantic temperament is sensuous and emotional; it is disposed, if anything, to magnify its impressions severally in the interest of " wonder " and so to exaggerate the apprehension of diversity incidental to its subject-matter. And as it is prompt to respond to the stimuli of experience, so it is eager to open as wide a range of representation as possible. As a result, romantic literature, in comparison with classic, is characterized by expansiveness and diffusion; it appears in content more abundant and variegated. At the same time, it loses, as though in compensation, much of the classic certainty and penetration; it is less significant and intelligible. In addition, its sentimental instability is constantly urging it to the pursuit of the uncertain, even the dubious, until in its curiosity and impulsiveness it finds itself attempting to express the inexpressible. Hence its abuse of suggestion. Its ambition is the manifestation of " life " and the emotions proper to it; its characteristic feat, the creation of a phantom or mirage of actuality.

All modern literature is preoccupied with fact; it is either scientific or romantic. The most alarming symptom of romanticism at present is its want of mind. No one can read our current *belles lettres* after those of the preceding century without being struck by their intellectual flaccidity. In subtlety and acuteness of thought, in comprehension of human nature and tradition, even in sheer common-sense and plain level-headedness, to say nothing of maturity of character, the writers of this age appear like children beside those of the eighteenth century. They seem to have no moral grasp — as Goethe said of Friedrich Schlegel, no inner *Halt*. With a plausible appearance of liberality in its programme — with its passionate appeal to the instinct of individual freedom and its spirited pleas for breadth and tolerance, romanticism has always been cursed by its impatience of discipline and restraint and its indulgence of dissipation and irresponsibility. To that sense of enlargement without which life is a drab and dusty chronicle there are but two conceivable means — dissipation and discipline. That the former is the more " natural " and spontaneous may be granted. It is the way of youth, which giving free rein to its impulses and feeding on self-deception, revels in its license to do as it likes. But the other is the way of understanding, which leads its followers through carefulness and control to self-possession and the power to do as they will. Between these two states, that of effortless abandonment to caprice and that of purposeful exertion — an interval which measures the difference between the green Goethe and the ripe, the Goethe of *Werther* and of *Iphigenie* — lies a limbo for him before whose eyes has dissolved the mirage of youth — a period of nostalgia and skepticism ere he finds himself capable of the higher and significant illusion of character through a settled and confirmed habit of the will —

The University of Nebraska Press wishes to express its thanks to Professor Keith M. Aldrich, Department of Classics, for supplying translations of the Greek passages; to Mr. Felix Atance, Department of Romance Languages, for translations of the French; to Professor William M. Bowsky, Department of History, for translations of the German; to Professor Lloyd Teale, Department of Romance Languages, for translations of the Spanish; and to Miss Lorna Heim for assembling the translations and preparing this section for publication.

Dedication: "For this alone, if anything, would have drawn back [the dead] and bound them to life: if they had been allowed to live together with those possessed of the same principles as themselves." Marcus Aurelius, IX.3.

GERMAN ROMANTICISM

p. 57: "What disorder! What clamor!"—Faust
p. 58: "The color sounded, the form resounded."
p. 64: "It belongs to the ever more formed contrast of the new time with the old, that one is never more one, but each is all."

p. 67 (top): *Talks on Religion*

p. 67 (bottom): "The solution of all riddles lies in the secret of love."

p. 70 (top): "Everything leads me back into myself."

p. 70 (bottom): "I meet only myself in an empty wilderness"

p. 74: "that poetry is the highest and last"

p. 75 (top): "What we call nature is a poem, that lies locked in a secret, wonderful writing."

p. 75 (bottom): "From the force that binds all being

The man frees himself, who vanquishes himself."

p. 79: "Being is, because we thought it,

The world lies in its gloomy splendor,

Into its dark pit there falls

A glimmer, which we brought with us."

p. 86: "Pedantry asks Fantasy

For a kiss; she directs him to Sin.

Shameless, without strength he embraces it

And she recovered from a dead child,

Named Lucinde."

THE IDEA OF GREEK TRAGEDY

p. 92: "I do not call art that which is a thing without reason."

p. 99: "The [things] before a tragedy."

p. 100: ". . . accomplishing through compassion

and fear the purgation of just such emotions." Arist. *Poetics* 1449^b.27-8.

p. 114: " . . . so as [to overrule] unwritten and steadfast laws of the gods. . . ." Soph. *Ant.* 454-5.

p. 115: ". . . [actions and words,] the laws of which are set forth, highfooted laws, born in the sky's air, whose only father is Olympus (no mortal seed generated them), and may forgetfulness never lull them to sleep; deity is great in them, and does not grow old." Soph. *Oed Tyr.* 865-72

p. 134: "I erred, I shall not deny it." Aesch. *Prom.* 268.

p. 154: "For I in future time, with bow and arrows unerring from my hand, shall avenge myself upon some other who comes to be dearest of men to her." Eur. *Hipp.* 1420-22.

CORNEILLE: THE NEO-CLASSIC TRAGEDY AND THE GREEK.

p. 160: "Let all die with me, madam: What matter
Who treads after my death the ground where I lie?
Will those illustrious ancestors perceive
The night of their tombs lit up by a new splendor?
Will they breathe the air where they will be brought back to life

By these descendants who will with difficulty follow in their steps,

And who perhaps will only dishonor them,

And carry on their blood only to degrade
it?

When we have lost the sun which lights
our way

This kind of life is highly imaginary,

And the briefest moment of a wished-for
happiness

Is preferable to such a cold and vain eter-
nity."

Surena, i., 3.

p. 161 (top): "Life is but a small thing and
sooner or later, what matter

Whether a traitor snatch it from me, or
age carry it away?

We die constantly; and in the sweetest
fate

Every moment in life is a step towards
death."

Tite et Bérénice, v., 1.

pp. 161-162: "I have often been asked at the court
which of my works I liked best, and I have
found that those who have asked were so
biased in favor of *Cinna* or *The Cid* that
I have never dared to declare all the fondness that I always have had for this play
[*Rodogune*], to which I would gladly give
my vote, had I not feared to fail somehow in the respect which I owed to those
inclined toward another choice. This

preference on my part is perhaps one of those blind inclinations which many fathers have for some of their sons over the others; perhaps there enters also some pride, in the sense that this tragedy, I think, belongs more to me than those which preceded it, because there are certain incidents which are of my own making, and had never been seen in the theater before; and finally, perhaps, there is some true merit, which makes this inclination not altogether unfair."

p. 162 (bottom): "Then to what avail are all these fabrications? Do they create the slightest bit more probability in the history which is overladen with them? They are not once probable for even themselves. Corneille showed off with that as if with very wondrous exertions of inventiveness; and he should have known that not the naked invention but the appropriate invention demonstrates a creative spirit."

p. 164: "I see that we who live are nothing but a phantom, a shadow without substance."

p. 172: "of whose dark thoughts
          Are always enclosed in a thick cloud,"

p. 173: "I erred, I shall not deny it."
          (Cf. supra, p. 134)

p. 174: " '[He] does not seem to me to be committing a crime,' he says, 'despite the fact that he kills his father, for he does not know him and all he does is to contest the right of way with somebody who attacks him with an advantage.' "

p. 175: "What would have happened if I had defiled the stage with the murder of a person as kind and virtuous as Iphigenia had to be?"

p. 176: "Thus, to charm us, tragedy in tears
Gave words to the grief of bleeding Oedipus,
Of Orestes the parricide it expressed the fears,
And, to entertain us, it brought tears to our eyes."

pp. 180-181: "It is so unlikely that there should occur, either in imagination or history, a quantity of transactions illustrious and worthy of tragedy, whose deliberations and effects can possibly be made to happen in one place and in one day without doing some little violence to the common order of things, that I cannot believe this sort of violence altogether impossible. There are admirable subjects where it is impossible to avoid some such violence; and a scrupulous author would deprive himself of an excellent chance of glory and the public of a good deal of satisfaction, if he were too timid to stage subjects of this sort for fear of being forced to make them pass more quickly than probability permits. In such a case I should advise him to prefix no time to his piece or any determinate place for the action. The imagination of the audience will be freer to follow the current of the action, if it is not fixed by these marks, and it will never perceive the precipitancy of events unless it is reminded and made to take notice of them expressly."

pp. 181-182: "I maintain, then, that one must seek this perfect unity as much as possible, but since it does not lend itself to all topics, I would then concede that action taking place in a single town may be considered as having unity of place. Not that I would want the stage to represent the whole town (this would be too vast), but only two or three distinctive places within its walls. . . . In order to rectify in some way this ambiguity of place when it is inevitable I would want two things done: first, that no change of location should occur in the same act, but only between acts, as in the first three acts of *Cinna*; second, that the two locations should not require different stage decorations, and that neither of the two should ever be named specifically, but only the general location where both occur, such as Paris, Rome, Lyon, Constantinople, etc. This would convey the illusion to the spectator, who, seeing nothing showing the contrast between the different locations, would not notice it, short of a malicious and critical consideration of which very few people are capable, the majority being too excited by the action taking place in front of them."

pp. 182-183: "The other scruple concerns the unity of place, which is accurate enough, since everything takes place in a room or a waiting room common to the apartment of both Felix and his daughter. It seems that propriety is somewhat strained in order to maintain this unity in the second act, in the sense that Pauline comes to this waiting room in order to find Severus, whose visit she should have awaited in her study. To this I answer that there are two reasons for her coming to him; first, to render a greater honor to a man whose wrath her father feared, and whom she had been enjoined by her father to influence in his behalf; second, to break off with more ease the conversation with him, by retiring to her own study, had he not been willing to depart at her command, thus escaping by this retreat from an interview dangerous for her, something she could not have done had she received him in her apartment."

pp. 183-184: "But, since people with opposing interests cannot in all likelihood set forth their confidences in the same place and since they are sometimes introduced in the same act, with connecting scenes necessarily carrying this unity along, a way must be found to make this unity compatible with a rigorous verisimilitude. . . . Juriconsults introduce fiction in law, and following their example, I should like to introduce theatrical fictions in order to create a theatre setting which would not be Cleopatra's apartment, nor Rodogune's in the play which bears that title, or Phocas', Leontine's, or Pulcherie in Heraclius, but a room with doors opening on the different apartments, and to which I would ascribe two privileges: first, that everyone who would speak there should speak with the same secrecy as if he were in his room, second, that instead of the normal procedure, in which decorum is served by having those occupying the stage seek out those who are in their studies in order to speak to them, the latter should be able to come to the stage without violating propriety, thus maintaining the unity of place and the continuity of the scenes."

p. 185: "The concept of illusion has caused great errors in the theory of art. It has often been understood as involuntary deception, as if the representation were real. . . . No, theatrical deception like anything poetic is a dream while awake, to which one gives himself freely. In order to bring this about the poet and actor must forcibly carry minds along; the calculated probabilities do not help to do that in the least."

p. 187: "I would prefer better still that he give his name,
And say: 'I am Orestes,' or else 'Agamemnon.' "

p. 188: "But what I liked best about it, was that I found it [the topic] extremely simple. [And he continues:] Nothing matters much in tragedy save likelihood; and what is the likelihood that there should happen in a single day a multitude of things which could hardly happen in several weeks? Some there are who think that this simplicity is a sign of small invention. They fail to notice that on the contrary all invention consists in making something out of nothing and that all this great mass of incident has ever been the recourse of those poets who have felt their genius too frail and scanty to hold their audience for five acts by *a simple action supported by the violence of the passions, the beauty of the sentiments, and the elegance of the expression.*"

p. 189: "The Count and D. Diégue quarrel as they come out of the palace: this could happen in the street; but having been slapped, D. Diégue cannot remain in the street giving expression to his grievance while waiting for his son to arrive, for he would be instantly surrounded by people and would receive the offers of several friends to take up his cause. . . . As the scenes are here, one may say that it is necessary sometimes to help the stage along and make up for the lack of what can not be reproduced. . . . Thus, through a theatrical fiction, one can imagine that D. Diégue and the Count, having left the palace, walk down the street wrangling and finally arrive at the house of the former, when he is slapped, and he is then obliged to go in and seek help."

p. 190: "If this poetical fiction does not satisfy you, let us leave D. Diégue in the public square, and let us say that the gathering of the people around him, and the offers made to him by the first friends met there, are circumstances which the novel must not forget, but that since those minor actions do not help the main action in any way, it is not necessary for the author to worry about them on the stage."

p. 191: ". . . The play is so involved that it demands a great effort of the mind. I have heard very intelligent people, and highly qualified men of the court, complain that the presentation of this play tired the mind as much as serious study. People have indeed liked the performance, but I think that they have had to see it more than once to understand it fully."

p. 192: "To preserve my honor and end my woe, Pursue him, slay him, and die after him."
Le Cid, iii., 3.

p. 193: "Had he a moment only delayed his defeat,

Rome would at least have been overcome
little later."

Horace, iii., 6.

pp. 193-194: "I love, I confess, this noble pride
That has never bowed to the yoke of love,
In vain Phedre honored herself with
Thesus' sighs:
As for me, I am prouder, and shun the
easy glory
Of winning a compliment offered to a
thousand others,
And entering a heart open at all sides,
But to bend an inflexible courage,
To bring pain to an insensitive soul,
To chain a captive astonished by his fet-
ters
Rebelling in vain against a yoke which he
loves:
That is what I want, that is what excites
me,
It was easier to disarm Hercules than
Hippolytus.
And, vanquished more often, and sooner
overcome,
Prepared less glory for the eyes which had
tamed him."

Phedre, ii., 1.

p. 194 (bottom): "Take this sword, fear nothing,
let your murderous arm
Strike a heart which was always yours;

In it your name will be seen; for it is there
    engraved."

Les Scythes, v., 5.

pp. 195-196: "When Heaven's commands have
    made us for each other,
    Lyse, then ours is an agreement soon made.
    His hand into hearts, by a secret power,
    Sows understanding before we perceive it;
    It prepares so well lover and sweetheart
    That their souls on hearing the mere name
        are moved and awaken:
    They esteem and seek one another and
        fall in love at the first moment;

    Any word exchanged convinces promptly,
    And not troubled by groundless fears,
    Faith anticipates the words before they
        are uttered.
    The tongue explains much with few words,
    While the eyes, more eloquent, reveal
        everything at a glance;
    And of whatever they both vying with
        each other, may instruct each other for
        us,
    The heart understands more about it than
        both of them can say."

La Suite du Menteur, iv., 1.

p. 196: "If I were forced to say why I like
    him, I feel I could not express it: There
    is, so it seems, beyond my speech and
    whatever I may say, some divine and fa-

tal power, mediating this union. It is not one, two, three, four, nor a thousand special considerations; it is I do not know what quintessence of all this blend, which, having subjugated my will power, forced it to immerse itself and get lost in his. I say lost, as a matter of fact, for it does not retain anything peculiar or intrinsic."

p. 197 (top): "Great things [truths], [says Sainte-Beuve], which are simple at the same time, have been said very early: moralists and poets of antiquity sketched and apprehended human nature in its main and broad features; it seems that they have left to the moderns only the task of discovering details and the luxury of refinement."

p. 197 (bottom): "The imitating slave is born and vanishes;
Night falls, the body remains, and its shadow flees."

RACINE

p. 209: "Let him to his own efforts join those of Hell,
I am master of myself as of the universe."

p. 212: "It is Venus in all her power grasping her victim."

p. 213 (top): "For my accomplishments have

been of suffering rather than of doing."
Soph. *Oed. Col.* 266-67.

p. 213 (bottom): "And let love, often struggling
with remorse,

Appear as a weakness rather than a virtue."

p. 215: "Everything is ready. They wait for me.
Do not follow me.

For the last time, farewell, my Lord.

Alas!"

p. 216: "Forever! Ah! My Lord, do you realize
How hideous that cruel word is when one
is in love?

In a month, in a year, how shall we endure,

My Lord, that so many seas will separate
me from you,

That the day will dawn and set

Without Titus being able to see Berenice,

Or I able to see Titus, during the whole
day?"

pp. 216-217: "Let us not go any farther, let us stop
here, dear Oenone.

I can no longer stand, my strength leaves
me;

Back in daylight again, my eyes are dazzled

And my trembling knees give way beneath me . . .

How oppressive these vain ornaments and
veils!

What importunate hand in tying these
  knots,
Has taken care to gather my hair over
  my forehead?
All is affliction and harmful to me, and
  conspires at my downfall . . .
Noble shining author of a wretched race,
You whose daughter my mother was
  proud to be,
Who perchance are shamed to see me in
  this plight,
Sun, I come to behold you for the last
  time!"

p. 219:   PHAEDRA

They love each other! By what spell have
  they deceived my eyes?
How have they met? how long? where?
You knew it: why did you let me be de-
  ceived?
Could you not inform me of their clandes-
  tine love?
Have they often been seen talking or look-
  ing for each other?
Were they wont to hide in the depths of
  the forest?
Alas! they saw each other freely:
Of their sighs Heaven approved the in-
  nocence;
They followed without remorse their am-
  orous leanings;
Every day rose bright and peaceful for
  them!
And I, sad outcast of the whole universe,

Hid away from the brightness of day and
  shunned the light . . . !

OENONE

What fruits will they enjoy of their vain
  love?

They shall not see each other again!

PHAEDRA

They will love each other forever . . .

Wretch! And I live! and endure the sight

Of that holy Sun from whom I have come!

I have for ancestor the father and master
  of gods;

Heaven and the whole universe are full of
  my ancestors:

Where shall I hide? Let us escape into
  the infernal night.

But what am I saying? My father holds
  the fatal urn;

Destiny, they say, has put it in his stern
  hands.

Minos judges in Hell all mortal souls.

p. 222 (top): "Life is but a small thing; and
  sooner or later, what matter

Whether a traitor snatch it from me, or
  age carry it away?

We die constantly; and in the sweetest
  fate

Every moment in life is a step towards
  death."

p. 222 (bottom): NERINE

Break the blindness in which you are
  seduced,

To see to what state it has reduced you.

Your country hates you, your spouse is faithless,

In such a disaster, what is left to you?

MEDEA

Myself.

p. 225 (top): "And Crete foaming with the minotaur's blood,"

p. 225 (bottom): "Ariadne to the rocks recounting the injustices [suffered by her]."

p. 226 (top): "They followed without remorse their amorous leanings;

Every day rose bright and peaceful for them!

And I, sad outcast of the whole universe,

Hid from the brightness of day, and shunned the light."

p. 226 (bottom): "My Lord, I come to you. For today finally

If you forsake me, who will help me?

Without kith or kin, forsaken and fearful,

Long a Queen in name, but in fact a captive,

And without having had a husband, a widow now,

My Lord, of my misfortunes these are the least."

p. 227: "He is a madman who prays for death. Better to live foul than die fair."

Eur. *Iph. Aul.* 1251-2.

p. 229 (first): "The laws pertaining to men."

p. 229 (second): "Nothing too much."

p. 230: "Unwritten and steadfast laws of the gods." Soph. *Ant*. 454-5

p. 231 (top): "unwritten laws." cf. supra

p. 231 (bottom): "To live well, to fare well they understand to be the same as to be truly happy."

p. 234: "For such insensibility is not human."

p. 238 (top): "No god pleases me whom I must admire by night." Eur. *Hipp*. 106.

p. 238 (bottom): "For the sins of his forefathers bring him before these [judges]."
Aesch. *Eum*. 934-5

p. 239: "Since it is the wish of Venus, of this deplorable blood
I die the last and the most wretched."

p. 252: "This purple, this gold, enhanced by his glory,
And these laurels witnesses yet of his victory."

p. 261 (top): "Unhappy example of a long constancy;"

p. 261 (bottom): "In the midst of perils a great heart is revealed.
Led by love what could friendship not perform?"

p. 262: "Let us not delay, let us march; and if I must die,
Let us die, dear Osmin, I, as a vizir, and you
As the favorite of such a man as I."

CALDERON

p. 306 (top): "the last peak of romantic poetry"

p. 306 (bottom): "Religious feeling, honest heroism, honor and love"

p. 313: "What are we to do? Will we slay our mother?"

Eur. *Electra*. 967.

p. 316: "Is this one of Don Pedro Calderón's plays in which perforce there is always a hidden lover or a woman with her face covered [to hide her identity]?"

p. 318 (top): "And so I come at a time when all my cadaverlike house is lying in the tomb of sleep";

p. 318 (bottom): "How wrong I was when turned into a fool by love and its violence, I reproached Antonio for loving that gypsy girl,
the one who took part in the greatest tragedy ever performed on the stages of the world!"

p. 322: "What is life? A frenzy.
What is life? An illusion,
a shadow, a fiction,
and the greatest good in it is very small:
for all life is a dream,
and dreams are merely dreams."

STRUCTURE AND STYLE

p. 352: "Character through habit."

Plato. *Laws*. 792ᵉ.

PB 1137